Resilient Cultures

Resilient Cultures:

America's Native Peoples Confront European Colonization, 1500–1800

John E. Kicza

Washington State University

Upper Saddle River, New Jersey 07458

Library of Congress Cataloging-in-Publication Data

KICZA, JOHN E.
    Resilient cultures: America's native peoples confront European colonization, 1500–1800
/John E. Kicza.
    p. cm.
Includes bibliographical references and index.
ISBN 0-13-093250-7
    1. Indians—Government relations.   2. Government, Resistance to—America.   3.
Indians—Cultural assimilation.   4. Latin America—Civilization—Indian influences.   5.
North America—Civilization—Indian influences. I. Title.

E59.G6 K53 2003
970.01—dc21   2002070002

Editorial Director: Charlyce Jones Owen
Senior Acquisitions Editor: Charles Cavaliere
Associate Editor: Emsal Hasan
Editorial Assistant: Adrienne Paul
Director of Production and Manufacturing: Barbara Kittle
Production Editor: Judy Winthrop
Project Liaison: Louise Rothman
Prepress Manufacturing Manager: Nick Sklitsis
Prepress and Manufacturing Buyer: Sherry Lewis
Marketing Director: Beth Mejia
Marketing Manager: Claire Bitting
Cover Design Director: Jayne Conte
Cover Art: Illustration of encounter between colonists and Indians in King Philip's War, 1675–1676.
Manager, Rights and Permissions: Zina Arabia
Interior Image Specialist: Beth Boyd-Brenzel
Cover Image Specialist: Karen Sanatar

This book was set in 10/12 Minion by Lithokraft II
and printed and bound by Courier-Stoughton.
The cover was printed by Lehigh.

 © 2003 by Pearson Education, Inc.
Upper Saddle River, New Jersey 07458

Printed in the United States of America

10 9 8 7 6 5 4 3 2 1

0-13-093250-7

Pearson Education Ltd., London
Pearson Education Australia Pty., Limited, Sydney
Pearson Education Singapore, Pte., Ltd.
Pearson Education North Asia Ltd., Hong Kong
Pearson Education Canada, Ltd., Toronto
Pearson Educación de Mexico, S.A. de C.V.
Pearson Education—Japan, Tokyo
Pearson Education Malaysia, Pte., Ltd.
Pearson Education, Upper Saddle River, New Jersey

To Adrienne and Andy

Contents

List of Documents   *xi*

List of Illustrations   *xiii*

Preface   *xv*

1 The Native Societies
of the Americas
Before Contact   *4*

2 The Coming of Humans
to the Americas
and the Agricultural Revolution   *4*

Sedentary Imperial Societies   6
Landholding Patterns and Forms of Production and Distribution   14
Empires and Warfare   19
Semisedentary Societies   23
The Primacy of Community and Lineage   27

Nonsedentary (or Nomadic) Peoples   *29*
The Native Population of the Americas on the Eve of Contact   *30*
Conclusion   *31*
Selected Bibliography   *32*
Endnotes   *33*

3 The Conquests and Initial Establishment of Colonies in Latin America   *34*

The European Setting   *34*
Iberia's Early Efforts at Exploration   *36*
The Spaniards in the Caribbean   *37*
The Organization and Functioning of Spanish Expeditions of Conquest   *41*
The Conquest of the Sedentary Imperial Societies   *47*
Differing Iberian Interactions with Semisedentary Peoples   *57*
Limited Iberian Success against Nonsedentary Peoples   *62*
Conclusion   *63*
Selected Bibliography   *64*
Endnotes   *65*

4 Colonial Spanish America and Its Impact on the Sedentary Imperial Societies   *67*

Spanish Colonists and Their Expectations   *67*
The Retention of Indigenous Provincial Organization   *70*
Fragmentation and Its Impact   *72*
Demographic Collapse and Its Consequences   *74*
Tribute and Labor Service Systems   *76*
Urban Indians   *78*
Race Mixture and Its Recognition   *80*
Creative Adaptations at the Local Level   *81*
Changes in Material Culture   *83*
The Christianization of the Native Peoples   *84*
The Role and Popularity of Religious Sodalities   *88*
The Cult of the Saints   *89*
Language and Cultural Change in Mesoamerican Communities   *90*
The Character of Native Revolts   *91*
The Impact of Eighteenth-Century Population Growth   *92*
Conclusion   *93*
Selected Bibliography   *94*
Endnotes   *96*

5 Native Response to Settlement
in the East and Southwest
in North America   *97*

Spain in Eastern North America   *97*
The Spanish Impact on the American Southwest   *100*
The French Arrival in Canada   *104*
The French Avoidance of Conflicts over Land and Authority   *108*
The Fur Trade and the Huron   *109*
French Warfare against the Iroquois   *112*
French Settlement along the St. Lawrence in the Eighteenth Century   *114*
The Canadian West and the Mississippi River Valley
    in the Eighteenth Century   *116*
The Dutch in New Netherland   *118*
The Dutch Fur Trade at Fort Orange   *119*
Dutch Settlement around New Amsterdam and Its Impact
    on the Native Peoples   *120*
Conclusion   *121*
Selected Bibliography   *123*
Endnotes   *124*

6 The British and the Indians
of Eastern North America   *125*

Early English Undertakings in North America   *126*
Jamestown and English Settlement in the Chesapeake   *126*
Puritan Settlement in New England and the Rapid Transformation
    of the Local Peoples   *132*
The Iroquois in the Eighteenth Century   *137*
The Carolinas in the Eighteenth Century   *143*
The Native Peoples West of the Appalachians
    until the American Revolution   *145*
Conclusion   *148*
Selected Bibliography   *149*
Endnotes   *150*

7 Spanish and Portuguese Interactions
with Tribal Peoples   *152*

Migration and an Enduring Frontier among the Maya
    of the Yucatan Peninsula   *153*
Muted Transformations among the Pacified Maya   *154*

The Portuguese and the Peoples of Brazil   *157*
Spanish Settlement among the Guarani of Greater Paraguay   *161*
The Formidable Araucanians of Southern Chile   *164*
Limited Spanish Success against the Nomadic Peoples
   of the Mexican Desert North   *165*
Missions in Spanish and Portuguese America   *167*
Conclusion   *171*
Selected Bibliography   *173*
Endnotes   *173*

8   Enduring Connections between the New World and the Old   *174*

The Movement of Peoples   *175*
The Movement of Diseases   *176*
The Movement of Animals   *176*
The Movement of Plants   *177*
The Movement of Precious Metals   *180*
By Way of Conclusion—Enduring Patterns in the Americas   *183*
Selected Bibliography   *185*
Endnotes   *186*

Bibliography   *187*

Index   *195*

List of Documents

Chapter 2
The origins and great migration of the Mexica   *15*
Prehispanic labor service patterns   *19*
The Aztec army at war   *22*

Chapter 3
Runaway native retainers in early Cuba   *42*
Manco's siege of Cuzco   *56*

Chapter 4
The petition to the King from the rulers of Huejotzingo   *71–72*
A Peruvian cacique's testimony about tribute payments in 1562   *76*
A colonial native chronicle asserts that the precontact Andean peoples knew
    Christianity   *87*

Chapter 5
Champlain's account of his 1609 voyage up the St. Lawrence   *106*
A Micmac comments about French and Indian cultures   *115*

Chapter 6

An encounter between Powhatan and Captain John Smith   *129*
An adoption ceremony among the Seneca   *140*
The devastation of incessant warfare on the Chickasaws in the 1750s   *146*

Chapter 7

Jean Léry's description of civil order among the Tupí   *159*
Alvar Núñez Cabeza de Vaca's description of the Guaycurú, an enemy tribe of
    the Guarani   *162*
Araucanian weaponry and tactics against the Spanish   *166*

List of Illustrations

Chapter 2

Major Indian cultures of Latin America in 1500 *7*
Chronology of Central Mexican history up to European contact *9*
Chronology of Central Andean history up to European contact *10*
An early colonial Mexican Codex depicting the Aztec migration myth *12*
Important sites in the Valley of Mexico on the eve of European contact *17*
Important towns and ethnic groups in the Andes, 500–1500 *20*
Indian tribes of Eastern North America on the eve of European contact *24*
The community of Secota in Carolina as represented
   by Theodore De Bry *26*

Chapter 3

The paths of Spanish conquest in the Caribbean and North America *38*
The paths of Spanish and Portuguese conquests in South America *44*
Aztec warrior attire *48*
An Indian's depiction of the capture, imprisonment, and execution
   of Atahuallpa *55*

Chapter 4

The political organization of the Spanish and Portuguese American empires
   around 1700 *68*
An Andean Indian's depiction of some Spanish-American cities in the early
   seventeenth century *79*

An indigenous map of the Mexican community of Cuzcatlan in 1580   *82*
A portrait of a native Andean noblewoman in the mid-colonial period   *85*

Chapter 5

Major Indian peoples and European bases in Eastern North America in the
    mid-seventeenth century   *98*
Samuel de Champlain fighting with Indian forces attacking the Iroquois
    stronghold of Ticonderoga   *107*
A depiction of the Iroquois town of Hochelaga   *113*

Chapter 6

A depiction of the Indian community of Pomeiock   *128*
European colonies and important Indian peoples in Eastern North America in
    the mid-eighteenth century   *138*
Eastern North America after the French and Indian War   *142*

Chapter 7

A Brazilian Indian family   *158*
Native peoples and Portuguese settlements of coastal Brazil, c. 1560   *160*
A plan of a mission in San Antonio, Texas   *168*
A Mission Indian flutist in Central South America, c. 1750   *170*

 # Preface

The native peoples of the Americas numbered many millions when they first came into contact with persons from the Old World, but they soon suffered grievous losses in population from their initial exposure to a variety of epidemic diseases. Native peoples also often experienced casualties from military conflicts with the European settlers or against other indigenous societies who were responding to the unprecedented upheaval caused by the establishment of the early colonies. However, the devastation and adaptation that were very much part of this process did not erase the physical or cultural presence of the Indian peoples who continue to thrive in many nations in both North and South America.

In Canada, the Iroquois flourish to this day, many practicing a distinctive religion that emerged over a century and a half after their initial contact with Europeans. In the eastern United States, over the past quarter century, native peoples have successfully asserted their rights to extensive bodies of land—or considerable compensation for the loss of them—under colonial treaties. Tribes once thought to have disappeared have in recent decades gained recognition of their existence from the federal government.

In Latin America, native peoples living on their own land have endured, even sometimes prospered, to the present day. Some millions of people still speak indigenous languages as their primary means of communication. Written records in these languages date from very early in the colonial period and are still routinely generated in Mexico, Guatemala, Peru, and Bolivia, just to mention some of the major Latin American cases. Native religious beliefs and rituals are widely practiced, sometimes having been incorporated into the Christian faith. A new generation of self-conscious indigenous intellectuals has recently emerged. Such individuals are currently changing the role of the Maya Indians in

Guatemala, for example. In southern Mexico an Indian revolt has brought about widespread questioning of national policy toward native peoples and the natural resources they control.

In Guatemala, a fragile peace has finally emerged, ending a thirty-year civil war that killed tens of thousands of Mayans and displaced many more. In the Amazon River basin in Brazil and Ecuador, hunting and gathering peoples who have never been firmly subordinated to national governments are fighting physically and legally to gain secure title to their traditional lands and prevent the intrusions of oil companies and gold miners. In the Andes, over the past half century, native villages have been asserting ownership as collectives over the lands they occupy, requiring the break-up of privately owned landed estates.

This book explores the impact of the colonization of the Americas on the indigenous societies. It is explicitly comparative and seeks to explain how native cultures were transformed and adapted creatively to the unprecedented pressures placed on them by the European settlements planted in their midst. It likewise notes the manifold ways in which the local indigenous peoples modified the course of colonial history, affecting the economies, cultures, and social patterns of the European settlers.

Acknowledgments

The composition of this book has consumed much of my time over several years. Its elaboration benefitted greatly from the support I received from Roger Schlesinger, the chair of my department and himself a student of expansion and cultural interaction in the early modern period. But its intellectual genesis dates back nearly a quarter of a century, to my doctoral studies at the University of California, Los Angeles, with the fine social historians and ethnohistorians of the colonial Americas, James Lockhart, Gary Nash, and James Henretta. They and their colleagues in these fields of history will readily recognize their stamp in the pages that follow, at least in the better parts.

I began to think through the themes in this work in a systematic fashion and in a dialogue with other interested scholars in the late 1980s, first at a NEH Summer Institute held at The Newberry Library in Chicago, Illinois, and then at The John Carter Brown Library at Brown University in Providence, Rhode Island. As the suggested readings that follow each chapter make abundantly clear, I have drawn upon the insights of a number of scholars. Notable among these are Rolena Adorno, James Axtell, and William Taylor.

Special thanks are owed to Michael Adas, who initially helped me shape this project, and to Lyman L. Johnson and Rebecca Horn, who provided a detailed and thoughtful page-by-page reading of the book manuscript that contributed greatly to its improvement.

I wish also to acknowledge the commentaries provided by Felipe Fernández-Armesto, Susan Schroeder, Eric Van Young, Sherry L. Smith, Donald L. Fixico, and several anonymous reviewers.

Resilient Cultures

1

Introduction

For the Europeans who explored and colonized the Americas after 1492, the two continents constituted a new world, but for the native peoples whose known histories dated back hundreds of years and whose physical presence extended back thousands of years, these vast lands composed an ancient and familiar world. They had long intimacy with the peoples and environments around them. Trading networks, political alliances, and cultural influences were often far-reaching. Though these peoples divided themselves into a great number of ethnic groups and a variety of political arrangements, they routinely interacted with the societies around them. The relative isolation that characterized many of them by the nineteenth century resulted from the most deleterious effects of European settlement and did not reach back into precontact times. In fact, oftentimes such isolation did not appear even in the early decades after conquest by Europeans. Rather, it developed only gradually.

The early European observers of the peoples and lands of this New World had a most imperfect understanding of them, and their political and cultural agendas often led them to portray what they perceived in a most slanted manner. But substantial parts of the lives and cultures of the native peoples in the prehispanic centuries can be comprehended through wise use of archaeological evidence, the statements of early colonists (which can be compared to each other to filter out the less likely possibilities), and the recorded commentaries of native spokespersons. Finally, and more commonly than is generally known, the natives

1

expressed their histories and views of the world in writings and record books they composed themselves, having gained a written form of native or European languages through contact with settlers and missionaries. Sometimes, however, histories survived in wood or stone carvings or in scroll-like picture books that were elaborated in the centuries before the European arrival.

Once colonists established themselves in the Americas, the documentary evidence explodes in volume and complexity. Now many voices, native and European, in agreement and in conflict, can be heard. The scholar's task then is to choose the best evidence or reconcile different versions.

This book is profoundly comparative. It contrasts native societies in both of the American continents in the period just before the arrival of Europeans there, and occasionally relates some history of the even deeper past. It considers the nature of the encounters between diverse indigenous and European societies. It also examines how the colonies developed in response to the character of the natives in their vicinity, the local environment and natural resources, and the economic potential that the regions offered. In some colonies, the settlers incorporated the natives into their societies, largely because of the nature of these indigenous cultures; in others, frontiers developed, often with significant commerce emerging between the peoples on either side, that transformed both of them. And in yet other colonies, the settlers sought to eradicate or expel the native societies, forcing virtually all of them to the other side of a boundary that the settlers respected only until they needed additional land.

Further, the incorporation of the Americas into the rest of the world promoted the creation of the first true worldwide economic trading system, with Europeans transporting commodities from the Americas to Africa or South or East Asia, where they exchanged them for yet other goods that they shipped back to Europe and sometimes to the Americas themselves.

This book is arranged as follows. Chapter 2 considers the range of Indian histories and cultures before the arrival of the Europeans and introduces some important institutions and practices that would endure and affect the character of cultural interaction throughout the colonial period. Chapter 3 examines the motives and expectations of the Europeans in light of their contacts with other non-European peoples. It looks at the very early colonization in the Caribbean and then turns to the successful Spanish conquests of the great Indian empires, the Aztecs and the Incas. Finally, it addresses the much more limited military success and sometimes failure that the Spaniards experienced against a variety of semisedentary and nonsedentary peoples. Chapter 4 offers a systematic treatment of the responses of the advanced sedentary peoples to conquest and colonization by the Spanish. It deals with the perceptions and expectations each had of the other and considers material and cultural transformations, as well as retentions. Chapter 5 shifts attention to the peoples of eastern North America, with emphasis on the native interaction with the French and Dutch colonies. Chapter 6 devotes itself to the considerable subject of indigenous interaction with and impact on the British North American colonies. It argues that different patterns prevailed in the northern and southern colonies. Chapter 7 considers the interactions of the Spanish and Portuguese colonists with the many semisedentary and nonsedentary peoples of Latin America. These interactions differed dramatically from those with the sedentary imperial peoples treated in Chapter 4, and the responses and adjustments of these tribal cultures were quite different. Chapter 8 addresses the Columbian exchange and the importance of American silver in the creation and maintenance of the first global economy. By way of conclusion, it then reflects on some of the central issues raised in the preceding chapters.

2

The Native Societies of the Americas Before Contact

The Coming of Humans to the Americas and the Agricultural Revolution

Humans first came to the Americas at least 15,000 and possibly as early as 20,000 years ago as part of the vast and long-lasting migration of peoples into northeast Asia and then across a strip of land subsequently covered by the Bering Sea, separating Siberia from Alaska (a region commonly termed "Beringia". Like their contemporaries in the Old World, for thousands of years these peoples subsisted primarily as big-game hunters. They spread across both continents and reached the southern tip of South America about 12,000 years ago.

As they dispersed, new languages and ethnic identities developed, leading over time to great cultural diversity and intense rivalries. At the arrival of the Europeans, North America alone contained over 200 languages.

With the inundation of Beringia, the American peoples lost contact with, and eventually knowledge of, the Old World. They were as ignorant of Europe and the rest of the globe as the peoples there were of them. The Americas were briefly and tentatively connected with the rest of the world before the time of Columbus when the Vikings explored the North Atlantic around 1000 A.D. Norse ships almost certainly reached Newfoundland on several different occasions, but they fought with the natives and were never able to establish a stable settlement.

4

With their decline in subsequent centuries, the Norse ended their expeditions into the western Atlantic. Because they left few written records, knowledge of their discoveries faded rapidly into vague legends that circulated in Northern Europe. Hence these early contacts had no effect on the later initiation of European exploration across the Atlantic at the end of the fifteenth century.

Around 8,000 years ago, in central Mexico and in the Andes, human societies quite independently began to domesticate plants and to improve their yields, commencing America's agricultural revolution. The primary foods cultivated in the Americas differed from those found in the Old World. Maize quickly emerged as the most important grain in the Western Hemisphere. While maize cultivation developed independently in several widely separated regions, it spread very slowly. Although it was grown in central Mexico as early as 7,000 years ago, maize did not appear in the American southwest until around 1500 B.C. The peoples of eastern North America did not adopt it until nearly 2,000 years later.

Maize was generally cultivated with beans and squashes, commonly in the same fields. Collectively these vegetables provided a nutritious diet. In the highlands of the Andes, where the climate prevented the cultivation of these crops, native peoples raised potatoes as their staple. On some Caribbean islands, along the Atlantic coast, and extending well into the interior, manioc—a tuber—constituted the primary agricultural product. After being soaked, drained, ground up, and baked, manioc flour rendered an acceptable bread with high caloric value. More than any other factors, the nature and productivity of a region's agriculture, in combination with its environmental setting, shaped the organization and material cultures of the Native American peoples.

These societies had no durable metal tools; they refined and shaped gold, silver, and copper, but never iron nor any other hard metal suitable for tools and weapons. Andean societies did refine copper alloys, but they could not match the sharpness and resilience of bronze and steel. The Americas also lacked large draft animals for use in hauling or plowing. The near absence of domesticated animals limited the use of manure to fertilize fields. So agriculture prospered only where the land was inherently fertile or where humans could be organized to construct massive public works projects, such as terraces, irrigated fields, or drainage adjustments, to put more land into cultivation.

Crops, animals, and even cultural attainments tended to spread rather slowly across the Americas. The two continents in the Western Hemisphere run primarily North–South, unlike Europe and Asia, which extend far more along an East–West axis. This latter orientation means that vast expanses of the Old World share common environmental and climatic conditions, whether the frigid north, the temperate central zone, or the warmer south of Europe that extend eastward into the Middle East and then Central and East Asia. These vast zones broadly shared common or similar plants, animals, diseases, and cultural practices. Even when societies widely separated along the same parallel of latitude cultivated different grains (such as wheat and rice) or raised different animals (perhaps cattle and yaks), they still shared roughly similar growing seasons, and hence could depend equally on agriculture for their sustenance or could domesticate large animals to provide power, meat, skins, and milk.

Such wide distributions of similar patterns and practices could not prevail as readily in the Americas, for the North–South orientation dictated that the natives of that Hemisphere lived in a wide variety of incompatible environmental and climatic zones. The Americas were even further divided by some sharply defining geographical features, such as the Rocky Mountains of North America, the extensive northern desert of Mexico, and the Andean chain that runs down the entire western side of South America.

In this much less conducive physical setting, the indigenous peoples could not readily adopt the crops, animals, and even cultural attainments of other peoples who lived in quite distinct or distant environments. As already discussed, maize spread slowly into and across North America because of the very different environmental settings that marked that continent. Only considerable adaptation enabled the peoples in one zone to adopt the crop from the inhabitants of another. Potatoes could not be readily transferred from their ecological niche in the upper elevations of the Andes. The buffalo of western North America could not pass across the massive desert to populate Mexico or Central America. Likewise, the llamas, alpacas, and vicuñas of the Andean highlands could not thrive in the quite distinct environments even found quite nearby. The great civilizations and empires of the Aztecs and Incas, although exact contemporaries of each other, seemed unaware of each other, or only in the most hazy fashion. Metallurgy proliferated throughout the Andes for many hundreds of years before it was finally introduced in Mexico.

Sedentary Imperial Societies

About 3,500 years ago, sedentary agricultural communities emerged in both Mesoamerica and the Andean zone. Mesoamerica refers to the region of central Mexico, southern Mexico, Guatemala, and parts of Belize, El Salvador, and Nicaragua. The Andean zone comprises the Andean highlands from northern Chile into Colombia, the coastal zone of Peru rendered fertile by narrow river valleys, plus the extensive High Plain that reaches into central Bolivia from the west. Each of these separate, massive regions contained peoples who shared broadly comparable high cultures. These culture zones relied on agriculture for the maintenance of their heavy population densities, although modest amounts of animal and fish protein complemented their diets. The steady, intense cultivation of land in these areas yielded reliable, substantial food surpluses, enabling a minority of people in each community to become full-time craft specialists, transporters and traders, priests, and professional military men. Hereditary local nobilities and ruling families arose within each ethnic group as well. Some of the most important ethnic provinces contained cities of substantial size: cities with populations in the tens of thousands were not unusual, and at least two cities with over 200,000 people arose in Mexico, the most densely settled region of size in the pre-Columbian Americas. These sedentary societies also constructed monumental architecture—palaces, temples, and pyramids—and elaborate, exquisitely laid out ceremonial and governmental complexes.

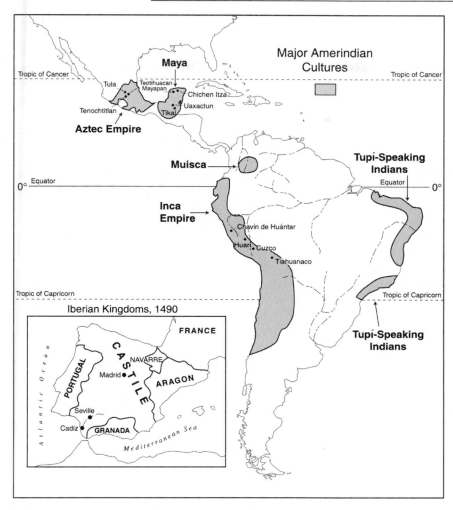

Major Indian cultures of Latin America in 1500 *(Mark A. Burkholder and Lyman L. Johnson,* Colonial Latin America, *4th ed. New York: Oxford University Press, 2001. Used by permission of Oxford University Press, Inc.)*

At least 2,000 years before the arrival of Europeans, the agricultural societies of Mexico began to organize themselves into states—political units with recognized boundaries administered by permanent officials who received incomes for their services, and with formal systems of justice, supervised by judges who imposed rulings and punishments dispassionately according to established codes of law. Mayan polities emerged in the area of the Yucatan Peninsula about two millennia ago. The Olmec civilization, located to the west of the Peninsula, predates the Maya by a millennium and may have developed its own political structures. State-organized Teotihuacán appeared in central Mexico 500 years after the Maya.

Organized states apparently emerged centuries later in the Andean region. Tiahuanaco, which clearly had state structures, appeared 1,500 years ago and ruled much of the central highlands for 5 centuries. Too little is known about such significant coastal cultures as Paracas, Nazca, and the Moche, all of which developed more than 2,000 years ago, to determine whether they had state structures.

No state-organized indigenous societies existed in North America when Europeans made their initial contacts in the sixteenth century. However, between 800 and 1500, a series of temple-mound builder cultures had proliferated throughout the greater Mississippi River basin and in the Southeast. These were characterized by urban sites centered around temple platforms and massive mounds constructed over many decades. Each of these sites was populated by thousands of residents, with the several largest containing some tens of thousands.

The city of Cahokia in southwestern Illinois, with its huge ceremonial mound, thrived between 1050 and 1200, numbering approximately 30,000 inhabitants, and dominating some 50 surrounding communities. Apparently the introduction of new varieties of maize and beans from Mexico had provided the additional nutrition needed to sustain this notable population increase. But all such early cities inevitably developed unhealthy living conditions due to the lack of efficient waste-disposal systems, exacerbated by the unprecedented population density. These deficiencies may have caused the collapse of such civilizations.

Sedentary societies were organized into ethnic provinces. A permanent council made up of representatives from the most distinguished noble families typically governed these politics. Each had a ruler whose power varied greatly from case to case. Sometimes these ethnic lords held virtually absolute authority and claimed descent from the gods, but other times they functioned more as spokesmen for their polities, and needed support from the noble families to carry out policies.

The cultural attainments of these sedentary agricultural peoples were manifold. Perhaps most dramatic were the many physical improvements that they carried out to put more land under cultivation and to improve crop yields. They terraced hills and mountainsides, dug canal systems, maintained intricate irrigation complexes, raised artificial fields alongside water sources, utilized decaying vegetation as fertilizer, and in lake regions, constructed fields along the shores just above the water line and used the currents to bring nutrients to the crops. These fields, called *chinampas* in Mexico and often misrepresented as "floating gardens" (they were built into the lakebeds and never floated), could render two to four harvests a year and supplied large amounts of food to urban areas, which otherwise would have had difficulty obtaining adequate food from the countryside.

The densely settled peoples also designed massive urban complexes and residential and ceremonial structures. Some 3,000 years ago, the Olmecs of Mexico, who inhabited the tropical coastal region along the Gulf of Mexico in parts of the modern states of Veracruz and Tabasco, had already constructed large and elaborate ceremonial centers that consisted of complexes of pyramids,

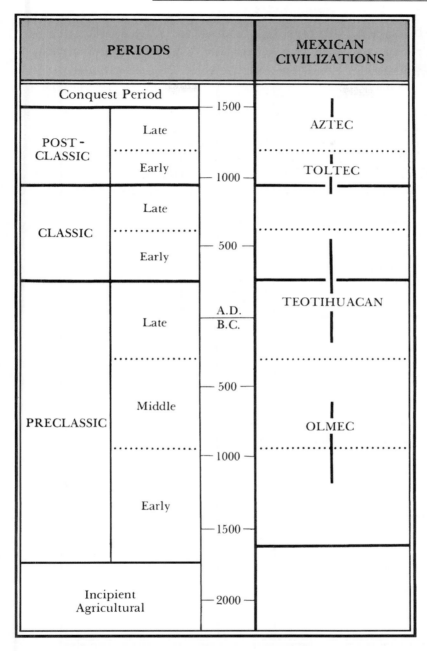

PERIODS			MEXICAN CIVILIZATIONS
Conquest Period		1500	
POST-CLASSIC	Late		AZTEC
	Early	1000	TOLTEC
CLASSIC	Late		
	Early	500	
PRECLASSIC	Late	A.D. / B.C.	TEOTIHUACAN
	Middle	500	
		1000	OLMEC
	Early	1500	
Incipient Agricultural		2000	

Chronology of Central Mexican history up to European contact
(Geoffery W. Conrad and Arthur A. Demarest, Religion
and Empire: The Dynamics of Aztec and Inca Expansionism,
New York: Cambridge University Press, 1984, p. 14.
Reprinted with permission of University Press.)

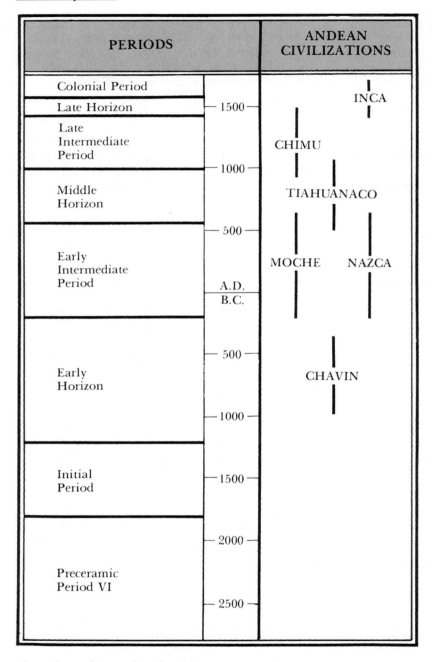

Chronology of Central Andean history up to European contact
(*Geoffery W. Conrad and Arthur A. Demarest,* Religion
and Empire: The Dynamics of Aztec and Inca Expansionism,
New York: Cambridge University Press, 1984, p. 87.
Reprinted with permission of University Press.)

mounds, altars, and mosaic inlaid floors. The scale and magnificence of Olmec monumental architecture reflect the Olmecs religious beliefs (to be motivated to erect these massive arenas of devotion), the ability to marshal regular agricultural surpluses to feed the thousands of builders of the sites (who required vast amounts of food, while not themselves being engaged in productive agriculture), and the stability and efficiency of social and occupational hierarchies (to build these structures over decades under the supervision of rulers and to require a variety of specialized artisans).

The civilization based in the enormous city of Teotihuacan that blossomed in central Mexico emerged some 2,000 years ago and thrived for more than 800 years. Teotihuacan contained dozens of temple complexes located over 20 square kilometers of territory. Far from being just a religious center, it constituted a city of around 200,000 people, who lived in more than 2,200 residential compounds apparently organized around kinship groups. Teotihuacan enjoyed a formal empire in central Mexico, but its cultural influence and trading circuits extended throughout virtually all of Mesoamerica.

Urban orientation characterized the societies in the sedentary agricultural zones of the Americas for many hundreds of years before the arrival of Europeans. Members of the first Spanish expeditions spoke admiringly of the cities of Mesoamerica and the Andes, noting the regularity of the streets and canals and the symmetry and quality of the large structures. Bernal Díaz del Castillo, who was a member of Cortés's expedition when it entered Tenochtitlan, the vast island capital of the Aztecs in 1519, remarked in his history of the conquest,

> Next morning, we came to a broad causeway and continued our march
> towards Iztapalapa. And when we saw all those cities and villages built
> in the water, and other great towns on dry land, and that straight and
> level causeway leading to Mexico, we were astounded. These great
> towns and *cues* (temples) and buildings rising from the water, all made
> of stone, seemed like an enchanted vision from the tale of Amadis (a
> famous late medieval romantic novel). Indeed, some of our soldiers
> asked whether it was not all a dream.[1]

The population of the largest cities in the Americas far exceeded that of their counterparts in Spain, and probably all cities in Europe except for London, Paris, and Rome. The Aztec capital of Tenochtitlan contained perhaps 250,000 inhabitants; Cuzco, the Inca counterpart, held around 60,000. Aquaducts provided clean water to the urban population, and dependable urban services removed both human waste and garbage safely away from contact with people and potable water sources. Pedro Sancho described Cuzco as follows:

> Most of the buildings are built of stone and the rest have half their
> facade of stone. There are also many adobe houses, very efficiently
> made, which are arranged along straight streets in a cruciform plan.
> Their streets are all paved, and a stone-lined water channel runs down
> the middle of each street.[2]

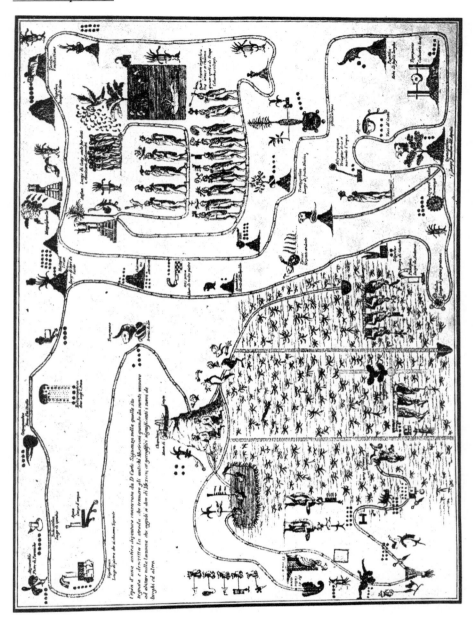

An early colonial Mexican Codex depicting the Aztec migration myth *(Geoffery W. Conrad and Arthur A. Demarest,* Religion and Empire: The Dynamics of Aztec and Inca Expansionism, *New York: Cambridge University Press, 1984, p. 21. Used by permission.)*

The sedentary peoples also devised scientific advances, including highly ac-curate annual calendars that were as accurate if not more than those of Europe at the same time. They made considerable use of numerical systems, generally with "twenty" rather than "ten" serving as the base number. Skilled astronomers, they understood and graphically represented the movement of the moon, sun, and stars. The peoples of central Mexico, though not those of the Andes, had devel-oped symbolic representation systems and illustrated long scrolls (called codices) that had begun to approximate a writing system based on letters and syllables. This tradition of writing probably explains why the peoples of Mexico quickly learned to write their own languages and hence their own literature and histori-cal records in the Spanish alphabet after the arrival of the Europeans. Michael Coe, Dean Snow, and Elizabeth Benson describe the complexity of Maya writing as follows:

> The Maya script was the only *complete* writing system in the ancient
> New World: that is, only the Maya could express in writing everything
> that was in their language. It was a complex mixture of ideographic and
> phonetic elements, similar in structure to certain scripts of the Old
> World, such as Sumerian, Egyptian, and Japanese. Since the system
> included a complete syllabary (i.e. a symbol for each syllable), they
> could in theory have written everything phonetically, but like the
> Japanese they did not because the ideographs continued to have
> immense prestige and probably even religious overtones.[3]

Because some pre-Columbian written sources have been preserved, we have learned about aspects of Mesoamerican history that examination of the physical remains of these civilizations alone would not have yielded. Instead, modern scholars compose accounts of these peoples that address rulers, dynas-ties, priests, migrations, the foundation and abandonment of cities, and military campaigns, among other topics.

The sedentary imperial peoples all developed profound and complex reli-gious systems, virtually always including a spectrum of gods, with each god iden-tified with certain attributes and natural functions. The gods of different ethnic groups generally resembled each other in important ways, but each society had one or two gods who were distinctive to it and who were worshiped with special fervor. People expected direct benefits from their gods, anticipating healthy births, good harvests, and military victories in return for the proper performance of religious rituals. Failures in important aspects of life would cause the devotees first to question whether they had followed proper ceremony and then even to doubt the effectiveness of the god being beseeched. Commoners were extremely devout and obedient to both their gods and their own secular rulers as long as events developed favorably, but a reversal of fortune could quickly make them question the rightfulness of either a god or a particular ruler.

In Mesoamerica the concept of time was very much caught up in religious belief. The peoples there believed that the gods had already created and destroyed four worlds, and they were living in the fifth age, whose survival was tenuous. Moreover, they were prone to think of time—and of the sequence of events embedded in it—as cyclical rather than linear. They sought to discern patterns in their individual and collective lives that had been prefigured in an earlier period to understand what was likely to occur next—or as important, what *should* occur next.

> The historical traditions that have survived say much about how the preconquest and conquest-era peoples of central Mexico viewed the workings of their complex society and cosmos. Their reality, as they conceived it, was acknowledged and understood as the outcome and hence the repetition of past events, by which it was endowed with the legitimacy of antiquity.[4]

Mesoamerican peoples, like many others in the Americas, practiced limited forms of human sacrifice, offering the lives of a few victims—typically the most valiant and respected—to their gods. The Aztecs, however, made human sacrifice the centerpiece of their worship to the sun god named Huitzilopochtli. The annual number of victims seems to have been in the thousands.

This practice should not be confused with cannibalism, the consumption of human flesh, which was very limited both in the number of peoples who practiced it and the types of occasions when it was permitted. The sedentary agricultural societies did not consume human flesh for nutrition. However, during certain rituals designated individuals ate small amounts of cooked human flesh. These were usually the remains of recently slain enemy warriors of exceptional valor. The belief was that their personal qualities were absorbed along with the flesh.

Landholding Patterns and Forms of Production and Distribution

Much of the agricultural land in Mesoamerica and the Andean zone was held collectively by individual communities, which would periodically redistribute it among their member households as they grew or shrank in size and as new ones were formed through marriage. These lineage-based communities that owned land collectively were called *calpullis* in Mesoamerica and *ayllus* in the Andes. The assigned plots seem to have been worked by individual households, though the community cooperated as a group during planting and harvesting. Further, if one household was short of food, the others shared with it to ensure that no residents starved.

Rural villagers, however, practiced private ownership of land as well, and many maintained individual plots beyond the boundaries of the central village lands that were held in common. In addition, nobles owned lands as individuals

The Origins and great migration of the Mexica

Juan de Tovar lived his entire life in Mexico. After entering the Jesuit order in 1573, some fifty years after the conquest of Mexico, he became noted for his preaching among the Indians and for his knowledge of their language, Nahuatl. He gathered indigenous historical writings and interviewed contemporary native scholars about the pasts of their peoples. From them he composed his own "Account of the Origin of the Indians Who Live in this New Spain According to their Histories," from which the following passages derive.

The Indians of this New Spain, according to the usual account given in their histories, proceed from two different nations: one of these they call Nauatlaca, which means "people who express themselves and speak clearly," unlike the second nation, which in those times was very savage and barbaric, and whose sole occupation was hunting. The Nauatlaca called them Chichimeca, which means "hunting people," those who live from that rude and rustic occupation; and they also call them Otomi. The former name was given them because they all dwelt among the crags and in the most rugged places of the mountains, where they lived like beasts, lacking any civilized traits and going completely naked. . . . By the time the Chichimeca had acquired some civilized traits and the land was colonized and filled with the six tribes already mentioned, three hundred and two years had passed since they left their caves and ancestral seats. Now those of the seventh cave, which is the tribe of the Mexica, arrived in this land; they, like the others, came from the lands of Aztlan and Teoculhuacan. They were a warlike and hardy people who fearlessly undertook great deeds and exploits, and were civilized and refined. They brought with them an idol whom they called Huitzilopochtli, which means the left claw of a bird of shining plumage native to their land, from whose feathers they make figures and other beautiful things. They declare that this idol ordered them to leave their homeland, promising that he would make them princes and lords of all the provinces which the other six tribes had colonized, a land abounding in gold, silver, precious stones, feathers, and rich mantles, and all imaginable wealth. . . . When they had reached this hill of Chapultepec, near the great lagoon of Mexico, they established their camp with no little fear and apprehension because it was within the frontiers of the Tepaneca, a famous people who at that time were masters over all the other tribes, whose chief city and court was called Azcaputzalco, meaning "anthill," owing to the large number of people it had, as has already been explained. The Mexica settled in this place and built their rude houses, preparing to defend themselves as best they might. They asked their god what they ought to do; he answered that they must await the event, that he knew what they were to do and would let them know in good time.

Source: Juan de Tovar, "Relación del origen de los Indios que havitan en esta Nueva Espana segun sus historias," trans. by Frances López-Morillas, in John H. Parry and Robert G. Keith, eds., *New Iberian World,* Vol. I (New York: Times Books, 1984), pp. 52, 55, 57. Reprinted by permission of Edward J. Joyce, trustee.

(really as representatives of their lineages) and supervised permanent retainers who worked exclusively for them.

Such important entities as government posts, priesthoods, temples, and the military had lands assigned to their support. Commoners routinely cultivated these plots as part of their rotary draft labor service (performing labor in predictable turns as directed by their leaders). The harvest was used to maintain the officeholder, religious structure, military unit, or the like.

In these sedentary societies, men dominated work in the fields, although women seem to have assisted them at particularly busy times such as planting and harvesting. Women operated the households, often clustered into residential compounds, prepared and stored foods, and wove cloth, a crucial function in their economies.

These cultures were highly patriarchal, practicing a doctrine of masculine priority in politics and household governance. The senior man in any family lineage generally headed up the group compound in which other members of his descent group resided. When a compound grew overlarge, it would spin off a new one, itself focused around another senior man from the same lineage. Wives did not invariably move into their husband's compound after marriage, though they did frequently. Sometimes the husband moved into the family compound of the wife, or more rarely they both moved to that of a distant relative of one of them. Individuals of both sexes often measured their descent lines through both their mother and father.

Mesoamerica differed greatly from the Andean zone in the distribution of goods. Mesoamerica had long enjoyed vibrant exchange systems and marketplaces, some local and others regional in scope, in which people bartered a great variety of goods and foods. These events were held regularly on certain days in different communities. Women dominated the local markets both as buyers and sellers; special long-distance merchants, who were predominantly men, monopolized at least some types of trade in high-value goods. While no currency ever developed as a standard medium of exchange, the value of trade goods was sometimes expressed in numbers of cacao beans (for they were rather uniform in size and greatly valued for the chocolate drink they rendered, a taste Spaniards quickly adopted after their arrival) and units of standard woven cloths.

Highly distinct ecological zones dominated much of the Andean region, imposed by the sharp verticality of that massive mountain range. Each elevation produced distinct commodities. For example, the Pacific lowlands produced cotton, the medium lowlands were suitable for maize cultivation, even higher elevations supported the cultivation of potatoes, and the highest arid plains afforded suitable pasture for llamas and alpacas. To avoid the uncertainty of trading with members of different ethnic and kinship groups, *ayllus* typically stationed to a branch at each distinct ecological zone. The exchange of vital goods then proceed to within the framework of the larger kinship group without reliance on outsiders. Hence the formal markets and long-distance trade and the larger process of open exchange between different localities and ethnic groups that long typified Mesoamerica were quite underdeveloped and tenuous in the Andes.

Important sites in the Valley of Mexico on the eve of
European contact *(Geoffery W. Conrad and Arthur A.
Demarest,* Religion and Empire: The Dynamics of Aztec and
Inca Expansionism, *New York: Cambridge University Press,
1984, p. 12. Reprinted by permission.)*

Monarchs governed the city-states that typified political organization in the ethnic provinces that dominated the sedentary agricultural zones. Although these rulers presented themselves as absolute dictators, in fact, they relied substantially on support from their extended kinship groups. These determined who would succeed to the throne, and they staffed many of the highest posts in the government. Royal family members appreciated that their own interests suffered when a weak ruler held power. They might lose parts of their empire, and consequently some of the tribute payments and labor service that produced most of their wealth. Therefore, they acted surreptitiously at times to remove flawed or ineffectual leaders. An early colonial chronicle from Mexico directly refers to such an act.

> During this time Tlacaelel (a revered, powerful member of the Aztec royal lineage) urged Tizoc (the emperor) to finish the building of the Great Temple because only a small part had been constructed. But before the work could begin, members of Tizoc's court, angered by his weakness and lack of desire to enlarge and glorify the Aztec nation, hastened his death with something they gave him to eat. He died in the year 1486, still a young man.[5]

Ascension to the throne did not generally pass to the late ruler's eldest son. Rulership more commonly passed from one brother to another until all suitable candidates within the generation had filled the post, whereupon it moved to the next generation, usually from uncle to nephew. Because noblemen in these societies had multiple wives (most of them arranged to establish political alliances), a royal family generally had a number of contenders—and considerable rivalry—for the throne. While the ruling family maintained the public image that the late ruler had chosen his successor before dying, considerable rivalry and coalition-building among the major contenders and their supporters seems to have preceded each transition. The victor sometimes had to execute disgruntled losers or face the possibility of revolts organized by them. Nonetheless, members of the royal lineage typically united when an external threat challenged their collective preeminence.

These political elites routinely demanded labor service from their subjects to construct and maintain the vast infrastructure—buildings, roads, bridges, religious complexes, irrigation works, terraces, and the like—of their provinces. The commoners delivered these services in rotation, working for a period of some months under the direction of community leaders. Their task completed, they returned home not be summoned again for a few years. This widespread practice can be termed rotary draft labor service. During their turn, workers expected to be treated well by the lords for whom they worked, receiving appreciation, housing, feasts, and drink. The participants viewed this as community service and reciprocal in nature. Rulers were expected to protect and sustain their people, leading the defense of their province if necessary and providing food from storehouses during times of shortage.

Prehispanic labor service patterns

In the mid-seventeenth century, some 125 years after the Spanish conquest of Peru, Father Bernabé Cobo, resident in that colony, set about to assemble material for a history of the New World, with considerable emphasis on the Andean region. He assembled a considerable library of information on the local peoples, which he used to compose a history of the Inca empire. In this passage, he describes the labor service system utilized by the empire.

Apart from the work the people did in place of tax or tribute by cultivating the fields and raising the livestock of the Inca and religion and by doing the other jobs and tasks that we have told about, they had to make a very great contribution of men and laborers for all of the jobs and work done throughout the kingdom for the service and utility of the king as well as for the republic. The taxpayers came to these jobs by turns of *mita* (as they say), when each person was called; and they all took part in the occupations and chores that the Inca and his governors assigned to them.

Source: Father Bernabé Cobo, *History of the Inca Empire,* trans. by Roland Hamilton (Austin: University of Texas Press, 1979), p. 231.

Empires and Warfare

The autonomous ethnic provinces of the sedentary agricultural zones produced both healthy surpluses of food and specialized craft goods, such as wood carvings, fine metalwork, and feather work, sometimes made into entire garments or headdresses. Rival ethnic states habitually launched military campaigns against each other to impose political control and to demand labor service and tribute payments in the form of stipulated amounts of scarce commodities or finely crafted goods. They rarely demanded basic agricultural products, for each people generally produced a surplus of the same items.

Pedro de Cieza de León, an inquisitive early settler of Peru, provides this description of the Inca method of expansion.

They marched from Cuzco with their army and warlike materials, until they were near the region they intended to conquer. Then they collected very complete information touching the power of the enemy, and whence help was likely to reach them, and by what road. This being known, the most effective steps were taken to prevent the succor from arriving, either by large bribes given to the allies, or by forcible resistance. . . . They sent chosen men to examine the land, to see the roads, and learn by what means they were defended, as well as the places whence the enemy received supplies. When the road that should be

Important towns and ethnic groups in the Andes, 500–1500
(*Luis Lumbreras, "Andean Urbanism and Statecraft" (C.E. 550–1450),
in Frank Salomon and Stuart B. Schwartz, eds.,* The Cambridge History
of the Native Peoples of the Americas, *volume III, South America,
part I, New York: Cambridge University Press, 1999. Reprinted by permission.)*

taken and the necessary measures were decided upon, the Inca sent special messengers to the enemy to say that he desired to have them as allies and relations, so that, with joyful hearts and willing minds they ought to come forth to receive him in their province, and give him obedience as in the other provinces; and that they might do this of their own accord he sent presents to the native chiefs.[6]

In Mesoamerica, empires reached back fully 2,000 years. In its central region, a succession of powerful empires emerged, each of which lasted hundreds of years. The last empire—the Aztecs—was conquered by Cortés's expedition in 1521.

The conquering powers did not normally demand that their newly subject provinces abandon their local cultures and distinctive ethnic identities, including their pantheons of gods. However, the conquered peoples considered the victorious power to have benefitted from the superiority of its primary god or gods, so often added one or two of the new gods to their existing set. Imperial centers even permitted subordinated provinces to retain their traditional ruling families. They utilized them to extract labor service and, in the case of Mexico, tribute payments of specialized products and craft goods from their people. Subject provinces often rose up against these impositions, and conquering states then had to use their armies to subdue them anew, and not just to expand the boundaries of the empire.

These densely populated states could amass enormous armies. They maintained expeditions that numbered in the tens of thousands in the field for months at a time, making use of storehouses they placed along their routes. However, organization of these armies was very hierarchical and inflexible. For example, when a unit's commander was killed or captured, his entire force withdrew from action, considering that it had failed in its mission. Commoners participated in campaigns as part of their expected labor service to the state. Hence most warfare occurred in the months that followed harvest. Some military powers established battalions of professional soldiers, but they were quite limited in number.

The approach to warfare stressed formal announcement of a campaign, quite limited use of battlefield tactics, the preservation of the opponent's cities, fields, and noncombatants, and—in combat itself—emphasis on the taking of captives over the slaying of the enemy. Certain exceptions must be acknowledged, however. For example, the Incas devastated the Cañari people located in the northern Andes. But as settlements and civilians were generally secure from attack, the sedentary peoples did not fortify their cities with walls and other defensive apparatus. The militaries made only very limited use of bows and arrows and lances, perhaps because the lack of metal tips made them rather ineffectual weapons in the large-unit operations that characterized warfare in these sedentary zones. The basic weapon was a carved wooden club commonly imbedded with obsidian or flint chips. Of course, as the Americas lacked horses, no cavalry existed.

The Aztec army at war

Diego Durán came to Mexico as a child shortly after the conquest and lived his life there as a Dominican friar. He was an acute student of Aztec culture and history, composing two massive books based heavily on indigenous writings. In this section from his detailed history, Durán gives a close account of an Aztec military campaign.

News came that the Huaxtecs had attacked and killed all the merchants and traders who were active in that area, leaving not one alive. Most of these men had come from Tenochtitlan and its provinces. . . . The news of the Huaxtec rebellion and the death of merchants, who had been cast from great heights into ravines below, was brought to Motecuhzoma [the first of that name, who ruled some fifty years before the one defeated by Cortés] by people of Tulantzinco. The king thanked them and ordered that they be attended well. Then he summoned Tlacaelel [his senior advisor] and asked him to send envoys to Tezcoco, Tacuba, Chalco, Xochimilco, and all the neighboring towns. Since the aggression had been directed at the people of all these cities, retaliation must be taken by all of them. They were ordered to prepare for war, to obtain provisions and all the necessary arms, tents, and fighting equipment that they would need for the conflict. . . . Then some seasoned warriors began to marshal the troops and prepare them for battle. These men, who had authority in thus ordering the soldiers, were very well armed and they carried staffs in their hands and wore headbands, long shell earrings, and labrets. . . . All these soldiers were ordered to lie down upon the earth with their shields and swords in their hands, as if in an ambush. There were about two thousand men from all the provinces, and in this way they were covered with grass until not a man could be seen. Then the captains and seasoned soldiers were formed into squadrons, and next to each experienced soldier was placed a youth, one of those new recruits who had never been to war before. Orders were given to the soldiers to take care of these younger men and give them protection. . . . Once the battle had begun, the Aztecs, seeing this ferocious, frightful enemy, and hearing the ghastly howls that issued from their throats--which made their hair stand on end--pretended to retreat. They went back to the place where the great warriors waited in ambush. When the enemy had entered the trap, the men concealed by the grass stood up and, with great fury, surrounded them, taking many prisoners and killing others. Not one Huaxtec escaped. Even the youths took many captives and all the prisoners were taken to Tenochtitlan.

Source: Fray Diego Durán, *The History of the Indies of New Spain*, trans. by Doris Heyden (Norman: University of Oklahoma Press, 1994), pp. 160, 161, 164, 165. Copyright © 1994 by the University of Oklahoma Press. Reprinted by permission.

Semisedentary Societies

Although the sedentary imperial peoples of the Americas attained the most complex civilizations, semisedentary peoples who practiced a less intensive form of agriculture imposed by the limitations of their natural environments inhabited much more territory in the two continents. They had to move their settlements to nearby fresh lands every few years and supplement cultivation with hunting, fishing, and trapping to round out their dietary needs. A major consequence of their limited agricultural output was a substantially lower population density than the fully sedentary peoples.

In North America virtually the entire region south of the Great Lakes and the St. Lawrence River and east of the Mississippi River was inhabited by semisedentary peoples. Given the general expanse of forests throughout this region before the coming of Europeans (though the types of forests varied considerably from one locality to another), the peoples who lived there—though representing a diversity of ethnicities and languages—shared a broadly comparable material culture and way of life and hence are commonly referred to as Eastern Woodlands Indians. (Do recall, however, that a series of densely populated and urban-based civilizations prospered in the Mississippi River basin and the nearby Southeast for centuries before they collapsed over the several hundreds of years before the arrival of Europeans.) West of the Mississippi, the land was much less forested and of significantly lower agricultural quality, so most of the peoples who inhabited its vastness were hunters and gatherers. Exceptions include the ancient agricultural societies situated in certain parts of the American southwest (today known as the Pueblos), and the societies located along the Pacific coast who thrived from fishing and some limited agriculture.

Semisedentary societies inhabited Central America south of the Mesoamerican-boundary and roughly the northern half of South America east of the Andes, the area that now encompasses much of Colombia, Venezuela, Brazil, and Bolivia. The vast Amazon River basin contained many such semisedentary peoples; it was much more densely populated than is the case presently. Even Chile and Paraguay included substantial semisedentary communities, though they were surrounded by less inviting terrain inhabited by hunters and gatherers.

Tremendous cultural variation existed among these semisedentary societies. They all practiced agriculture, but their dependence on it varied greatly according to the local environmental setting. Also, those peoples situated near the complex civilizations of the sedentary agricultural zones were inevitably influenced by their cultural achievements. Such was not the case among those who lived in areas more distant and less accessible to these complex societies.

Semisedentary societies did not generally attempt permanent improvements, such as terraces or raised fields, to increase agricultural productivity. Rather, they depended almost exclusively on swidden agriculture (also known as slash and burn). With swidden agriculture the members of an entire community cut down the brush and small trees in a certain area and then burned them. The site was then suitable for cultivation, with the ash providing fertilizer.

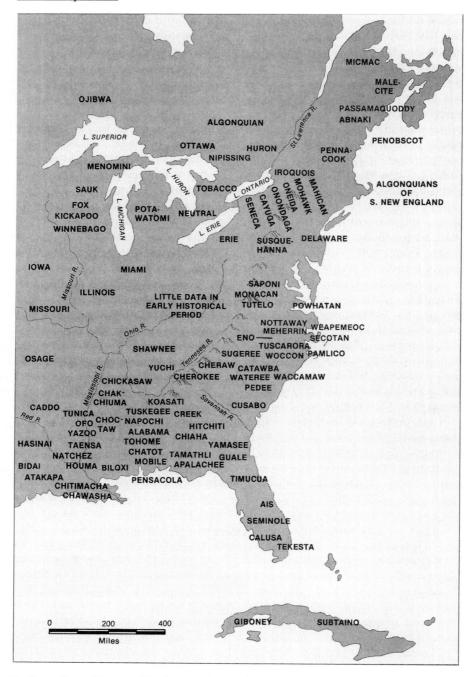

Indian tribes of Eastern North America on the eve of European contact
(*Gary B. Nash,* Red, White, and Black: The Peoples of Early North America,
*3rd ed., 1992. Reprinted by permission of Pearson Education, Inc., Upper Saddle
River, NJ.*)

Generally, such a field provided three to five years of good harvests before output declined drastically because of the decrease of nutrients in the soil. The community then moved to the next promising location a short distance away and carried out the same procedure. The process continued time after time within a circumscribed zone until the earliest cultivated area was once more fully overgrown with foliage that could be cut down, burned, and cultivated anew, a period of time usually around twenty-five years. Thus the community's mobility took place within a well-delimited region within boundaries that the community and nearby groups recognized (which is not to say that a rival might not encroach on it or raid into it). Hence all these periodic community migrations took on a predictable character, following a certain circuit that would take the inhabitants to fields that they or their parents had worked about a generation before.

The many semisedentary peoples scattered across such vast and distinctive territories developed a great variety of social and cultural practices. Among the Eastern Woodlands peoples of North America, the men worked to clear and burn down fields, but only women actually cultivated the crops, generally working in gangs in the fields and assisting each other with child care.

Anthony F. C. Wallace describes the practice of agriculture among the Seneca people of the Iroquois Confederation as follows:

> The responsibility for carrying on this extensive agricultural
> establishment rested almost entirely on the women. Armed with crude
> wooden hoes and digging-sticks, they swarmed over the fields in gay,
> chattering work bees, proceeding from field to field to hoe, to plant, to
> weed, and to harvest. An individual woman might, if she wished, "own"
> a patch of corn, or an apple or peach orchard, but there was little reason
> for insisting on private tenure: the work was more happily done
> communally, and in the absence of a regular market, a surplus was of
> little personal advantage, especially if the winter were hard and other
> families needed corn. In such circumstances hoarding led only to hard
> feelings and strained relations as well as the possibility of future
> difficulties in getting corn for oneself and one's family.[7]

Perhaps because they produced most of the nutrition, women enjoyed considerable political power in some of these semisedentary societies. They had to approve policies and diplomatic arrangements worked out by chiefs before they could be implemented. Lineage was measured through the female line, and residence in longhouses and family compounds was organized around one's relationship to the senior female who headed the residential complex. When daughters married, their husbands moved into the longhouse with them. Divorces were common and easily arranged. Unmarried sons remained in their mother's house. The senior female of the clan assigned men's work and their participation in blood feuds on its behalf. Men spent great amounts of time away from their villages and families, hunting, trapping, fighting, and conducting diplomacy, all of which took them into the uninhabited countryside.

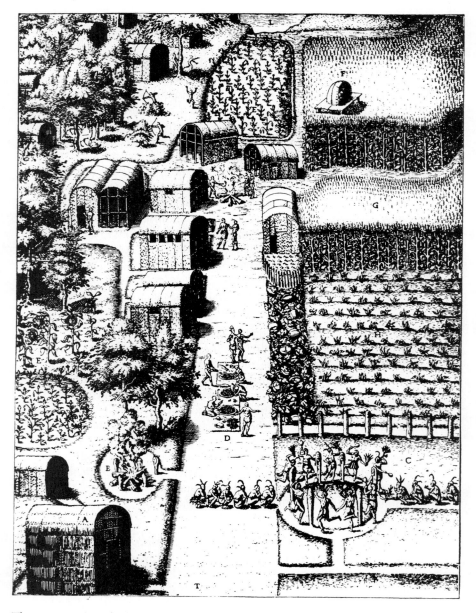

The community of Secota in Carolina as represented by
Theodor De Bry *(Ernest and Johanna Lehner,* How They
Saw the New World, *New York, Tudor Publishing Company, 1966.)*

Such arrangements were present in South America as well, most particularly among the Guaraní in what is now Paraguay. There, too, women dominated

agriculture, headed lineages, organized work and warfare, and had considerable voice in political deliberations.

The decreased nutrition that this way of life provided, together with the required periodic movement of the community, determined that semisedentary peoples maintain a significantly lesser population density than the fully sedentary peoples. Further, semisedentary societies had somewhat less occupational and social elaboration. Few if any full-time artisans and other specialists could maintain themselves; virtually everyone engaged in agriculture most of the time. As there were few specialized craft items or local commodities, trade among communities was rudimentary and regular markets as they existed in Mesoamerica were little known.

Some semisedentary peoples practiced cannibalism for nutrition. The most notorious were the Caribs of the southern Caribbean islands and the northern shoreline of South America and the Tupinambá located along the Atlantic coastline of Brazil. Most of their victims were captives taken in raids by one settlement against another as part of longstanding campaigns of vengeance against traditional enemies.

The Primacy of Community and Lineage

Few social institutions or loyalties existed above the village level. In fact, even the community endured a certain instability, as lineages within it might spin off to found their own hamlets. The numerous semisedentary societies in the Americas never organized themselves into states with true political structures and institutions. At the time of the European arrival, the most complex alliance among such peoples was the Iroquois confederation of five tribes who saw themselves as sharing a common ethnicity. But this confederation functioned primarily as a nonaggression pact among the participants. It provided neither for coordinated military operations in the event of warfare against other peoples nor for a council of representatives from the five tribes to set policy.

Some civilizations that had once been sedentary agricultural and state organized in character later became semisedentary and tribally organized after their cultures faded due to some combination of famine, environmental exhaustion, disease, and warfare. Such was the case with the Mississippi mound builders, but an even more dramatic episode caused the dissolution of the highly accomplished Maya civilization.

This civilization—never an empire—in southern Mexico and Guatemala thrived for well over a millennium before it collapsed in the ninth century A.D. Its achievements include writing, sophisticated mathematics and astronomical knowledge, and the construction of substantial, beautiful cities and ceremonial centers in the rugged jungle of the Yucatan Peninsula. In the classic period at least several cities had populations that numbered in the tens of thousands. The integrated cultural sophistication, urban focus, and dynamic trade networks of the classic Maya were based on substantial agricultural engineering, using networks of canals and raised fields. When the Maya abandoned these agricultural

complexes because of the still incompletely understood combination of in-
ternecine warfare, famine, and internal revolts during the ninth century, they did
not disappear.   In fact, some ethnic provinces, such as Mayapan and Chichen
Itza, endured over subsequent centuries, but they were nonetheless pale imita-
tions of the previous broad-based civilization.

Most areas reverted to village-based, subsistence-oriented, swidden agriculture (in other words they became semisedentary), and ceased to calculate
their calendars and to write their histories (enterprises that must have been the
domain of the elites who were repudiated in the collapse). Likewise the cities and
ceremonial centers lost their purpose and were left to become overgrown. With
the abandonment of artisan craft and regional commodity production specialization, the elaborate trade systems (and market towns, transporters, and merchants that had been sustained by them) dried up.   Hence when Europeans
arrived in the region of the Maya, they were mystified by such great, overgrown
temples, palaces, and complexes lying ignored throughout the peninsula in the
midst of scattered, locally oriented, villages.

Communities of semisedentary peoples tended to be led by chiefs who
spoke for their people and who led rituals and war parties but who lacked political authority. Instead, these communities—desperately needing to maintain internal cohesion—practiced consensus politics, wherein virtually every family
had to agree to any important decision. Chiefs could not insist on tribute payments or labor service from their people. No permanent nobility existed. Chiefs
were selected for particular diplomatic or military campaigns, but their authority did not generally persist after their conclusion. Nor could the offspring of
chiefs anticipate succeeding their fathers.

While warfare against other lineages, communities, and sometimes entire
tribes was common (perhaps endemic) among the semisedentary peoples, conquest, long-term subordination, and the delivery of tribute or labor service were
unknown.   These societies provided no basis for empire—each community
would have to be subjugated in turn, and its members could always flee into the
hinterland. As among the sedentary imperial societies, the warfare of semisedentary peoples typically involved few casualties and did not emphasize the taking or
destruction of the opponent's community or the slaughter of noncombatants.
Groups undertook warfare to right a perceived wrong or injury inflicted on them
by outsiders or to enable their men to gain honor and status through their military accomplishments. (As all of the peoples in a given region produced essentially the same basic goods and few if any specialized or luxury items, the
possibility of plunder did not incite attacks.) The men of a lineage or a community assaulted their counterparts in the forest or open country. The rugged countryside lent itself to ambushes and quick retreats. Greater prestige was afforded
to the capture of an opponent than killing him, even though the commonality
with which these peoples used bows and arrows—when compared to sedentary
societies—made them more lethal.   Some of these groups, particularly in
more tropical areas, used poisoned arrows, the single indigenous weapon the
Europeans would truly fear.

Captives brought back to the village were usually ritually tortured to death
(in the process, supposedly righting the wrong inflicted) or were—somewhat less

often, it seems—adopted into the lineage to replace the person whose death or injury engendered the warfare in the first place. Many societies in both North and South America adopted outsiders—and sometimes entire remnant communities or tribes—into their midst, a practice often witnessed (and probably more often needed) when the arrival of Europeans brought with it both more deadly warfare and the decimation of entire villages and tribes.

Nonsedentary (or Nomadic) Peoples

Lands unsuitable for any kind of cultivation—deserts, plains (whose hard-packed soils would require plows for productive agriculture), high mountains, and some tropical zones—were inhabited by nonsedentary (or nomadic) peoples. These rugged peoples lived rudimentary lives based on hunting and gathering. Completely dependent on the unimproved resources of their surroundings, the nomadic bands could not achieve a substantial population density. They clustered in small bands organized around descent groups and moved about within a circumscribed area, as the seasons and animal migrations dictated that grains, berries, nuts, and game could be found. (The most notable exception to this general pattern is the extensive desert region in the North American Southwest, where such complex cultures as the Anasazi and the Hohokam thrived for centuries, practicing extensive agriculture through careful use of the limited water sources.) Most of the hunters and gatherers of North America west of the Mississippi River except for some close to the Pacific Ocean fit this description, as do those in or near the Arctic region. So also do those of the deserts and mountains of northern Mexico and of the pampas and scrubland of Argentina, western Brazil, and eastern Bolivia. The northern and southern extremes of Chile also contained such peoples.

The nonsedentary peoples had no craft or social differentiation, only task specialization by gender, with the men as hunters and warriors and the women as gatherers and food processors. Their inherent mobility required that they have few possessions, and of course they erected no permanent structures. Highly egalitarian, they selected leaders for particular war campaigns or diplomatic undertakings, after which they enjoyed no special authority. Nor was there a special rank of priests; any man who felt that he had spiritual or healing powers could be accepted as a shaman as long as he found persons who accepted him as such.

With their ruggedness, mobility, knowledge of the land and climate, and stress on ambush, bows and arrows, and killing rather than capture in warfare, these nomadic tribes were formidable opponents against each other—for they typically had deep-set animosities against at least some of their neighbors—and against any semisedentary or sedentary peoples near whom they might reside. Of course, the nonsedentary would raid, loot, and withdraw, but they could not conquer and subordinate. However, sometimes a nomadic band ventured into a sedentary zone and remained; numerous such migrations are recorded (and, of course, semisedentary peoples could do much the same thing). They served as mercenaries in warfare and were assigned to live on marginal lands by the sedentary people they served. Over time, they became increasingly acculturated to the more sedentary way of life, but they might retain special pride in their origins and exploits in battle and hence a distinctive history and sense of themselves as a people. This process is well recorded in Mesoamerica, where the Mexica—the most powerful group in the Aztec alliance—were one such group.

> When they first arrived, the Mexicas, like the Chichimecs of Xolotl and even the early Toltecs, were by all accounts part-civilized and part-nomad. After settling in the Valley of Mexico, they would at times proudly proclaim their Chichimec, or nomad, ancestry, while at others they laid equal stress on their descent from the city-dwelling Toltecs. More probably, like so many of their neighbours, they were a fusion of two elements, migrant and sedentary.[8]

Migration of bands, villages, and complete ethnic groups was common in the history of the Americas, as was the reorganization of communities and the formation of new ones from disparate parts. The migration of groups and the creation of new communities seem to have long been characteristic of Andean societies; the Inca empire used the practice to its own advantage, locating contingents of friendly peoples among those with a heritage of hostility to the empire. The prehispanic Americas constituted a dynamic world in which new communities and alliances were constantly being formed.

The Native Population of the Americas on the Eve of Contact

I have left discussion of the population of the Americas on the eve of the arrival of the Europeans to last because of the impact that agriculture has on population densities. Sedentary peoples enjoyed much more substantial populations than semisedentary ones (and particularly large ones because of the commonality of urbanism among the fully sedentary societies of the Americas) and that in turn semisedentary peoples greatly outnumbered nonsedentary ones.

The population of both continents probably totalled approximately 60 million persons on the eve of contact with the rest of the world. The zone of greatest population was Mexico, with up to 20 million people. The Aztec empire embraced the majority of them. The Andean region, with more rugged country though agricultural as well, contained perhaps 12 million, with a very high percentage of them part of the Inca empire. The Caribbean and Central America were inhabited primarily by semisedentary peoples, yielding populations of around 5 million each. South America outside of the Andes contained mostly semisedentary peoples in its northern and central parts and nonsedentary ones more in the south, totalling altogether around 9–10 million people. North America held perhaps 7 million inhabitants, 5 million of those in what became the United States and an additional 2 million or so in what became Canada. Of these over two-thirds lived as semisedentary peoples east of the Mississippi River—the Eastern Woodlands Indians. The peoples of the western plains were, of course, largely dependent on hunting and gathering for their subsistence.

Two notable factors help to explain the significant population density achieved by the American peoples. First, maize was the primary grain cultivated in very substantial parts of both continents. It yielded more calories per acre than did any of the grains in the Old World at the same time. Second, having been cut off from the Old World for over 10,000 years, the Americas avoided exposure to some of the worst epidemic diseases that regularly ravaged other parts of the world.

Some comparison with figures for other parts of the world in 1500 is revealing. Europe west of Russia totalled 60–70 million; China alone reached 100–150 million. The Indian subcontinent totalled 75–150 million. All of Africa had a population of 36–72 million. The regions of most intensive agricultural cultivation in the Americas—central Mexico and some parts of the Andes—attained population densities that rivalled those of the Eastern Hemisphere's most populated regions located in China and the South Asian peninsula.

Conclusion

This portrait of the salient features of the vast number of distinct societies in the Americas before the arrival of Europeans demonstrates that it was truly an ancient land containing peoples who had a profound sense of their own history and intense pride in and identification with their particular ethnic identities. Some of the most famous native confederations and empires that the first colonists encountered—the Iroquois, Powhatans, Aztecs, and Incas, for example—proved to be relatively recent developments, ranging from several decades to several centuries of age when initially discovered. But these rather recent phenomena had built on centuries, even sometimes millennia, of cultural practices, interactions, and historical development in both North and South America. For if the peoples of the Americas possessed ancient histories and traditions, they were likewise dynamic, adaptable, and opportunistic by nature. Just a few of these precursors from earlier centuries include Cahokia, the Anasazi, the Olmecs, and the Moche. The nature of this study prevents mention of numerous advanced pre-Columbian civilizations that thrived for centuries, influenced enormous territories, and left behind extensive physical remains, and sometimes a record of their histories.

Their agricultural achievements and environmental settings (of course, inextricably interconnected) dictated the broad characteristics of the peoples of the Americas more than any other factors. The grouping of widely dispersed and ethnically distinct native societies into the encompassing classifications of sedentary, semisedentary, and nonsedentary, therefore, provides one of the fundamental units of organization of this present work. The substantial population density that characterized many areas in the Americas reflects the productive and cultural accomplishments of the inhabitants. Even certain semisedentary regions, such as central Colombia, the Amazon River basin, the major islands of the Caribbean, and the Mississippi River basin extending into the American southeast, are now understood to have maintained dense populations, with sizable communities and religious sites common in many areas.

Thriving, vigorous, and productive in the late fifteenth century, the peoples of the Americas had no reason to be cowed by the arrival of explorers and settlers from lands never imagined. Though afflicted in many cases by the devastating impact of colonization, the indigenous cultures responded creatively and dynamically, both shaping the colonial societies installed and adapting their own to their best advantage. Their histories over the subsequent five centuries, the first half or so of which is related in this volume, demonstrate time and again the validity of describing these peoples as "resilient cultures."

Select Bibliography

Adams, Richard E. W. *Ancient Civilizations of the New World.* Boulder, CO: Westview Press, 1997.

Berdan, Frances F. *The Aztecs of Central Mexico: An Imperial Society.* New York: Holt, Rinehart and Winston, 1982.

Boone, Elizabeth Hill. *Stories in Red and Black: Pictorial Histories of the Aztecs and Mixtecs.* Austin: University of Texas Press, 2000.

Clendinnen, Inga. *Aztecs: An Interpretation.* Cambridge, England: Cambridge University Press, 1991.

Coe, Michael, Dean Snow, and Elizabeth Benson. *Atlas of Ancient America.* New York: Facts on File, 1986.

Conrad, Geoffrey W. and Arthur A. Demerest. *Religion and Empire: The Dynamics of Aztec and Inca Expansionism.* Cambridge, England: Cambridge University Press, 1984.

Davies, Nigel. *The Ancient Kingdoms of Mexico.* Harmondsworth, England: Penguin Books, 1983.

Fiedel, Stuart J. *Prehistory of the Americas.* Cambridge, England: Cambridge University Press, 1987.

Hassig, Ross. *Aztec Warfare: Imperial Expansion and Political Control.* Norman: University of Oklahoma Press, 1988.

Hassig, Ross. *War and Society in Ancient Mesoamerica.* Berkeley: University of California Press, 1992.

Josephy, Jr., Alvin M., ed. *America in 1492: The World of the Indian Peoples Before the Arrival of Columbus.* New York: Alfred A. Knopf, 1992.

Lucena Salmoral, Manuel. *America 1492: Portrait of a Continent 500 Years Ago.* New York: Facts on File, 1990.

Morris, Craig and Adriana von Hagen. *The Inka Empire and Its Andean Origins.* New York: Abbeville Press, 1993.

Richter, Daniel K. *The Ordeal of the Longhouse: The Peoples of the Iroquois League in the Era of European Colonization.* Chapel Hill: University of North Carolina Press, 1992.

Rountree, Helen C. *The Powhatan Indians of Viginia: Their Traditional Culture.* Norman: University of Oklahoma Press, 1989.

Rouse, Irving. *The Tainos: Rise and Decline of the People Who Greeted Columbus.* New Haven:

Yale University Press, 1992.

Salisbury, Neal. *Manitou and Providence: Indians, Europeans, and the Making of New England, 1500–1643*. New York: Oxford University Press, 1982.

Sharer, Robert J. *The Ancient Maya*. 5th ed. Stanford: Stanford University Press, 1994.

Spalding, Karen. *Huarochirí: An Andean Society Under Inca and Spanish Rule*. Stanford: Stanford University Press, 1984.

Wallace, Anthony F. C. *The Death and Rebirth of the Seneca*. New York: Vintage Books, 1972.

Endnotes

1. Bernal Díaz, *The Conquest of New Spain,* trans. by J. M. Cohen (Hammondworth, England: Penguin Books, 1963), p. 214.

2. Pedro Sancho, *An Account of the Conquest of Peru,* trans. by Philip Ainsworth Means (New York: Cortes Society, 1917), p. 192.

3. Michael Coe, Dean Snow, and Elizabeth Bishop, *Atlas of Ancient America* (New York, Facts on File, 1986), p. 118.

4. Susan D. Gillespie, *The Aztec Kings: The Construction of Rulership in Mexica History* (Tucson: University of Arizona Press, 1989), p. 209.

5. Fray Diego Durán, *The History of the Indies of New Spain,* trans. & intro. by Doris Heyden (Norman: University of Oklahoma Press, 1994), p. 307.

6. Pedro de Cieza de León, *The Second Part of the Chronicle of Peru,* trans. and ed. by Clements R. Markham, The Hakluyt Society, first series, No. LXVIII (New York: Burt Franklin, nd), pp. 47–48.

7. Anthony F. C. Wallace, *The Death and Rebirth of the Seneca* (New York: Vintage Books, 1972), p. 24.

8. Nigel Davies, *The Ancient Kingdoms of Mexico* (Harmondsworth, England: Penguin Books, 1983), p. 169.

3

The Conquests and Initial Establishment of Colonies in Latin America

The European Setting

Europe in the mid-fifteenth century was far from the dominating continent that it would become in a couple of centuries. Europe was in fact one of the weakest, most fragmented, and troubled regions in the Old World. It was on the defensive against the dynamic Ottoman empire, which dominated the Islamic Middle East. The Ottomans controlled the eastern Mediterranean Sea and could cut Europe off from the silks, porcelains, spices, and other prized items brought overland from the Far East. After capturing Constantinople in 1453, Ottoman forces invaded the Balkans and penetrated well into Eastern Europe, eventually taking Budapest and even besieging Vienna (though unsuccessfully). Otranto on the southern tip of Italy also fell to them for a brief time in 1480.

Europe itself was economically stagnant. It had lost a third of its population, some 30 million people, in the second half of the fourteenth century due to the Bubonic Plague. Even before the plague hit, the continent had suffered from famine, and these afflictions continued. It enjoyed no economic advantages in the quality or types of goods produced or in the techniques utilized to craft them. But Europe had begun to improve on ship designs and navigational systems that it had adopted from Islamic traders of the Middle East. Similarly, Europe improved the printing press, originally invented in China. Very importantly, Europe began to develop firearms, both muskets and artillery, initially incorporated from foreign sources as well.   Perhaps this willingness to experiment and to adopt technology and techniques developed in other lands constituted Europe's primary advantage against its competitors.   Nonetheless, as Europe began to expand overseas, it possessed only the most tenuous of military and naval advantages and none in the quality of its products nor in the manner of their manufacture.

The relatively weak countries of Europe frequently warred against each other, but generally gained little enduring advantage or profit from their victories.   For example, France and England were preoccupied and debilitated by their Hundred Years War, which only ended in the mid-fifteenth century.   In time, competition among European countries for trade and colonies would spur continual overseas expansion and technological innovation.   But in the early sixteenth century European rulers did not even dream of enjoying such power over other parts of the world.   Indeed, they were preoccupied with holding onto power and resisting the incursions of Muslim states.

Nor did religious zeal fuel overseas expansion, though it certainly colored and justified many of the efforts, and some of the individuals involved had strong religious motives.   The Catholic Church's capacity to initiate continent-wide campaigns such as the Crusades had faded centuries before, and the papacy itself was quite weak.   Even the efforts of the Catholic countries of Portugal, Spain, and France to convert the peoples they subdued across the seas were more often a secondary, rather than central, motive for their enterprises.   This is not to say that their faith was insincere, only that it was not the primary inspiration for expansion.   The bitter, traditional rivalry between Catholicism and Islam, though, did give an anti-Muslim tinge to much of Europe's early expansion, especially to that by Spain and Portugal (together known as Iberia). Their agents expressed the hope that successful exploration might strengthen Catholic Europe against the Muslim Middle East.

In 1518, the Protestant Reformation permanently split Europe into hostile, competing religious spheres, further weakening it and slowing its economic expansion somewhat.   Further, the Protestant powers that participated substantially in the colonization of the Americas—England and Holland—were not at all preoccupied with overseas missionary activity, for it was not yet an integral part of the Protestantism that they practiced.

In the second half of the fifteenth century, two major world areas other than Europe appeared better positioned to develop overseas empires.   One of them, the Ottoman empire, could have readily expanded on the well-established, Muslim-dominated trading networks between East Africa and the Indian subcontinent.   However, it instead concentrated on a more extractive system that focused on agriculture and the taxes that could be reliably derived from it.   Its military strategy against Europe also increasingly emphasized attacks over land rather than naval campaigns.

The other major world region with the capacity to expand overseas was China.   That vast country was economically and culturally quite self-sufficient and its rulers generally viewed the oceans as dangerous zones, replete with pirates and leading only to contact with backward foreigners. Unlike Europe, China was typically organized into a single unified state. In fact, this vast and quite homogeneous land had recently come under the control of the Ming dynasty (1368–1644). Having overthrown the Mongols, who had ruled China after invading it from the north, the new dynasty sought to insulate China from any new foreign threats.

Nonetheless, one of the first Ming emperors did send out several massive fleets (each with dozens of ships and thousands of men) under the admiral Zheng He between 1405 and 1433. These ventured to South Asia and as far as the coast of east Africa. But these expeditions proved costly and yielded little immediate profit, so the emperor, influenced by conservative court officials, ordered them to cease. No further explorations were undertaken by the government or by the merchant class, which was closely regulated by the government.

Iberia's Early Efforts at Exploration

Spanish merchants and provincial lords began to send fleets into the Atlantic early in the thirteenth century. Most of these efforts were small in scale, directed against well-known ports and towns in north Africa held by other European nobles or their Muslim counterparts. But in the mid-fifteenth century, Spain finally undertook the subjugation of a non-European, non-Muslim people on its own territory with the conquest of the Canary Islands off the coast of northeast Africa. Canary inhabitants were pastoral peoples, the population in the tens of thousands organized into distinct, rival ethnic groups. Their limited technology did not include firearms or even metal tools and weapons.

The several most populated islands were conquered only slowly over time, ending in 1496 with the defeat of Tenerife. Most of the expeditions were funded by their organizers and by merchants. The monarchy provided no direct support, only some tax exemptions, concessions, and land grants. Further, the bulk of these rewards were distributed only if a conquest proved successful. Many expedition leaders (called *adelantados*) ended up with substantial debts. The peoples of the Canaries used their intimate knowledge of the rugged, mountainous landscape to evade the expeditions and then to ambush the Spanish with rocks and bows and arrows when they became overextended or careless. Though the natives avoided pitched battles, the lengthy campaigns still caused considerable attrition from imported diseases and combat fatalities.

The Spanish enslaved many of the survivors, but sold few away from the islands. Most became house servants for colonists. Some male colonists lived with the daughters of native leaders. The commanders of successful expeditions were designated the first governors of the islands, with the privilege of rewarding their followers with grants of land or labor service from the new subjects. Each commander soon established a city to serve as his capital. Neither the crown nor the expedition leaders considered conversion of the natives to Christianity to be a high priority.

The Spaniards in the Caribbean

The uniqueness of the 1492 voyage of Christopher Columbus under the auspices of the monarchs of Spain can be easily overstated. Many ships ventured well into the Atlantic in the fifteenth century, including British fishing boats that sailed far into the northern seas. Despite the fame he has enjoyed, Columbus only accelerated the European discovery of the Americas by perhaps a decade. (A Portuguese fleet under Cabral bound for India around the Cape of Good Hope discovered Brazil quite independently in 1500.) The primary impact of the Columbian voyage was to make Spain the first European colonizing nation in that part of the world and hence to make much of the New World "Spanish America." Spain had virtually free rein in the Americas until the early seventeenth century. England and France were preoccupied with competition within Europe. Spain explored a great part of both American continents and settled in the most lucrative and attractive regions, leaving the less desirable to later colonists from other nations.

Early Spanish domination in the Americas came about because the other major Atlantic naval power of the time, Portugal, reached India about the same time that Spain arrived in the Americas and subsequently devoted its modest resources to the immediate wealth (and consequent worries and demands) provided by exclusive trade with Asia. As a consequence, for about three-quarters of a century, Portugal only paid enough attention to Brazil to make sure that no other European nation seized it.

Columbus's initial description of the natives, as reconstructed from his journal by his contemporary Bartolomé de las Casas, is revealing, seeming to reflect the perceptions and concerns of many of the early explorers.

> They do not have weapons, or even know about them, because when shown a sword they grabbed it by the blade and cut themselves out of ignorance. They do not have any iron; their arrows are a kind without metal, and some of them have points made from the tooth of a fish, and others have other things. They are fairly tall and good looking, well made. They should be good and intelligent servants, and I believe that they could be converted into good Christians, for it does not appear that they have any other religion.[1]

His emphasis is on their level of technology, especially their military capacity, their appearance, their potential servility, and the likelihood that they would accept Christianity, which implied accepting the European way of life as well. They certainly had their own religion, which Columbus could not recognize for it was so different from Christian practices.

Only five months after Columbus conveyed word of his discovery to the monarchs—Spain being still divided into separate kingdoms—the next expedition set out to establish a major colony in the Caribbean. (If Columbus thought that he had actually encountered Asia—a debatable point—he was one of few so deceived.) The Spanish crown appointed Columbus governor over this fleet of

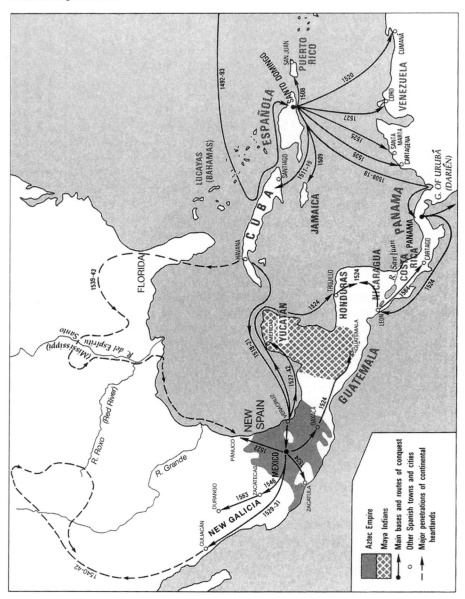

The paths of Spanish conquest in the Caribbean and North America
(Lyle A. McAlister, Spain and Portugal in the New World, 1492–1700,
Minneapolis: University of Minnesota Press, 1984. Map 2.
Reprinted by permission.)

seventeen ships containing about 1,500 men (no women were included in this
venture).

As was typical, the Spaniards immediately founded a city as the political and social center of their new colony of Hispaniola. After a couple of false starts, they established Santo Domingo in 1496. As in Spain, the leading citizens of the community composed the city council (*cabildo*), the fundamental local political institution.

The successful development of this first colony in the Americas—as would be the case with every one that followed, regardless of which country founded it—depended on the production of a profitable colonial export, that is, an item of high unit value that could survive long weeks of shipment over the ocean without deterioration, and for which a dependable market existed in Europe (even with high transportation costs attached). Those colonies that produced such goods would attract substantial immigration, develop towns of some size and occupational variety, and support the economic growth of outlying provinces. In the early years of colonization in the Americas, precious metals—gold and silver—and sugar alone served this role. Over their history, the American colonies would discover only a few other commodities with these qualities. Those colonies that lacked such reliable trade items could not carry on a vigorous trade with the Old World and, as a consequence, would not attain much beyond a subsistence level of living, unable to import many manufactured items of quality and fashion from Europe.

This need for a profitable colonial export commodity and the virtually universal desire of immigrants to improve their standard of living in their new settings largely explain the "gold rush" mentality displayed by Spanish colonists in the sixteenth century and by other European settlers upon their arrival in the Americas in the years following.

Most of the early colonists dispersed into the countryside of Hispaniola to look for sites offering up the promised gold dust and setting up rudimentary placer mines. During the first several decades, the colonists also erected sugar mills and plantations, but with little success. Sugar production and marketing required substantial start-up capital, considerable technological capacity (refining sugar from raw cane is a complex task that requires equipment), dependable suppliers of slaves from the African mainland, and networks to market the sugar products throughout Western Europe. Local Indians died so quickly in such great numbers from disease and abuse that they could not provide the dependent labor force that was so crucial to the formation of a major sugar plantation zone. Spain lacked the reliable market networks, financiers, and traders in African slaves to establish such a complex production and distribution system. Even the Portuguese in Brazil enjoyed only a modicum of success in the sugar industry until the Dutch, with their advanced trading and financial networks, became involved in the early seventeenth century.

The inhabitants of the several towns established on Hispaniola created a demand for agricultural products as well. Some of the better-off colonists established farms and ranches near these communities, where they soon began to market grains, vegetables, cattle, and swine.

The Tainos, a semisedentary people organized into chiefdoms, inhabited most of the major Caribbean islands. They initially accommodated themselves to the few thousand colonists and did not undertake massive armed resistance, although one chief did destroy the first Spanish community, Navidad, seemingly because its inhabitants became abusive. To speak of an initial "conquest" era in the Caribbean is thus inappropriate. But this situation would not long endure, largely for two reasons: a growing Spanish demand for tribute and forced Indian labor, and a rapid die-off of the natives, primarily from epidemic disease.

The Spaniards in the countryside exacted increasing amounts of food from the Tainos, plus workers to search for gold. In the face of such impositions, some communities rose up in resistance. In 1494 a *cacique* led his community in revolt, burning a fort and killing ten Spaniards. A retaliatory expedition devastated the village and forced the many captives into slavery. Another local revolt broke out a few years later, but the Spaniards rapidly suppressed it with many casualties among the insurgents. The colonists, however, suffered few losses from these uprisings, for the natives failed to coordinate their attacks. But their growing refusal to cultivate crops brought about a famine that affected both Spaniards and Tainos as early as 1496. Some Indians fled into areas outside of Spanish control, but the majority remained and were decimated by epidemic disease.

Hispaniola had a population of perhaps three million people in 1492. By 1500, the part of the island effectively colonized contained less than 20 percent of its original numbers. By 1550, nearly all of Hispaniola's native inhabitants had died. As early as the first decade of the sixteenth century, the Spaniards ventured to the other large islands near Hispaniola—Cuba, Jamaica, and Puerto Rico-to raid for Indian slaves to replenish Hispaniola's decimated labor force.

Despite the violence and depredations of the colonists, epidemic diseases previously unknown in the Americas caused the vast majority of Indian deaths. The very earliest Spanish explorers may well have transmitted influenza to the natives. This disease was seemingly unknown among the native Americans, probably because of the lack of swine in aboriginal America (swine serving as the incubation reservoir for flu). Smallpox and measles followed within a few years to become the primary killers.

Our knowledge of the native peoples of the Caribbean suffers considerably from the Spanish lack of curiosity about them. Few witnesses wrote much about the indigenous cultures. European colonists typically cared little about understanding native ways and organization. The primary exception is Catholic missionaries. (The Protestant faiths hardly cared to evangelize before the late eighteenth century.) However, their interest generally derived not from an appreciation of the natives among whom they lived, but from a desire to convert them more effectively and to detect backsliding and enduring paganism more easily.

In the Caribbean, and later carried over to the mainland, the Spanish imposed three distinct forms of labor service on the natives: draft laborers; personal retainers; and slaves. The colonists typically demanded draft labor service from the islands' inhabitants. This division of natives among the participants in any successful expedition was called *repartimiento*. The recipients did not own their workers, who were not legally enslaved. Nor did they have total and immediate authority over them; repartimiento workers remained under their own ethnic lords (*caciques*), who were expected to maintain their people in a peaceful and well-governed state and to provide groups of workers in rotation from their populations. Those settlers who received this privileged access to free labor were the most likely to prosper. On the mainland among denser indigenous populations, this labor allocation system blossomed and became institutionalized under the name of *encomienda,* with the holder called an *encomendero.*

Typical of Europeans of that time, Spaniards believed that prominent people should be surrounded by personal retainers, a labor category distinct from house servants. The indigenous nobles in chiefdoms (found on the large islands and in many parts of the mainland) and in the state-structured provinces (found in Mesoamerica and the Andes) also maintained such retainers. They constituted a distinct group from the commoners and lived in separate communities under their own rulers. The Spaniards rapidly incorporated a number of these retainers (called *naborías* after an Arawak word that they adopted in the Caribbean) into their retinues, and the practice expanded when they reached the mainland.

Finally, as the population of Hispaniola plummeted, the colonists began to raid nearby islands to capture slaves. Native slavery was a very secondary labor institution in most areas the Spaniards colonized on the mainland. Like the people enslaved on the islands, they were typically outsiders brought forcibly into a region, never members of local societies.

The Organization and Functioning of Spanish Expeditions of Conquest

As long as Spanish colonization focused on the Caribbean basin, the Americas produced little wealth (the amount of gold found was meager) and attracted little interest in the home country. Caribbean settlement was just one enterprise among many that the country was pursuing in Europe and overseas. Spain did not devote great attention to the New World until it established colonies on the mainland, where it found valuable resources and densely populated native societies: Hernando Cortés's conquest of the Aztec empire was easily the most galvanizing event.

The slowness with which the Spaniards moved to the mainland—fully 25 years passed between the establishment of the first colony on Hispaniola in 1494 and the arrival of Cortés's expedition in Mexico in 1519—reflects the typical Spanish pattern of full settlement of a newly discovered area and also the considerable ignorance regarding the Aztecs among the peoples of the major Caribbean islands. The Spanish, conditioned by the prolonged "Reconquest" of their homeland from the Muslim Moors, had a distinctive approach to the discovery of new lands that first revealed itself on the Canary Islands, replicated itself in the Caribbean, and was successfully transferred to the American mainland; it has been termed the full-settlement model.

Runaway native retainers in early Cuba

In 1533, some twenty years after the Spanish takeover of Cuba, colonial authorities raided encampments of fugitive native workers in the woods and mountains, bringing back four men and three women. The following is the testimony of one of the captives.

Later Manuel de Rojas ordered the interpreter, under the conditions established by his oath, to speak with another Indian who had been captured at the *rancho* [camp] and summoned before him, asking him his name, whose *naboria* he was, and how long he had been a rebel. . . . The Indian replied that his name was Alexo, that he was from Inagua in the province of Guantanavo and that he was the *naboria* of the factor Fernando de Castro. He said he had been a rebel for four years, having gone to Guama's *rancho* with captain Juan Perez, and that he had been a fugitive until now, when he was captured by the Christians with the other fugitives. He was ordered to ask the Indian if after running away he had taken part in the murder of any Spaniard or peaceful Indian or the burning or plundering of any huts or had done any other injury . . . he replied he had not. He was ordered to ask the Indian how many people from Guama's *rancho* remained in the woods. He said ten men with one youth and five women with five children, and that he believed they would return there for food, because they do not have it anywhere else, since after captain Diego Barba had defeated them, they had been accustomed to living there and had no plans to settle anywhere else. Thus they had stayed nearby and got their food there, and he believed the other fugitive Indians would do the same and would not go anywhere else. He was ordered to ask the said Indian whether or not he had seen Juan Perez or Guama kill anyone or steal from anyone . . . he replied that he had not seen them do anything, but that it was known at the *rancho* that Guama had killed many Indians from the *rancho*, taking them outside by deception, and that he had killed his brother treacherously with an ax while he was sleeping and this was widely known among the Indians of the *rancho*. He said that Alexo had been with the said Guama until now and is called Guamayry (?) and is now captain of the other rebels.

Source: "1533 Interrogation of Indian runaways in Cuba," trans. by the editors, in John H. Parry and Robert G. Keith, eds., *New Iberian World*, Vol. II (New York: Times Books, 1984), pp. 354–355. Reprinted by permission of Edward J. Joyce, trustee.

In the typical pattern, the Spaniards organized privately funded expeditions (*entradas*) into new territories. If they conquered the inhabitants or discovered a valuable resource, they then established a capital city in its heartland and constructed family mansions as near to the main plaza as they could. The crown almost invariably named the expedition leader as the first governor (such successful ventures had to be rewarded and hence encouraged), and the new governor proceeded to reward his supporters with land grants and exclusive claims to the labor of local Indians. The colonists searched for precious metals, conducted trade, and set up commercially oriented rural estates to supply the capital city and also any provincial centers that might emerge. They established a complex and enduring society in the new colony, and the wealthier members likely never joined in another expedition. But latecomers to the colony from the home country and those Spaniards who just did not succeed economically in the colony constituted a ready population to staff new expeditions into unknown territories. A certain Esteban Rodríguez Cabeza de Vaca participated in eleven separate *entradas* over a twenty-year period.

In many ways, Cortés's venture represents Spain's first true effort at conquest in the Americas, its organization and operation harkening back to patterns from the Reconquest in Spain and the subjugation of the Canary Islands. The social composition and organization of these expeditions substantially shaped the process of early colonization. In general, neither the monarchy nor any government body in Spain organized or funded these ventures. The role of the government in Spain was commonly limited to giving official sanction to these undertakings, which were organized, funded, and equipped locally in the colonies. Some colonists launched expeditions without prior government sanction and only received authorization upon their return.

Almost all of the early *entradas* on the mainland originated in Cuba or in Panama. Once an island or region was subjugated, it in turn served as the base for future campaigns, with the last effectively settled area serving as the site for organizing subsequent expeditions beyond the frontier.

> Thus the colonization of Puerto Rico, Jamaica, and Cuba originated in Hispaniola. The conquest of Mexico and De Soto's campaign across southeastern North America began in Cuba. Hernán Cortés's victory over the vast Aztec empire in 1521 inspired a dramatic expansion in the number of *entradas* undertaken over the next quarter century or so. It led directly to the conquests of the Yucatan, Guatemala, and even the Philippines. Francisco Vázquez de Coronado's trek began there also, to be followed about a half century later by more successful expeditions to the north. Francisco Pizarro's expedition to Peru led to others into Ecuador, southern Colombia, Bolivia, Chile, and northern Argentina, as well as into a number of fiascos in tropical jungles or endless plains.[2]

These expeditions were not organized as military enterprises, with ranks and a strict hierarchy of authority under the ultimate aegis of the government. Rather, they were voluntary associations freely entered into by all parties. Indeed these *entradas* were commonly referred to as *compañías* (companies), as they were risk-taking economic ventures for all involved. An expedition was commonly organized by a person of stature in the colony who wished to gain the status and wealth that accrued to one who conquered a new province. He already had the standing and resources to attract supporters and to finance a significant part of the undertaking. In other words, the *adelantado,* or expedition leader, was typically a *baquiano,* an experienced Indian fighter who had already spent many years in the Indies.

The leader had three major tasks to complete in organizing an expedition: to assemble a cadre of reliable lieutenants to whom he could delegate authority

The paths of Spanish and Portuguese conquests in South America
(Lyle A. McAlister, Spain and Portugal in the New World, 1492–1700,
Minneapolis: University of Minnesota Press, 1984. Map 3.
Reprinted by permission.)

over the 150–500 men who usually made up the rank-and-file; to recruit the participants themselves; and to finance and supply this large enterprise. Each *adelantado* looked to family members (broadly defined) and people from his home district in Spain for his associates. Francisco Pizarro even journeyed back to Spain to recruit several half-brothers and others from his native province before he commenced the conquest of Peru.

Assembling the manpower was difficult in some aspects and simple in others. As a rule, the members of an expedition were certainly willing to risk their own lives and to act ruthlessly toward their opponents. However, once they became wealthy and established members of the newly formed colonial society, they proved reluctant to join any new ventures. They were already comfortable with their gains and elevated social rank. Hence it is quite inappropriate to refer to these expeditionaries as "adventurers," a term too often used to distinguish early Spanish colonists from their counterparts from other countries.

But some people in the colonies—newcomers and the dissatisfied—were anxious to join. Certain persons invariably arrived too late at a newly established colony or for some reason did not share in its prosperity. They were happy to join a new undertaking—and the people well situated in the colony were equally happy to see these potentially disgruntled troublemakers move on.

Participants in expeditions signed on for a share of any booty that the venture might gain. Typically, a man equipped with armor and weapons generally received a full share, whereas a man with no equipment received only a half share. Horses were so important on these endeavors that a horseman received two shares. The *adelantado* was entitled to a number of shares, and he assigned his trusted associates a substantial number as well. The crown claimed a fifth of any treasure that the expedition gained before all those with shares or any other claims on the returns of an expedition divided it up.

The *adelantado* typically invested all or a substantial part of his wealth in the undertaking, for it had to be adequately supplied with food, equipment, armaments, and perhaps even ships. Local merchants and other businessmen provided the rest of the goods, charging high prices—and even higher ones if they took the risk of accepting payment after the success of the undertaking. Many expedition members formed companies with local colonists—and even with each other—to finance their participation. An *entrada* thus typically resulted from the efforts of many residents of the colony rather than being a centrally directed effort sponsored and organized from the home country.

The participants rarely had prior military experience in Europe. Few among them, including the leaders, had previous careers as professional soldiers. Examination of the members' backgrounds reveals a wide variety of social types, with a substantial number coming from the broad middle sector of Spanish society; urban areas were over-represented compared to the countryside. The high nobility and the desperately poor did not participate. The only women who went along were the wives or concubines of leading participants and sometimes the Indian companions of ordinary members. Social groups heavily represented include *hidalgos* (local gentry), professionals such as medical practitioners, clerks, and notaries, merchants, artisans, mariners, along with a scattering of blacks, mulattoes, and foreigners (Portuguese, Greeks, and Italians, most often). With the exception of the foreigners and the people of African ancestry, the English, Dutch, and French settlers of North America largely shared these same social characteristics.

The expeditionaries did not receive military training nor were they organized into strict ranks. They did not need to use tightly coordinated tactics nor assault fortified cities. Even their use of artillery and firearms (*harquebuses*) was very limited in most campaigns. The *adelantado* usually divided the men into four or five contingents under the command of his associates. The cavalry, which generally numbered no more than 25, operated as an autonomous unit most of the time. The commanders could not apply strict discipline, but overt disobedience commonly brought punishment (whippings and the like) and unsuccessful mutinies resulted in the execution of at least some of the ringleaders.

But lacking the authority and ordinances of the government or a formal military apparatus, and leading a force of volunteers whose primary motivations were economic, the *adelantado* had to cajole and entice as much as threaten and punish. He had to keep his men motivated and united. Thus most leaders consulted frequently with their men to explain their strategies and to remind them of the wealth and glory that awaited them if successful. Despite intense factionalism of every sort and occasional uprisings, most members understood that disunity threatened their survival in this hostile setting and were willing to stand by their commanders as long as some promise of success remained or the force was under the threat of attack. But when an expedition continued on deep in the interior without any glimmer of reward or relief, mutinies could be expected.

The most notorious mutiny occurred in 1560–1561 on Pedro de Ursúa's expedition into the upper Amazon basin. Lope de Aguirre organized the assassination of Ursúa and installed a man named Fernando de Guzmán as his replacement. As the Spaniards moved farther downstream, discipline collapsed and brawling resulted in some deaths. Aguirre became suspicious of Guzmán and slaughtered him and others he thought disloyal. Installing himself as *adelantado,* he wrote a notorious letter to the king, challenging his authority. But when Aguirre reached the coast of Venezuela, his force of 230 Spaniards, down from the original 370, was surrounded by colonists loyal to the monarch and taken captive. Aguirre was killed during the struggle.

Typically, only a small number of expeditionaries returned to Spain; instead they tried to entice relatives and friends to join them in this land of greater promise. In sum, then, nothing distinguished the *conquistadores* from other early Spanish colonists, except that they journeyed to the new land early enough to join in the overthrow of the native rulers. They came from the same spectrum of social groups and shared the same economic goals. Members of successful expeditions commonly remained in the new colonies and involved themselves in its economic development. Some of them invariably constituted a substantial segment of the initial social elite. By having served in these acclaimed military victories, moreover, the participants and their offspring enjoyed a privileged status in these early colonial societies. Some members of later generations of *conquistador* families persisted in their claims to social and political priority. But the other colonists—now numerous and influential—rejected their pretensions so many years after the now dimly remembered conquests and were usually supported by imperial administrators.

Spanish expeditions had extremely different initial interactions with indigenous societies depending on whether the latter were sedentary, semisedentary, or nonsedentary. The Spaniards experienced a greater range of interactions and outcomes with the semisedentary peoples than with those of the other two classifications. This chapter will now consider the character of Spanish military encounters and their levels of success against peoples from each of these classifications.

The Conquest of the Sedentary Imperial Societies

The most profound irony of the conquest era is that the vast and powerful indigenous sedentary empires proved the easiest for the Spanish to subdue. The nature and meaning of warfare among these peoples (outlined in the preceding chapter) goes far to explaining why this was so. These states could routinely muster massive armies of tens of thousands of men and keep them in the field for months at a time using warehouses of foods that they maintained for just this purpose. Despite this, warfare was characteristically controlled and ritualized so that it caused limited loss of life on the battlefield and did not involve the destruction of crops or settlements or the slaughter of noncombatants. Battlefield tactics focused on disabling and capturing individual opponents instead of killing them or relying on coordinated actions by military units. To kill or capture the opposition's commander caused the immediate surrender or withdrawal of his forces; even individual units ceased fighting when their leader was killed or their standard seized. Finally, these armies preferred weapons that were not very lethal in nature. Javelins and arrows were launched only at the beginning of battle and were discarded in favor of close combat between individuals with clubs edged with obsidian chips. These were more likely to disable one's opponents and render them captives for later sacrifice on temple altars than to kill them.

The Spaniards conducted warfare in a manner typical of European societies of their time. The purpose of battle was to destroy the opposing force's fighting capability and will to resist. This meant not only killing as many of your opponents as possible but also disabling their organizational structure. Further, despite much rhetoric about limiting warfare to formal combat between armies, European forces commonly burned crops and settlements and took captive, and sometimes slaughtered, noncombatants.

All European expeditions enjoyed a decided military technological advantage over the natives of the Americas. They carried metal weapons—generally swords, but sometimes lances and pikes—and metal helmets and armor. This technological advantage meant that unless fighting in constricted places such as mountain passes or narrow city streets, European combatants could predictably defeat their native opponents equipped with clubs and flint-tipped or fire-hardened arrows and lances. They did not fear fatal injuries, because helmets protected their heads from crushing blows and the Indians had few weapons that could inflict penetrating wounds.

Aztec warrior attire *(Ross Hassig,* Aztec Warfare: Imperial
Expansion and Political Control, *Norman; University of
Oklahoma Press, 1988, p. 89. Cliché Bibliothèque nationale de
France, Paris.)*

When facing the great armies of the Aztecs and Incas in open countryside,
the Spaniards made little use of their light artillery—small cannon that could be
carried by two men—or their harquebuses. No defensive structures needed to
be knocked down, and the firearms were so inaccurate and slow-firing against
these massed forces that they were of limited utility. In fact, when the Spaniards
used projectiles against the Inca and Aztec armies, they far preferred crossbows,

whose bolts were deadly, highly accurate, and more rapidly fired in the sixteenth century.

Even Aztec sources recorded the natives' adept response to firearms and cannon. Book Twelve of the *Florentine Codex*, written after the conquest by central Mexican natives in their own language, Nahuatl, reports:

> But when the Mexicans could behold and determine where the gun [shots] and bolts would strike, no longer did they follow a direct course. Only from side to side would they veer; only sideways, at a slant, they traveled. And when [those on land] also already saw that the big gun was to fire, they all fell to the ground; all stretched out on the ground, and lay flat.[3]

In his discussion of a battle against the Tlaxcalans in central Mexico, Díaz del Castillo notes how the Spaniards coordinated swordplay and the firing of crossbows and harquebuses. He also remarks on the natives' failure to make effective use of their tremendous advantage in manpower:

> The crossbowmen were warned to use their supply of arrows very carefully, some of them loading while the others were shooting. The musketeers were to act in the same way, and the men with sword and shield to aim their cuts and thrusts at the enemy's bowels, so as to prevent their coming as close to us as they had done before. . . . Their charging swordsmen were repelled by stout thrusts from our swords, and did not close in on us so often as in the previous battle. . . . The Indians were charging us in such numbers that only by a miracle of sword-play were we able to drive them back and reform our ranks. One thing alone saved our lives: the enemy were so massed and so numerous that every shot wrought havoc among them. What is more, they were so badly led that some of their captains could not bring their men into battle.[4]

Another tremendous advantage the Europeans enjoyed was their cavalry. Spanish expeditions commonly had only about 25 horses with them, but these were enough to give them a decided edge against peoples who always fought on foot. The natives quickly overcame their initial fear and confusion about men on horses, but the cavalry's real advantages remained.

For example, during the conquest of Peru in 1536, an Inca force of some tens of thousands isolated roughly 200 Spaniards in Cuzco and placed them under close siege. Pedro Pizarro, the half-brother of the *adelantado* Francisco, and two other horsemen had been surprised while on patrol and surrounded by a vastly superior force. Nearing exhaustion, they were rescued when a contingent of ten Spanish horsemen heard the sounds of the struggle. Charging into the Incas in an organized formation, they proved unstoppable. They rescued their colleagues, while suffering some serious wounds, but only one casualty. This occurred when one of the riders dismounted to fight on foot and was subsequently separated from the others and surrounded.

The horsemen could always scout enemy positions and formations. Hence the Spanish were typically well informed about the deployment of their opponents and were therefore very difficult to surprise or ambush. The cavalry enabled the Spaniards to launch an attack on their enemy's flank or rear faster than they could respond. The horsemen tried to avoid fighting as individuals. Instead they charged into the enemy's ranks in closed cohorts of at least several, stabbing with lances and trampling their defenseless opponents. They wove back and forth, disrupting the enemy's formation and cohesion instead of standing still and fighting one against one. Finally, units of horsemen could protect injured and exhausted footmen who were vulnerable to being overrun after long hours of combat by holding off their opponents, enabling them to rest, dress their wounds, and withdraw in good order if necessary.

Díaz del Castillo gives a good depiction of the use of cavalry in the campaign against the Tlaxcalans.

> As we marched along, we decided that the horsemen, in groups of three for mutual assistance, should charge and return at a trot, and should hold their lances rather short; and that when they broke through the Tlascalans' ranks they should aim at the enemies' faces, and give repeated thrusts, so as to prevent them from seizing their lances. If, however, a lance should be seized, the horseman must use all his strength and put spurs to his horse. Then the leverage of the lance beneath his arm and the headlong rush of the horse would either enable the rider to tear it away or drag the Indian along with him.[5]

Cortés faced an Aztec empire that embraced probably over ten million people and Pizarro an Inca one of around eight million. But they did not have to vanquish all those people, for the two imperial centers each controlled many millions of people who rankled at their subordination, had never lost their distinctive ethnic identities, and repeatedly rose up against rule by outsiders. Once the *entradas* displayed an ability to fight the imperial powers effectively, many provinces rushed to join their side, or at least determined to stay neutral in the struggle. In fact, in the case of Mexico, Cortés was himself approached by a coastal people, the Cempoalans, who sought his assistance to throw off Aztec rule, offering him support from a league of disgruntled provinces. As described by Cortés's secretary, Francisco López de Gómara, the Cempoalan headman related his scheme.

> He said, however, that Tlaxcala, Huejotzingo, and other provinces of the country, together with the Totonacs of the mountains, were enemies of Moctezuma [the Aztec emperor] and, moreover, had heard something of what had happened in Tabasco [a Spanish military victory against a coastal Mexican people]; that, if Cortés so desired, he would make a league with all of them that would be so strong that Moctezuma would not be able to stand against it.[6]

So the Spaniards had to conquer only the imperial centers, not entire empires. Further, some of the subordinated provinces offered the invaders shelter, supplies, porters, and the other logistical support. What they did not provide, however, were armed combatants, except for a few exceptional battles. It was not that these societies did not want to fight their old enemies; they were anxious to do so. Rather, the Spaniards did not hold them in high regard as fighters, for they fought in the same manner as the ruling states, whom the Spaniards routinely defeated. They even feared that native combatants would get in their way during engagements.

Díaz del Castillo, in his blunt manner, says as much several times in his account. One passage states:

> The first thing we did was to get our Tlascalan allies off the causeway
> [that led from the mainland to the Aztec island capital]. They were very
> numerous, and the Mexicans, being cunning, would have liked nothing
> better than to see us obstructed by our friends. Thus they made fierce
> attacks on us from two or three directions, hoping to catch us between
> them and cut some of us off. So if we had been impeded by the
> Tlascalans we should not have been able to fight them everywhere.
> Once our allies were no longer hampering us, we retired to our camp
> without ever turning our backs but always facing the enemy.[7]

When the Aztecs and Incas first learned of the Spaniards entrance into their territories, they displayed no great fear. After their conquest, Inca informants disclosed to the victors that they had initially considered them to be raiders from the sea and that they had intended eventually to take them captive. The Aztecs held the foreigners in somewhat higher regard, perhaps because they had seen Spanish ships which had coasted Mexico and knew of some of their military victories to the south. They may also have considered them potentially to have supernatural qualities, though by no means to be gods. Overall, the peoples of Mexico regarded the Spaniards under Cortés as outsiders in the same way as they considered all native groups not of their province. They did not stress the exoticness or "otherness" of these new persons. Rather they regarded the invaders' aims to be virtually the same as those of the leading Aztec emperors.

As James Lockhart, a preeminent scholar of the Nahuas, the native peoples of central Mexico, comments,

> The Nahuas continued to see the world as they had before, divided be-
> tween the altepetl [the Nahuatl term for an ethnic province] group and
> all outsiders, be they indigenous or Spaniards.[8]

Regardless of their first impression, Montezuma's envoys soon learned from Cortés that he was the representative of a powerful, previously unknown, monarch and wanted to meet with the Aztec emperor. The Aztecs from then on responded to him accordingly, seeking, largely unsuccessfully, to attain certain goals. They wanted recognition of the equivalent status of the two empires and their rulers, offering to send precious goods to the Spanish monarch in return for proper diplomatic relations and an agreement that the foreigners would never seek to enter the Aztec empire. They feared that if the Spaniards ventured into the heartland of the empire, they would attract support from subjugated provinces already prone to rebel. But once Cortés's men penetrated deep into Aztec territory, its rulers sought several times to take the invaders captive in order to ascertain their intentions and to operate from a situation of control.

The expeditions against the two native empires both utilized a longstanding Spanish practice. They captured the headman and ruled through him for as long as possible. Thus shortly after entering Tenochtitlan, Cortés seized a surprised Montezuma in his own throne room and took him back to the Spanish headquarters where he was put in chains. Pizarro's force ambushed Atahuallpa, the Inca emperor, and his royal guard as they arrived for a meeting with the Spaniards. Both *adelantados* then ruled the empires peacefully through their royal captives for some months, an approach that over time proved unsustainable. For the ruling families came to understand that the Spaniards would not withdraw and that acceptance of the prevailing situation meant the end of their authority. Hence they began to disobey the orders of the emperors and even to organize revolts. (Profound divisions developed among the ruling families of subject provinces as well over whether to side with the Spaniards.)

This situation led to the considerable irony of the captive emperors turning to the Spaniards to enforce their orders and to suppress uprisings led by fellow members of the royal family. But even this situation could endure for only so long before both of the emperors were totally repudiated. Montezuma was rejected and stoned by his former subjects. Pizarro executed Atahuallpa after he had lost his usefulness and might himself have organized a rescue attempt. In both cases, once this period of peaceful control ended and the imperial families understood the implications of continued Spanish rule, they rose up in violent resistance. The two imperial capitals had to be conquered anew by the Spaniards, this time not by stealth and manipulation but rather through pitched warfare.

In fact, trapped for a while in the Aztecs' island capital, Cortés's force was almost annihilated in mid-1520. The city's narrow streets, squeezed between houses and canals that ran crisscross through the city, neutralized most of the Spaniards' usual military advantages. López de Gómara provides a graphic description.

> Cortés sallied forth on one side and another captain on the other, each
> with two hundred Spaniards. The Indians attacked them furiously,
> killing four and wounding many, while losing few of their own, for they
> took shelter in the houses near by, or behind the bridges and wells. If
> our men attacked in the streets, the Indians promptly cut the bridges; if
> they attacked the houses, they were badly hurt by the blocks and stones
> hurled from the rooftops; if they retreated, they were closely pursued.
> Their own house was fired in many places; a good part of it was burned,
> and the fire could not be put out until rooms and walls were pulled
> down upon it.[9]

But the Spaniards managed to escape the city in the dark of night, fleeing across a causeway, though with the loss of about two-thirds of their force of over a thousand men. The battered and depressed survivors began to march toward the safety of their allied province of Tlaxcala, but after two weeks, at Otumba, they confronted the entire Aztec army assembled to finish them off. After a long day of fighting, even in these desperate circumstances, the Spaniards prevailed—and with relative ease. This battle demonstrates in compelling fashion the overwhelming military superiority Spanish expeditions enjoyed against native armies except when certain extraordinary circumstances prevailed.

The battle of Otumba shows that the coordinated swordplay of the footmen, when combined with repeated charges by detachments of cavalry in an open area, made the Spaniards virtually invincible against even huge, well-organized, and deployed native armies. Having lost their muskets and artillery and most of their crossbows during the flight from Tenochtitlan, the Spaniards could not fire projectiles of any sort in this engagement.

Díaz del Castillo gives us a particularly gripping description of the battle.

> We saw them beginning to surround us. Our horsemen, charging in
> bands of five, broke their ranks. And then, commanding ourselves most
> heartily to God and the Blessed Mary, and calling on the name of our
> patron St James, we charged them all together. It was a destructive bat-
> tle, and a fearful sight to behold. We moved through the midst of them
> in the closest quarters, slashing and thrusting at them with our swords.
> And the dogs [Mexicans] fought back furiously, dealing us wounds and
> death with their lances and their two-handed swords. And the field
> being level, our horsemen speared them at their pleasure, charging and
> retiring and charging again. . . . and to record Cortes' instructions to us
> who were in the thick of the enemy that we must aim our cuts and
> thrusts at distinguished chieftains who all wore great golden plumes and
> rich armour and devices.[10]

After some hours of battle, Cortés and several other horsemen charged the litter bearing the Mexican commander-in-chief and slew him. The native forces thereupon withdrew in dismay. As related by López de Gómara,

> When the Indians saw their standard and its bearer fall, they dropped
> their banners to the ground and fled, for such is their custom in war
> when their general is killed and their standard knocked down.[11]

After some months of recuperation and rearmament in Tlaxcala, the Spaniards returned to the Valley of Mexico in early 1521 to place Tenochtitlan under siege, a common strategy in European warfare. They had learned from their bitter experience fighting in the confined streets of the capital the previous year. The Spaniards largely refrained from advances directly into the heart of the city, where they could be cut off and attacked from above and all sides. Actually, they made a couple of such attempts, which were so nearly catastrophes—

including the near capture of Cortés—that they finally decided to cease such forays and to turn to a systematic siege. To cut off the island city, the Spaniards had to take command of the huge lake. They did so by building thirteen small ships called brigantines, each carrying 25 men (twelve of whom were rowers) and a small cannon, plus a sail. These soon took control of the lake, sinking many of the canoes laden with food and fresh water that tried to resupply the city.

Cortés slowly came to the painful realization that to capture the magnificent city, he would have to level it. Thus each day the Spanish took part of a causeway or a block or two of the city through hard combat and then held it while their native allies demolished the structures and filled the canals with their rubble, effectively transforming the city into the flat, open area in which Spanish fighters operated so effectively. This process went on for a couple of months until the Aztec defenders were forced onto swampland and the emperor (now Cuauhtemoc, a nephew of Montezuma) was captured trying to flee in a canoe. The empire had fallen and would remain securely in Spanish hands through the several centuries of the colonial period.

No treatment of the final siege and fall of Tenochtitlan would be complete without consideration of another contributing factor: epidemic disease, specifically smallpox. When the Spaniards returned to the Aztec capital for the final campaign in early 1521, traveling ahead of them was smallpox, brought to Mexico by one of the men who arrived to supplement Cortés's force. In this densely settled territory that had never suffered exposure to the disease, the epidemic spread like wildfire, and the afflicted perished in very high numbers because so many people were sick at the same time that few remained to provide even basic care. In besieged Tenochtitlan, the devastation was tremendous; even the Spaniards expressed some regret at the horrible situation they witnessed on the other side of the barricades. Nonetheless, because the Aztecs were still able to mount such a spirited and enduring defense and did not surrender until they were decimated, the epidemic seems contributory to but not determinative of the Aztec defeat. After all, the Spaniards enjoyed similar military success against the Inca empire without epidemics playing a role during the campaign.

In the Andes, after Pizarro's expedition captured the Inca emperor Atahuallpa in 1532, the Spaniards ruled through him and his successor, Manco Inca, with relative peace until 1536. But by then Manco appreciated that the Spaniards would never cede him true sovereignty over his people and that they had come to the Andes to stay, for more arrived with every ship. He determined to eliminate them, beginning with the capital of Cuzco, far in the highlands. A rather small number of Spaniards lived there separated from the majority who dwelled along the coast, particularly in the new capital Pizarro had founded in 1535, Lima.

At the end of April, Manco led his secretly gathered army of over 100,000 men against the 190 Spaniards of Cuzco, 80 of whom had horses, and their approximately 500 Indian allies. Although the Inca army initially invaded the city and cornered the Spaniards in one section of it, within two weeks the defenders had driven all of the Incas out of its confines. Though cut off for the next year, this small number of Spaniards kept their attackers out of the city—and in

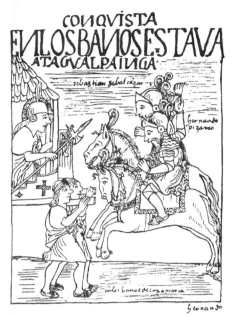

(a) *Atahuallpa being carried from the baths*

(b) *Atahuallpa on his throne*

(c) *Atahuallpa in prison*

(d) *Execution of Atahuallpa*

An Indian's depiction of the capture, imprisonment, and execution of Atahuallpa *(Huamán Poma,* Letter to a King: A Peruvian Chief's Account of the Life Under the Incas and Under Spanish Rule, *Christopher Dilke, Co., New York: E. P. Dutton, 1978, p. 112. Reprinted by permission of the Royal Library of Copenhagen.)*

Manco's siege of Cuzco

Titu Cusi Yupanqui, the eldest son of Manco Inca, ruled the refugee Inca state of Vilcabamba from 1557 to 1571. Despite his refusal to subordinate himself to Spanish rule, he routinely dealt with colonial and church officials, even accepting a priest into his community and becoming baptized. He wrote one of the few native accounts of the conquest of Peru, and in this selection treats his father's attack against the Spaniards in Cuzco in 1536.

The next morning at nine o'clock, all the Spaniards were organized into squadrons in the plaza of Cuzco, their numbers not being known, except that it is said that there were many men and that they had many blacks with them. Then there came into view all around Cuzco, a huge number of Indians, blowing whistles and trumpets and shouting loudly enough to terrify the whole world. In all, there were more than 400,000 Indians, . . . And when the Spaniards saw so many Indians following them, they turned their horses and made a circuit around a mountain that was called Queancalla, attacking the Indians in the rear where Vila Oma [an Inca commander] was, the latter having climbed up with all his men and fortified himself in the fortress of Cuzco that was called Sacsahuaman. There they fought strongly and took the four gates of the fortress, while from the walls, which are very strong, the Indians threw down many boulders and launched arrows, darts, and lances, which badly injured the Spaniards. With these boulders, they killed Juan Pizarro and two blacks as well as many of the Indians who were helping them. When Vila Oma's men ran out of boulders and other ammunition, the Spaniards were able with divine assistance to enter the fortress and seize it, killing many of the Indians inside, while others threw themselves from the walls.

Source: "Titu Cusi's account of Manco's rebellion," trans. by the editors, in John H. Parry and Robert G. Keith, eds., *New Iberian World,* Vol. III (New York: Times Books, 1984), pp. 143, 144.

general on the defensive—the entire time. They suffered fewer than 20 casualties, with most of those occurring during the 2 weeks during which they drove the Incas out of the city.

The Incas also attacked Lima, but were easily repelled. They did, however, gain firm control over all the mountain passes leading into the highlands, thus cutting off Cuzco from Spanish relief columns. The Spaniards could not overcome native attacks when winding their way up narrow mountain trails, where they could not maneuver as groups or use their cavalry advantage effectively and where the Incas could ambush them from above.

Once the defenders of Cuzco had driven the native army out of the city through swordplay and cavalry charges, routine patrols by horsemen forced the Incas to remain on the defensive, and even to locate themselves several miles from the city, while the Spanish footmen hardly had to fight again. Instead they acted as support personnel for the cavalry. The Spaniards also utilized terror tactics, killing any women taken captive and sometimes cutting off the right hand of captured warriors before sending them back to their encampments. The Spanish cavalry operated so freely and with such impunity that patrols regularly penetrated far into the countryside to gather foods and animals.

The Incas meanwhile suffered from defections—many of their troops were farmers who returned home to care for their crops—and from a divided leadership. With rivalries still rampant within the royal family, two of Manco's brothers went over to the Spaniards with their followers. Ultimately, in mid-1537, a Spanish force of 500 men returning from an unsuccessful expedition to the south into Chile lifted the siege. The Inca army dissolved before these reinforcements, the uprising collapsed throughout the Andes, and Manco with a few followers fled to the east into the tropical tangle of the Amazon headwaters. Spanish control over the Andean zone would never be threatened again, despite certain local and regional revolts, and in 1572, Tupac Amaru, the last claimant to the title of Inca emperor, was captured at his Amazon jungle headquarters and taken to Cuzco to be executed.

Differing Iberian Interactions with Semisedentary Peoples

The military advantages the Spaniards enjoyed against the sedentary imperial peoples did not prevail in the same way against the continent's many semisedentary societies. They could not seize a single imperial center and thereby command a vast region, for the semisedentary peoples often did not owe allegiance to any entity beyond their individual communities. Some did develop confederations in response to the European challenge, but they did not exist before contact. Each community had to be defeated in turn and, often, then effectively occupied, for these peoples would assert their independence anew as soon as the Spaniards had departed. Discussing the difficulties the Spaniards encountered with the Maya of the Yucatan Peninsula, Inga Clendinnen remarks,

> That first task of conquest proved difficult. Although they spoke a common tongue the Maya were not politically united: indeed, the Spaniards were long puzzled to discover any stable political groups in the country. . . .
> They learnt that a town which had once welcomed them with gifts might on the next entry greet them with arrows. Even more bewildering, if less dangerous, that order was sometimes reversed. More frustrating, expecially for Spaniards, who at least officially placed a high value on the binding power of oaths, the Maya seem to suffer from selective amnesia. Treaties and agreements were forgotten when the actual physical presence of the Spaniards was withdrawn, leaving battles to be fought and submissions to be exacted all over again. It seemed that, for the Maya, oaths were written in water.[12]

Even the countryside worked against the Spaniards. Most semisedentary peoples lived in forests, and the foreigners had difficulty moving through the overgrown hinterland, which was conducive to ambush and flight. Entire communities would disappear into the backcountry for years at end, practicing their swidden agriculture in a new setting.

Nor did native warriors stand and fight to the death or capture. Instead they commonly utilized stealth and flight. They chose the battleground—or even attacked by surprise—and when at a disadvantage, they scattered into the rugged hinterland. They could not sustain a heavy loss of life, given their much lower population densities. While they sometimes battled man-to-man from fixed positions, for example, Mayan societies just as often fought from cover with bows and arrows, and they were quick to flee if their several volleys did not disrupt their opponents. Their arrows generally had little impact on the Spaniards, for they lacked metals to use as arrowheads. Consequently, the Spaniards soon abandoned their heavy body armor, except for their helmets, in favor of quilted cotton padding which they draped over themselves and their steeds. This padding proved sufficient to stop arrows and provided greater coolness and freedom of movement. Even successful ambushes that forced the Spanish to withdraw rarely caused them many casualties.

The hardship of travel through difficult terrain and the futility of these endeavors, rather than military defeats themselves, caused many expeditions to withdraw. In tropical regions with inadequate supplies of food and water, the combination of famine and disease plagued *entradas* more than enemy attacks. For instance, Diego de Rojas, an Indian fighter of long experience, led an expedition of 200 men all over northern Argentina from 1542 to 1546 and discovered nothing of value. Rojas died under suspicious circumstances during the venture. His successor was assassinated after two more years of unrelenting failure. The survivors then split formally into two groups, both of which returned to Peru.

The primary weapons that the Spaniards had used against the sedentary empires—swords and cavalry—were much less effective against peoples who did not fight in open areas and who avoided lengthy close combat. While the horse certainly still constituted an advantage, horsemen were rarely able to attack en masse into enemy formations. Likewise, swordsmen proved largely ineffective in the hit-and-run warfare characteristic of these areas. Thus the Spaniards turned increasingly to the use of their own projectiles—musket balls and crossbow bolts.

Another fundamental problem confronted organizers of Spanish *entradas* in areas inhabited by semisedentary peoples: the recruitment and retention of adequate men to hold the area. Typically, the initial expedition was well manned and equipped, but after it suffered losses and discovered neither exploitable resources nor peoples that could be translated into wealth, it would withdraw from the area. Subsequent *entradas* attracted fewer backers and participants. Eventually, these campaigns became wars of attrition, with a rather small contingent of committed Spaniards fighting a native population, itself undergoing disruption and decimation from the combination of combat and epidemics.

A frequent outcome was for a good number of the surviving natives to accept subordination to the colonists, whose own numbers would not increase notably because of the region's economic unattractiveness. The unsubdued would live on the other side of a frontier, which would shift from time to time but generally remained in place for an extended period—as these zones tended to face stagnant situations after their initial colonization. But even the unconquered natives resided in rudimentary settlements with more primitive economies and cultures than had been the case before the arrival of the Spaniards. Each side carried on some level of trade and cultural exchange with the other and engaged in military raids as well, if conditions warranted.

While the encounters between the Spaniards and the Inca and Aztec civilizations resulted in rather similar conquests, those between the Iberians and the semisedentary chiefdoms produced a considerable range of outcomes. The Maya of the Yucatan ended up reduced in number, with the survivors living in small communities on either of two sides of a frontier, as would a large number of the Tupinambá communities in Portuguese Brazil. But the Araucanians of Chile and the Guaraní of Paraguay had very different experiences.

The Araucanians organized perhaps the best extended military resistance to the Spanish of any of the agricultural peoples of the Americas. They controlled the southern third of Chile and actually expanded into the southern part of Argentina until the armies of the two countries finally defeated them around 1880. An expedition commanded by Pedro de Valdivia colonized central Chile in 1541, founding the capital of Santiago and a string of secondary cities. The Spaniards imposed rotary draft labor service (the *encomienda*) on nearby indigenous communities, who initially accepted the alien presence without violence, and began to look for gold. But in the 1550s, the Araucanians of central Chile rose up in a series of rebellions, killing a number of colonists (including Valdivia, who was captured and tortured to death), and forcing the remainder into palisaded settlements. Chile ceased to be a favored destination of Spanish immigrants. The Spaniards were able to reassert preeminence in the center of the country, but the south—beyond the Bío-Bío river—remained in the hands of the Araucanians, who stayed permanently in a state of arms.

The colonists would occasionally raid across the river, but had little success beyond the taking of some captives which they sold as slaves in Peru. Just as frequently, the Araucanians attacked the Spanish zone, destroying crops, burning down farmhouses, and sometimes even destroying communities. Despite this, central Chile became a well-established and thriving colony, with a complex economy and social structure. The colonial government responded to these frequent raids from the south by establishing a string of forts (*presidios*) along the frontier staffed by regular soldiers (usually lower-class colonists), as well as missions to try to convert the resolutely independent Araucanians, largely without success. All this cost a great deal of money, more than colonial Chile could afford, so Spain provided annual subsidies drawn from the prosperous mining economy of Peru.

The southern Araucanians (also termed Mapuches) responded to the Spanish pressure in very innovative fashion. They incorporated the horse into their way of combat, with one man guiding the steed and another behind him firing arrows. They used lengthy pikes to thwart Spanish charges, letting the horses or horsemen impale themselves by their own impetus. The Mapuche learned to use firearms from renegades and captives and even to make their own gunpowder. They also shifted from the cultivation of maize to wheat, as the latter had a shorter growing season and was thus less vulnerable to Spanish raids.

The Mapuche evolved politically as well. What had been a very decentralized society, with small communities having complete autonomy over their own affairs, developed a tradition of permanent (or at least long-term) war chiefs to govern affairs. This transformation gradually became a confederation to coordinate military matters complete with an unprecedented sense of constituting an Araucanian nation, that is, an ethnic province with a distinctive shared history and interests, and not just a common language.

By the eighteenth century, mounted Mapuche parties had crossed the Andes and subdued or expelled the native peoples of southern Argentina. They raided the stockraising establishments close to Buenos Aires, and prevented the Argentines from settling far south of that city. In the late 1870s, the militaries of Chile and Argentina took the southern parts of their countries away from Mapuche control and forced the survivors onto desolate reservations through the use of repeating rifles, barbed wire, and the telegraph.

Not all Spanish engagements with semisedentary peoples revolved around military subjugation. In a fascinating exception, the colonists and the native people of Paraguay entered into a close and enduring alliance against attacks from surrounding nomadic peoples. This colony emerged out of perhaps the most dramatic Spanish failure at large-scale colonization: the 1535 effort led by Pedro de Mendoza to establish a settlement at the mouth of the Río de la Plata. Some 1,300 people, including a substantial number of women, offloaded at a disease-ridden spot expecting to discover abundant silver, but instead found only meager subsistence. The peoples of the pampas, warlike nomadic bands, inflicted many casualties, and after just a few years, the 350 or so surviving Spaniards fled up the river, searching for a place of safety.

They installed themselves in a fertile region and founded the city of Asunción at the juncture of the Pilcomayo and Paraguay rivers, a thousand miles from the mouth of the La Plata. This area was inhabited by the Guaraní people, a branch of the Tupian peoples who inhabited much of central South America (including Brazil). But the semisedentary Guaraní were frequently attacked by nomadic peoples who populated the rugged, less fertile country that surrounded their territory, particularly to the north and west. Over the first quarter century of settlement, the Spaniards regularly assisted the Guaraní in warfare against their opponents and in return the Guaraní integrated them into native society as headmen.

As Guaraní society was organized around senior females, Spanish colonists accrued power and labor by affiliating themselves with as many of these women as possible. The female relatives of the Spanish consorts (who rarely became their wives) performed most agricultural labor, and the males constituted a dependable fighting force, and also sometimes laborers. Because few additional Spaniards immigrated to Paraguay, within a couple of generations virtually every Spanish child there was biologically a *mestizo* (person of mixed Spanish-Indian ancestry), but the better-off continued to consider themselves Spaniards, and only commoners were termed *mestizos*.

Portuguese colonization in South America in the sixteenth century was fundamentally shaped by the character of its Indian peoples, most of whom were semisedentary. Whereas colonization in the Americas constituted Spain's primary overseas venture, in the sixteenth century Brazil was a very secondary objective relative to Portugal's other enterprises. In 1498 a Portuguese fleet had already successfully voyaged to India to trade. Over the next few decades, Portugal would establish armed trading posts (*feitorias*) in India, Southeast Asia, and the Spice Islands and establish contact with both China and Japan.

For thirty years after 1500, when a Portuguese fleet under Cabral discovered Brazil, the country hardly paid any attention to this new territory. The only immediately exportable resource that Brazil offered was dyewoods. While Spain had quickly turned to the full settlement approach in the Caribbean, in Brazil the Portuguese continued the mercantile patterns that characterized their operations elsewhere in the world. As James Lockhart and Stuart B. Schwartz state,

> The system of private initiatives and royal contracts had been employed by the Portuguese in Africa, and in many ways the techniques of the dyewood trade paralleled those previously used to extract gold, ivory, and slaves from West Africa. Small forts or trading stations were established in suitable landing sites, often islands, and a few men under a *feitor*, or manager, stayed behind to staff them. During their stay, the Portuguese would induce local Indians to cut dyewood trees and deliver the logs to the fort in return for trinkets and European trade goods. Arriving ships could thus be sure of finding cargoes of dyewood logs waiting at the trade forts.[13]

South of the Amazon River basin, most of Brazil was inhabited by semi-sedentary Tupian-speaking peoples who lived in autonomous small communities that cultivated manioc. They lacked any central political authority. As among the Eastern Woodlands peoples of North America and the Guaraní of Paraguay, women performed the bulk of agricultural labor and had considerable status and authority. The men hunted, conducted diplomacy, and fought the community's enemies. The Tupians responded warmly to the Portuguese requests that they harvest dyewoods for deposit at their trading posts. Such work was similar to what was already expected of men in this culture and the people were anxious to receive the cloth and the iron tools and weapons that the Portuguese provided in exchange.

But the situation began to change in the 1530s, for Portugal's European rivals, especially the French, contested its control of Brazil. Portugal realized that it had to establish a substantial presence in the colony to retain it. Between 1533 and 1535, the Portuguese crown distributed the colony in fifteen sections (called *donatários*, or grants) divided along east–west lines to private individuals, who were mostly local gentry and experienced expedition leaders. Lacking the resources to develop Brazil, the monarchy left it to private individuals. The crown

granted recipients of donatary grant considerable jurisdiction and taxation authority plus the right to make land grants in their territory. Most recipients
lacked the funds to develop their grants and let them languish. A few, though,
did endure, in particular those in which settlers had established good relations
with the local natives.

From the earliest days certain Portuguese had chosen to stay—or had been
marooned—in Brazil when their ships departed. These men resided with local
women, and they and their mixed-race children (called *mamelucos* in Brazil) became vital intermediaries between Portuguese settlers and local native groups. In
the south, what became the province of São Paulo developed precisely because
Portuguese immigrants established households with mixed-race or native
women and integrated themselves into their cultures, even assisting the local
peoples in warfare. Portuguese and foreign merchants eventually invested in
sugar plantations there. The Northeast province of Pernambuco also prospered
in the second half of the sixteenth century when its proprietor and settlers followed the same strategy with the coastal peoples they settled among. However,
they enslaved Indians from the interior to provide most of the labor on the sugar
plantations they established; few Africans had yet been brought to Brazil. But the
enslavement of Indians had inherent limitations and could not endure indefi-
nitely as the primary labor institution in a large-scale sugar industry. The natives
were too few in number, often died from imported epidemics, or fled into the familiar backcountry. In their culture, agricultural labor was a female activity and
these people found European production techniques and implements to be quite
alien.

Limited Iberian Success against Nonsedentary Peoples

The Iberians also encountered nomadic bands who lived in the deserts,
plains, and jungles of the Americas. In general, the Europeans quickly withdrew
from these areas once they ascertained the lack of exploitable resources and the
character of the inhabitants. Hence they did not become significant zones of colonization until some centuries later. These regions were not conducive to agriculture, and the indigenous population was small in number, resilient in warfare,
and resistant to forced labor service. Sixteenth-century Spanish expeditions
journeyed across the North American plains, the Amazon drainage basin, and the
South American pampas, but withdrew because of their lack of appeal. Spanish
colonists congregated in Mesoamerica and the Andean region for their exploitable resources and numerous laborers.

But one major exception existed: northern Mexico, an arid and rugged
countryside that included major silver deposits. By the 1550s, colonists had
begun to establish mining camps throughout the area. These were sufficiently
large and well-defended not to be overrun. However, native bands sometimes
raided them as well as the ponderous wagon trains that connected the mines with
heavily settled central Mexico.

To combat these attacks, the colonial government utilized the same methods that had worked so well in the center of that country: formal *entradas* manned by recent recruits. But these slow, heavily equipped expeditions failed utterly. Nomadic bands simply avoided them, except to inflict sudden ambushes from time to time. The natives, generally called *Chichimecs* by natives and Spaniards alike, quickly learned the Spanish style of warfare, and even began to develop stronger leaders to coordinate their activities, some of whom had lived among the Spaniards.

The colonial government responded to this problem in two ways. First, it sponsored the colonization of certain sites in the north by contingents of pacified sedentary peoples from central Mexico. It established new municipalities and granted them special privileges and economic concessions. The intention was that these successful agricultural communities would influence the hunting peoples to adopt a more peaceful and sedentary way of life. This did not occur, but these settlements endured and retained their distinctive indigenous culture through the remainder of the colonial period.

Second, the government established a string of forts in the north, generally located by small towns and manned by (sometimes poorly) paid soldiers. To survive, these men conducted raids to capture hostiles and sell them as slaves in central Mexico. They also established small farms near their forts to provision themselves. Thus these soldiers often became permanent settlers after they left active service. The Spanish commanders began to stress mobility and small-unit actions with emphasis on musket fire rather than swordplay against these bands of hunters and gatherers that attacked from ambush and fled when beleaguered.

Though helpful, these strategies did not pacify the north. Each new viceroy in the second half of the sixteenth century denounced his predecessor's ineptitude and began a new offensive, which was rarely any more successful. Finally, in about the last decade of that century, the colonial government began a new approach that proved more successful. It dispatched envoys to inform the hostile bands that if they formed peaceful communities and accepted missionaries, the government would provide them with some wagonloads of European goods each year. A number of these bands, which were suffering to some extent from incessant warfare and from the ravages of epidemic diseases, accepted these terms. But as Spanish settlement extended farther into the north over the years, yet other campaigns were pursued against similar peoples. This process continued until the end of the colonial period, when it was still ongoing from California to Texas.

Conclusion

The *conquistadores* who defeated the great empires of the Aztecs and Incas should not be distinguished from the other early colonists in Spanish America. They had the same backgrounds, abilities, motives, and assets. The "conquerors" just found themselves in situations where extended combat (or combat readiness) was required. Once they had prevailed, they became in most respects indistinguishable from the others who arrived early on, but had avoided combat.

Although the expeditions against the Aztecs and Incas captured the emperor and ruled through him for some time, in both cases they ultimately had to defeat the imperial center led by members of the ruling family in grueling combat. Only when thoroughly defeated in warfare did the imperial dynasties acknowledge the permanent subordination of themselves and their peoples.

The native societies invariably viewed the Europeans through their traditional cultural lenses. They did not consider them as gods, or even as particularly alien beings who could not be understood and should be held in awe. Instead, they commonly understood them to be quite similar to themselves in their goals, expectations, and values. Indigenous rulers were quick to negotiate with the strangers and to seek to make use of them for their own ends. Overall, the Indians did not regard the Europeans as especially "other" ("otherness" being an often bandied-around concept that is not supported by the evidence), nor did they become passive and slow to respond to the new, unexpected situation. Native leaders commonly proposed alliances and strategies with the Spanish expeditions. At times, they clearly manipulated the intruders for their own ends without the Spanish commanders understanding how they were being used.

In actual combat against the armies of the sedentary imperial states, the Spanish made little use of their numerous, and otherwise important, native allies. They could not match the *conquistadores* in close combat that required small-unit tactics and reliance on sword-fighting complemented by periodic cavalry charges. However, the situation was totally different in campaigns against the many semisedentary and nonsedentary peoples. While cavalry and metal weapons remained important—indeed, most of the tribes who resisted the military onslaught most successfully incorporated both metal weapons and horses into their arsenals—the Spanish attackers relied on gunfire and long-term alliances with certain native peoples who provided guides, intelligence, and now also warriors. Indigenous fighters were far more valuable in campaigns that depended on rapid advances, surprise and ambush, and the exchange of projectiles. The Spanish commanders appreciated the additional manpower as well, for it often proved difficult to recruit an adequate number of Spanish participants in ventures that promised few Indian laborers or riches at their end.

Finally, those peoples who successfully resisted Spanish advances and established enduring frontiers with the colonial societies, as well as those well beyond the frontiers who came into little direct contact with Europeans, experienced significant cultural change. European trade goods, animals, plants, diseases, cultural practices, and religious perspectives all penetrated these societies to some extent.

Select Bibliography

Clendinnen, Inga. *Ambivalent Conquests: Maya and Spaniard in Yucatan, 1517–1570.* Cambridge, England: Cambridge University Press, 1987.

Flickema, Thomas. "The Siege of Cuzco," *Revista de Historia de América, 92* (July–Dec. 1981), pp. 17–47.

Guilmartin, Jr., John F., "The Cutting Edge: An Analysis of the Spanish Invasion and

Overthrow of the Inca Empire, 1532–1539," in Kenneth J. Andrien and Rolena Adorno, eds., *Transatlantic Encounters: Europeans and Andeans in the Sixteenth Century* (Berkeley: University of California Press, 1991), pp. 40–69.

Hassig, Ross. *Mexico and the Spanish Conquest.* London: Longman, 1994.

Hemming, John. *The Conquest of the Incas.* New York: Harcourt Brace Jovanovich, 1970.

Hemming, John. *Red Gold: The Conquest of the Brazilian Indians, 1500–1760.* Cambridge, MA: Harvard University Press, 1978.

Kicza, John E., "Patterns in Early Spanish Overseas Expansion," *William and Mary Quarterly,* 3rd series, *49*:2 (April 1992), pp. 229–253.

Lockhart, James. *The Men of Cajamarca: A Social and Biographical Study of the First Conquerors of Peru.* Austin: University of Texas Press, 1972.

Lockhart, James. ed. and trans. *We People Here: Nahuatl Accounts of the Conquest of Mexico.* Berkeley: University of California Press, 1993.

Marchant, Alexander. *From Barter to Slavery: The Economic Relations of Portuguese and Indians in the Settlement of Brazil, 1500–1580.* Baltimore: Johns Hopkins University Press, 1942.

Padden, Robert Charles, "Cultural Adaptation and Militant Autonomy among the Araucanians of Chile," *Southwestern Journal of Anthropology, 13*:1 (Spring 1957), pp. 103–121.

Powell, Philip Wayne. *Soldiers, Indians, and Silver: The Northward Advance of New Spain, 1550–1600.* Berkeley: University of California Press, 1952.

Sauer, Carl Ortwin. *The Early Spanish Main.* Berkeley: University of California Press, 1966.

Service, Elman R. *Spanish–Guaraní Relations in Early Colonial Paraguay.* Ann Arbor: University of Michigan Press, 1954.

Thomas, Hugh. *Conquest: Montezuma, Cortés, and the Fall of Old Mexico.* New York: Simon & Schuster, 1993.

Wilson, Samuel M. *Hispaniola: Caribbean Chiefdoms in the Age of Columbus.* Tuscaloosa, AL: University of Alabama Press, 1990.

Endnotes

1   Fray Bartolomé de las Casas, *Historia de Las Indias* (Mexico City: Fondo de Cultural Económica, 1951), vol. I, p. 204.

2   John E. Kicza, "Patterns in Early Spanish Overseas Expansion," *William and Mary Quarterly,* 3rd series, 49:2 (April 1992), p. 245.

3   Fray Bernardino de Sahagún, *Florentine Codex: General History of the Things of New Spain; Book 12 - The Conquest of Mexico,* trans. Arthur J. O. Anderson and Charles Dibble, (Santa Fe: School of American Research, 1955), p. 84.

4   Bernal Díaz, *The Conquest of New Spain,* trans. by J. M. Cohen (Hammondworth, England: Penguin Books, 1963), pp. 148–149.

5   Díaz, *The Conquest,* pp. 141–142.

6   Francisco López de Gómara, *Cortés: The Life of the Conqueror by his Secretary,* trans. and ed. Leslie Byrd Simpson (Berkeley: University of California Press, 1966), p. 74.

7   Díaz, *The Conquest,* p. 373.

8   *We People Here: Nahuatl Accounts of the Conquest of Mexico,* ed. and trans. by James Lockhart, Repertorium Columbianum, Vol. 1 (Berkeley: University of California Press, 1993), p. 21.

9   López de Gómara, *Cortés,* p. 211.

10   Díaz, *The Conquest,* pp. 303-304.

11   López de Gómara, *Cortés,* p. 225.

12   Inga Clendinnen, *Ambivalent Conquests: Maya and Spaniard in Yucatan, 1517–1570* (Cambridge, England: Cambridge University Press, 1987), pp. 24–25.

13   James Lockhart and Stuart B. Schwartz, *Early Latin America: A History of Colonial Spanish America and Brazil,* (Cambridge, England: Cambridge University Press, 1983), p. 182.

4

Colonial Spanish America and Its Impact on the Sedentary Imperial Societies

Spanish Colonists and Their Expectations

The fundamental division of the indigenous societies of the Americas into sedentary, semisedentary, and nomadic peoples greatly conditioned their interaction with colonists and colonial governments. This chapter treats the complex changes that took place among the sedentary agricultural peoples of Mexico and the Andes due to Spanish colonization. A later chapter examines the far different interactions and transformations that characterized the semisedentary and nonsedentary peoples elsewhere in Latin America, including those between the Portuguese and the native peoples of Brazil. The Spanish alone had the good fortune to encounter and subjugate the two zones of advanced sedentary peoples in the Americas—central Mexico and the Andean region—and most people think of these places when they envision the Spanish colonial presence in the New World.

Spaniards did not flood into the Americas. In fact, up to 1650, more than 100 years after the two great conquests, perhaps only 450,000 had come to the colonies. The vast majority of these immigrants settled in Mexico and Peru, where precious metals and the labor potential of large indigenous populations offered the promise of wealth. The Spanish historically have been a very urban-oriented people, and this pattern carried over into the New World, where they

The political organization of the Spanish and Portuguese American empires around 1700 (*Lyle N. McAlister, Spain and Portugal in the New World, 1492–1700, Minneapolis: University of Minnesota Press, 1984. Map 6. Reprinted by permission.*)

founded cities almost immediately upon their arrival in each new region. In every Spanish colony, the great majority of colonists lived in the cities. Sometimes, as in the case of Mexico City, they took over a long-established indigenous urban center—the former Tenochtitlan, capital of the Aztec empire. Other times, as in the case of Lima in 1535, they founded a totally new city because its setting was more inviting than any existing native one. As the vast majority of Indians remained in their rural villages, their contacts with the European population—and hence the possibilities for acculturation—continued to be limited.

Nor did the Spaniards (or colonists from other countries, for that matter) have any great curiosity about native cultures. Almost to a person they came to the Americas to make a better life for themselves than they could hope to achieve back in Spain. Most, at least during their first years in the colonies, aspired to return eventually to Spain, though in fact few did. These immigrants also lacked any sense of cultural relativism, and saw the vanquished Indians as inferior sorts hardly worth attention, except perhaps for how their existence might be accommodated within Christian doctrine. A few friars who came to the early colonies systematically explored the values, practices, and histories of some of the native peoples, generally as part of their efforts to evangelize them. But overall, colonists, whether landowners, merchants, priests, or government officials, hardly thought about the character of the people they now lived among. Few laymen in the first century of colonial rule wrote extended studies of native culture, with one notable exception. In the 1530s and 1540s, Pedro de Cieza de León composed a four-part work on the history and culture of the Incas and their conquest by the Spaniards based on his travels throughout the Andes and questions posed to the natives.

The economies of the major colonies of New Spain (Mexico) and Peru focused on silver mining and commercial agriculture, with thriving, autonomous mercantile and transportation spheres complementing these fields of enterprise. In most settings and throughout much of the colonial period these industries incorporated only a limited number of natives as permanent workers. However, they often utilized Indians as temporary laborers in work gangs, supervised by their own ethnic leaders.

No Spanish individual or agency argued that the existing native social and political organization should be destroyed and replaced by another model. The intent of Spanish policy from the beginning was to govern indigenous peoples by utilizing indigenous political structures and social hierarchies. The Spanish sought only to eliminate the upper levels of Aztec and Inca imperial administration. They left lower-level traditional ethnic lords in place.

But in Peru, the Spaniards were even slower to remove the imperial structure than in Mexico. Pizarro did not seek direct authority over the native population until the 1536 revolt led by Manco Inca. Even after this rebellion, the Spanish recognized the imperial pretensions of some Incas in limited ways. Andean peoples slowed the process of dismantling Inca imperial power because they long retained a benign memory of Inca rule. Several times hundreds of years after the overthrow of the Inca empire, Indian rebels galvanized popular support in the highlands by casting themselves as the rightful heirs to the Inca throne.

The Retention of Indigenous Provincial Organization

Spanish colonists well appreciated that the Incas and Aztecs had construct-ed vast empires out of ethnically distinct provinces, and sought to retain these larger political structures, while turning them to their own advantage. Most colonial efforts to regulate the native population or to utilize its labor power and resources were based on long-established indigenous practices. The most funda-mental indigenous organizational principle that the Spanish exploited was the ethnic province, or city-state. Most aspects of Spanish rule over the peoples of Mesoamerica and the Andes used this structure. An Indian province, whether assigned to an individual Spaniard early in the colonial period as a reward (an *encomienda*) or later on to a government functionary to administrate (a *corregimiento*), usually corresponded to this jurisdiction. Such indigenous provinces also became the basis for Catholic parishes established in the Indian countryside.

Spanish authorities expected local indigenous political leaders to mobilize their people to fill the labor drafts and to pay the tribute payments required under the new colonial order. Spanish administrators did not seek to systemati-cally reorganize native communities or modify prevailing *calpulli* and *ayllu* pat-terns. They did expect the Indians to reorganize their local ruling bodies to fit the Spanish model of a municipal council (*cabildo*), with magistrates and coun-cilors. Initially, this caused little disruption, as communities adapted in part by rotating offices among members of their traditional ruling elites. In 1580, the community of Yecapixtla located south of Mexico City reported that its *cabildo* consisted of a governor, three *alcaldes,* and six "ancient noble elders." Before con-tact, many native communities had been divided into four districts, each with its own nobility. In the 1540s, the large indigenous province of Cuernavaca, also south of Mexico City, rotated its governorship among its highest-ranked nobles. Four subordinate governors served under him, one from each of the communi-ty's major districts.

Charles Gibson describes the limited impact of the conquest on the Mexican province of Tlaxcala.

> In general the effect of the conquest upon Tlaxcalan society was to re-duce sharply its numerical population but not markedly to alter its in-ternal composition. In the forms of social life the Tlaxcalans, like many other Indians, survived the "shock" of the conquest. Nothing in Spanish government after 1530 or before the last quarter of the century prevent-ed them from creating a vigorous, prosperous society, based ultimately on pre-conquest forms but developed further through many post-con-quest techniques and institutions.[1]

The 1560 Petition to the King from the Rulers of Huejotzingo

Each traditional ethnic province retained its distinct identity under Spanish colonial rule and typically sought to portray itself to the government in the best possible light. In this petition originally written in Nahuatl some forty years after the conquest of Mexico in an effort to gain a reduction of their tribute allotment, the rulers of the Province of Huejotzingo seek to highlight and in the end exaggerate their community's unique contributions to the Spanish cause. The rhetorical hyperbole is typical of formal native Mexican discourse.

Our lord sovereign, before anyone told us or made us acquainted with your fame and your story, most high and feared universal king who rules all, and before we were told or taught the glory and name of our Lord God, before the faith reached us, and before we were Christians, when your servants the Spaniards came to us and your Captain General don Hernando Cortés arrived, although we were not yet acquainted with the omnipotent, very compassionate holy Trinity, our Lord God the ruler of heaven and possessor of earth caused us to deserve that in his mercy he enlightened us so that we took you as our king, to belong to you and become your people and subjects; not a single town here in New Spain surpassed us, in that first and earliest we threw ourselves to you, we gave ourselves to you, and furthermore, no one intimidated us, no one forced us into it, but truly God caused us to deserve that voluntarily we adhered to you, so that we gladly received the newly arrived Spaniards who reached us here in New Spain for we left our homes behind to go a great distance to meet them; we went twenty leagues to greet Captain don Hernando Cortés and the others whom he led. We received them very gladly, we embraced them, we saluted them with many tears, though we were not acquainted with them, and our fathers and grandfathers also did not know them; but by the mercy of our Lord God we truly came to know them. Since they are our neighbors, therefore we loved them; nowhere did we attack them. Truly we fed them and served them; some arrived sick so that we carried them in our arms and on our backs, and we served them in many other ways which we are not able to say here. Although the people who are called and named Tlaxcalans indeed helped, yet we strongly pressed them to give aid, and we counseled them not to make war; but though we so admonished them they made war and fought for fifteen days. But we, when a Spaniard was afflicted, without fail at once we would manage to reach him, like no one else. We do not lie in this, for all the conquerors know it well, those who have died and some now living. And when they began their conquest and war making, then also we well prepared ourselves to aid them, for out came all of our war gear, our arms and provisions and all our equipment, and we not merely named someone, we went in person, we who rule, and we brought all our nobles and all of our vassals to aid the Spaniards. We helped not only in warfare, but also we gave them everything they needed; we fed and clothed them, and we would carry in our arms and on our backs those whom they wounded in war or who were very ill, and we did all the tasks in preparing for war. And so that they could fight the Mexica with boats, we worked hard; we gave the Spaniards the wood and pitch with which they built the boats. And when they conquered the Mexica and all their adherents, we never abandoned them or left them. And as they went to conquer Michoacan, Jalisco, and Colhuacan, and at Pánuco and Oaxaca and Tehuantepec and Guatemala, (we were) the only ones who went along while they conquered and made war here in New Spain until they had finished the conquest; we never abandoned them, in no way did we hold back their war making, though some of us were destroyed in it, nor were any of our subjects left, for we did our duty very well. But as to those Tlaxcalans, several of their nobles were hanged for making war poorly; in many places they ran away, and often did poorly in the war. In this we do not lie, for the conquerors know it well.

Source: "Letter of the council of Huejotzingo to the king, 1560," trans. by the editors, in Arthur J. O. Anderson, Frances Berdan, and James Lockhart, eds., *Beyond the Codices: The Nahua View of Colonial Mexico* (Los Angeles: UCLA Latin American Center, 1976), pp. 181–183. Copyright © 1976 The Regents of the University of California. Reprinted by permission.

Fragmentation and Its Impact

The Spanish takeover of the sedentary imperial peoples did bring with it two dramatically transforming processes: one—fragmentation—largely unintended by the authorities; and the other—demographic collapse—never intended and little understood even at the time. After the conquest, traditional community and provincial leaders had to respond to the demands of colonial officials from a totally different culture that had no understanding of the logic and meaning behind their established forms of organization. Their relationships with Spanish authorities were not tempered by the patterns of intermarriage or the gift-giving and mutual feasting that had characterized precontact imperial arrangements.

The colonial system inflicted its greatest damage to the cultural and physical infrastructure of the indigenous cultures. The Incas and Aztecs supported not just empires, but also enormous shared culture zones: civilizations. These were fragmented to the provincial, and sometimes the local, level under Spanish rule, as the natives could no longer openly and freely transfer their traditional beliefs, practices, and products within a much larger region. The new rulers sought to eradicate indigenous imperial ideologies and religions. Hence the larger culture zones that characterized Mesoamerica and the Andean zone faded, to be replaced by an increasingly bifurcated world: a Spanish colonial sphere and a native one, which itself was divided internally into a number of smaller, largely autonomous ethnic zones. This sharp division was mitigated somewhat in Mesoamerica, though hardly in the Andes, by the early establishment of interprovincial trading networks that exchanged European items, and increasingly traditional native products, over long distances. While most native markets were local in character, this ever-expanding commerce touched on native communities, particularly those on or near to trade routes. But, of course, while this process brought more villages into contact with each other, it did so within the framework of the Spanish colonial economy and culture, not an autonomous indigenous one.

Spanish rule also dismantled the institutional structures of native religion at both the imperial and provincial levels. The realms of native religion that had once stressed gods, belief structures, and rituals across the civilizational zone, or even within the individual ethnic province, were dismantled under Spanish rule, replaced to some extent by Catholicism. So even religious belief and practices became localized to a considerable degree. Indigenous protests and rebellions against the colonial order were almost always organized at the community level and dedicated to the rectification of purely local problems.

In the Andes perhaps more than in Mesoamerica the precontact civilization had depended heavily on social and physical engineering, which involved the migration of groups from one location to another, and the construction of tremendous irrigation and terracing projects to ensure the harvest and storage of food surpluses. These surpluses resulted from the political infrastructure that had connected all of the diverse environmental zones and communities in the province. Under the colonial system, such intricate and vital structures were ignored and fell rapidly into disrepair. The sad result was that much of the cultural adhesion that had connected physically separated villages together and had integrated them into a larger entity disappeared, never to be replaced or reassembled. Agricultural production plummeted and native communities became more self-sufficient and separated from each other than ever before. The isolated Indian village of the colonial period, living at a rudimentary level, was a result of this disregard; it did not predate the conquest.

During the colonial period, the native population shifted their primary political identification to their individual municipalities, away from the ethnic province, once so important in the precontact period, and from the larger ethnic or language group. Indigenous rulers above the local level had been stripped of power, and sometimes incorporated into the Spanish colonial social hierarchy. In either case, they no longer held political authority over a large ethnic group, nor were they disposed to protect or mobilize their former subjects.

The native communities themselves contributed to the political fragmentation. In the precontact period, the individual communities within each ethnic province essentially enjoyed equal status, without headtowns and subject villages. However, in Spain, a headtown-subject village hierarchy of settlements constituted the fundamental principle of provincial political organization. Hence, colonial authorities expected and encouraged indigenous communities to arrange themselves along hierarchical lines. Many native towns gained recognition as headtowns from the colonial government, designating outlying communities as subject to them. Over time, the subject communities increasingly resented their subordinate status and petitioned for recognition as headtowns. These efforts often succeeded, with the result of greater decentralization through the creation of more autonomous indigenous political units.

Demographic Collapse and Its Consequences

Separated from the rest of the world for well over ten thousand years, the Americas had developed a quite distinctive—and generally healthier—disease environment. They had been insulated from the major epidemic diseases that regularly plagued the Old World, particularly smallpox, measles, typhus, and even perhaps influenza. (Malaria and yellow fever entered the hemisphere from Africa, probably with shipments of black slaves, making tropical regions in the Americas far more unhealthy than previously.) The peoples of Europe and much of the rest of Afro-Asia had developed natural antibodies that afforded them heightened resistance from repeated exposure to these epidemics generation after generation. Consequently, while these diseases killed the most vulnerable of their victims, usually the very young and very old, the great majority of adults recovered intact and resumed productive labor and human reproduction. Hence the detrimental impact of such epidemics was minimized and the basic configurations and functions of the affected society were preserved.

But the peoples of the Americas had developed no such natural resistance. When infected by an active carrier of one of these epidemic diseases—generally a person recently arrived from Spain—virtually the native population of an area became horribly sick, for the infection spread unrestrained among them. And as nearly everyone in a community fell sick at the same time, no one was available to provide even basic care, causing far greater numbers of fatalities. The Spaniards, like all Europeans of the time, were ignorant of the germ theory of disease. They were mystified as to why so many natives took ill and died, while they themselves developed only mild cases, if they became sick at all. They put forth a variety of explanations that ranged from the Indians being physically particularly weak vessels to divine punishment. Some Spaniards even argued that god meant to punish the rapacious colonists by depriving them of a subservient labor force.

The rates of population loss were horrendous. By the time that Cortés's expedition left Cuba for Mexico in 1519, the Caribbean natives constituted only a small fraction of their precontact population. The indigenous peoples on all the major islands disappeared by 1550. In central Mexico, a population probably over 20 million in 1519 declined to barely 1.25 million in 1650. Similar precipitous die-offs struck most areas in the Americas, from Central America to Chile.

The highland areas of the Andean zone experienced somewhat lower mortality because the coldness of higher altitudes retarded the virulence of disease and because the smaller number of Spaniards who settled in this region diminished the spread of contagion. In regard to Peru after its initial contact with the Spaniards, Noble David Cook writes

> The overall decline was approximately 93 percent for the century following contact between the European and Andean inhabitant. The collapse along Peru's coast was total. The native resident was almost completely wiped out and was replaced by the Spanish colonist and

African slaves. Only migration of highland Indians toward coastal haciendas [landed estates] and urban centers prevented extinction of Indian influence on the coastal strip. On the coast remaining Indians were transformed, as they became part of the lower level of colonial Hispanic society. By contrast, the sierra [highland] Indian was not decimated by the expansion of Europe in the sixteenth century. In spite of disease and outright exploitation by the Spaniards, the highland Indian persisted.[2]

Overall, population loss was greater in tropical zones than in temperate ones. Hunting-and-gathering societies resisted decimation better than their agricultural counterparts, because their lesser population density diminished rates of transmission. And, understandably, those regions that received the greatest number of European settlers suffered more than those that did not. Settlement rates were greatest in those areas with mineral wealth and substantial native populations, such as central Mexico and the southern Andes.

The agricultural peoples of the Americas commonly suffered roughly a 95 percent decrease in their population over approximately the first century of systematic contact with colonists. Their populations then began to recover, though only moderately. Much of Spanish America witnessed a gradual increase in the indigenous population in the second half of the colonial period, the 150 years after about 1650. This population growth heightened competition for fixed resources, transformed labor systems, and brought about greater migration out of native communities.

Without this tremendous reduction in the native population in the first centuries after contact, the degree of acculturation to Spanish ways within indigenous society would have been greatly diminished. The Europeans, and their culture, would have had less transforming impact on a much larger native population that constantly reinforced its own traditional beliefs and practices, particularly as the Spaniards did not commonly reside within indigenous communities.

In the late sixteenth and early seventeenth century, when population decline was at its worst, colonial officials sporadically enforced a policy of *congregación,* the consolidation of native populations into the larger towns in each ethnic province. This policy was intended to better administer, monitor, and convert the residents. The concentration of the population also had the unintended effect of accelerating the spread of epidemic disease. Finally, it made large stretches of abandoned land available to Spanish rural estates.

These consolidations of native populations respected traditional ethnic boundaries: people from two or more distinct groups were never combined. Further, they remained organized into their customary *calpullis* and *ayllus* and under the authority of their traditional lords. But even then, many people drifted back to their old settlements after just a few years, for the Spaniards did not monitor compliance once the initial relocation had taken place.

Tribute and Labor Service Systems

Many Spanish demands placed on Indian commoners, including tribute and labor service, continued or elaborated the practices of indigenous empires in the precontact period. Tribute payment in kind channelled through community leaders was a familiar concept in Mesoamerica, although it was unprecedented in the Andes, where all exactions had been in the form of labor service. The colonial government demanded the payment of a modest annual tribute in cash from each Indian adult male collected as a lump sum from community leaders. This required native communities to raise crops or animals to sell in the cities to raise the money, or individual Indians to enter the Spanish colonial economy temporarily as wage earners to pay their personal shares. Colonial revenue collectors sometimes incarcerated the leaders of communities unable to make their stipulated payments or seized their property to cover the deficit.

The Spaniards, like the imperial indigenous societies that had preceded them, also demanded rotary draft labor service from their subject peoples.

A Peruvian cacique's testimony about tribute payments in 1562

The Spanish colonial government periodically conducted reviews (*visitas*) of administrative districts to assess conditions and the conduct of its own officials. In one of these conducted in 1562 in the Province of Huánaco, a *cacique* was asked about tribute payments under the Incas and the Spaniards and responded as follows.

With regard to the sixth paragraph, concerning whether they presently pay tribute in the manner they did to the Inca and the rest, he said that they do not at present pay tribute to their *encomendero* [a Spaniard who received their tribute and labor service] as they did to the Inca, because now they make the cotton cloth and harvest the cotton on their *chacras* [cultivated fields]. They give wheat, which they did not give before, growing it where they used to grow the maize; and they give everything else that is included in their tribute assessment. . . . At present they find it harder to give the tribute than they did in the time of the Inca, because then there were many Indians and now there are fewer, and also because they give the tribute in cloth every four months and the Indian women and men are occupied spinning, weaving, and making it during the necessary time. Sometimes they do not have the time to go and cultivate their fields, since each married Indian has to provide a piece and a half of the cloth and a strip of blanket each year; and it takes the husband and wife four months to do the spinning and weaving for this, during which time they work in other things, hiring themselves out to work or cleaning their *chacras* and those of their *encomendero.* If they worked continuously on cloth without doing anything else it would take them three months to make their share of it.

Source: "1562. Testimony of a cacique before a *visitador,*" trans. by the editors, in John H. Parry and Robert G. Keith, eds., *New Iberian World,* Vol. IV (New York: Times Books, 1984), p. 372. Reprinted by permission of Edward J. Joyce, trustee.

Something around one-sixth of the adult males of each community under the supervision of a local leader had to work for Spanish enterprises, providing unskilled labor as a gang, usually for around six months. They then returned to their community and another group replaced them. Labor service characteristically consisted of the construction of roads, bridges, and buildings, transport, and labor on rural estates or in mining enterprises. Payment was nonexistent or token. Colonists certainly benefitted from this subsidized unskilled labor, but tribute labor was totally unsuitable for the performance of skilled or highly demanding tasks.

The indigenous peoples found this labor service very onerous, especially because of the tremendous population loss over the first century of the colonial period. Colonial officials did not regularly update community censuses, so communities typically had to provide a constant number of laborers despite the decline in numbers from epidemics and migration. Facing deteriorating circumstances in their home communities, males—occasionally with their families—sometimes chose to remain with the Spaniards for whom they worked, and as a result became more skilled and acculturated to Spanish ways. In Peru, others frequently opted to migrate to other native communities, because rotary draft labor service was expected only of people who lived in their home communities. In their new settings, these migrants avoided labor service, but they were also deprived of access to land and other resources. Over time, however, many migrants married local women and were thereby incorporated into the community, at least to a certain extent.

Another classification of native workers lived on the domains of ethnic lords disassociated from these rural communities. Yet others were slaves or permanent retainers of individual Spaniards; some also became free-wage laborers in colonial towns. Indian slavery was quite uncommon in colonial Mesoamerica and the Andean zone, but not because of any particular moral repugnance toward the institution. Rather, it was expensive compared to the inexpensive workers available through draft labor systems, and even at times through free wage ones. Further, it is quite difficult to enslave members of a society in their native territory; slaves are characteristically outsiders dependent on their masters. The few Indian slaves in such heavily settled regions as central Mexico and the Andes were typically war captives seized far away along the frontier against hunting-and-gathering peoples.

Both the Inca and Aztec nobility—and the Spanish nobility back in Europe—commonly utilized permanent personal retainers in their households and properties. These people were maintained by the noble household, worked only for it, and often identified closely with it. In the colonial world, Spaniards called these permanent retainers *naborías* (the Spanish adoption of an Indian word from the Caribbean) and they often enjoyed better working conditions and higher status than the commoners residing in native communities.

Urban Indians

Over time an increasing number of natives abandoned their communities to migrate into the Spanish colonial world as free laborers, often in the cities, but sometimes on haciendas (rural estates) or mining enterprises. In cities, some Indian workers resided in the central Spanish districts. There they worked as household servants, lower-level craftsmen, transporters, and unskilled laborers. These individuals typically became very acculturated to Spanish ways, for they worked for and among Spaniards, spoke to them in Spanish, and produced goods and services for them. Many became so acculturated that they eventually passed themselves off successfully as *mestizos,* or persons of mixed European descent. Even those who did not pass as *mestizos* frequently married persons of mixed racial descent, in part because people so classified were exempt from tribute payment and labor duty, with their children consequently classified as non-Indians.

Over time, outlying neighborhoods composed primarily of Indian migrants and their descendants ringed the major cities of Mesoamerica and the Andean region. Most of these peoples lived day-to-day, picking up what work they could. The men worked on construction crews and as unskilled day laborers. The women worked as domestic servants, market women, or laundresses. Migrants in these neighborhoods did not acculturate to Spanish ways with the same rapidity or thoroughness as those who lived in the central city, as they typically experienced less systematic contact with the European population. However, as the migrants belonged to different native ethnic groups, they developed a more generalized urban "Indian" cultural identity, for they could not maintain their distinctive original cultural beliefs and practices with such small numbers from each ethnic group. Language, foods, religious beliefs and ceremonies became increasingly standardized. John K. Chance describes what happened to members of these diverse ethnic and language groups in the southern Mexico city of Antequera (now Oaxaca City).

> What little population increase the city saw during the seventeenth century resulted primarily from the in-migration of Indians from the Valley [of Oaxaca] and the surrounding region. This process brought a further deterioration of ethnic distinctions among the urban Indians and a blurring of the division between principales [notables] and macehuales [commoners]. Antequera's service needs created a demand for the Indians' skills and labor, and they assimilated to Spanish urban society with little difficulty, though they continued to form a relatively closed and highly exploited ethnic group.[3]

With time urban Indians learned the Spanish language and Spanish tastes and techniques. But in other ways they remained very Indian, particularly in their choices of food, drink, and dress. And as they worked for wages, they came to constitute a substantial market for native products, such as beverages and clothing, shipped to the cities from rural villages. So Indian communities and

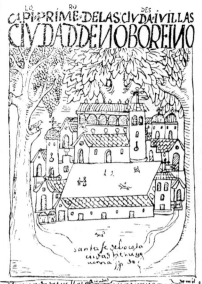

(a) *Bogotá*

(b) *Quito*

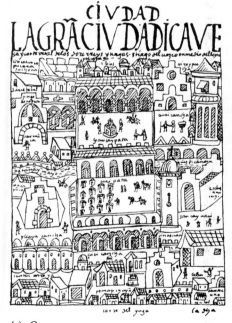

(c) *Cuzco*

(d) *Lima*

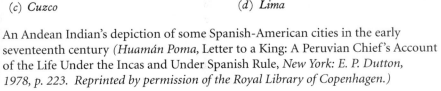

An Andean Indian's depiction of some Spanish-American cities in the early seventeenth century *(Huamán Poma,* Letter to a King: A Peruvian Chief's Account of the Life Under the Incas and Under Spanish Rule, *New York: E. P. Dutton, 1978, p. 223. Reprinted by permission of the Royal Library of Copenhagen.)*

businessmen—and even some Spaniards who appreciated the profits to be earned in this market—became suppliers of native goods to this growing population.

Race Mixture and Its Recognition

Throughout Latin America, but particularly in these vast zones inhabited by sedentary agricultural peoples, notable amounts of race mixture took place, and—just as importantly—the mixed-race offspring were recognized by all as different and occupying something of an intermediate rank between Spaniards and Indians. This process of race mixture, termed miscegenation or *mestizaje* in Spanish, began in the earliest years of colonization because of the relatively few Spanish women who migrated to the Americas in this period. The pattern of Spanish settlement in which Spaniards lived surrounded by native peoples— different from British North America, where the English continually pushed the vast majority of native peoples beyond the frontier—also promoted miscegenation.

The recognition of mixed racial groups was fostered by their substantial numbers in colonial cities coupled with the large number of respectable, decent-paying occupational positions they filled in the Spanish colonial economy. These positions appeared because of substantial long-term economic expansion and the limited number of Spanish immigrants available to fill the many available slots. Thus many *mestizos* and other *castas* (a term that referred collectively to all persons of mixed racial descent) were employed as artisans, store clerks, labor-gang supervisors, transporters, and the like.

These *castas* were largely Hispanic in culture, and typically spoke Spanish. They dressed in Spanish style and commonly ate wheat bread, the Spanish staple, rather than maize tortillas. In urban settings, most lived in the Spanish rather than Indian districts. Finally, as ethnic classification broadly determined one's social standing and life possibilities, many urban Indians aspired to become classified as *mestizos* and *mestizos* as Spaniards.

Testimony in a court case about Alberta María de los Dolores reveals how this shift from "Indian" to "*mestizo*" status could occur. She and her husband, Marcelo de los Santos, were born in Santiago Tlatelolco, an Indian neighborhood on the outskirts of Mexico City around 1700. After their marriage, they resided for some years in various Indian *barrios* on the edge of the city and regularly came into the center to sell goods in its marketplaces. After her husband's death, Alberta María moved to an apartment near the city center and continued to peddle wares in the streets. When Spanish authorities brought her to trial for selling love potions, some witnesses identified Alberta María as a *mestiza*, others as an Indian. Her own daughter identified herself as a *mestiza*, despite both of her parents being listed as Indians on their baptismal certificates.

Spanish authorities recorded many such cases of "passing," and ethnic mobility increased as time passed. Urban society was too complex and fluid to accurately trace everyone's ancestry, and the economy was so dynamic that new positions frequently opened up in the higher occupational ranks. Further, economically successful Indians sometimes married *mestizas*, and successful *mestizos* likewise married local Spanish women. In both cases, their offspring could generally claim the higher ethnic status enjoyed by their mothers.

Creative Adaptations at the Local Level

The native peoples responded dynamically to the imposition of the colonial regime. Many communities learned how to manipulate Spanish regulations and procedures to their own advantage. Numerous natives exploited the unprecedented opportunity now presented them to engage in commerce and other forms of enterprise. Steve J. Stern comments about the people of Huamanga in early colonial Peru.

> As usual, the Indians, rather than isolate themselves from these economic developments, sought to take advantage of new trends and opportunities. Individually and collectively, Indians incorporated the search for money and commercial advantage into their daily existence, and for their own benefit. To be sure, native societies had to find ways to earn money if they were to pay the money tributes owed to the encomenderos [individual Spaniards to whom the indigenous provinces owed tribute and labor service]. The early documentation, however, offers evidence which belies the conclusion that native societies participated reluctantly in the commercial economy just to gather monies needed for tribute. On the contrary, communities displayed an open, aggressive—even enthusiastic—attitude.[4]

Native society in rural areas retained many continuities with the precontact period, and most cultural adaptions were incorporated without great disruption to established ways, and certainly without radically transforming the ethnic group's traditional identity and cultural values. The Spaniards prohibited only three functional groups in indigenous society from practicing their occupations: professional military men, priests, and long-distance merchants. Most soldiers in traditional native warfare had been commoners fulfilling their labor service in the form of a military obligation. However, provinces also typically created a small cohort of professional soldiers organized into an elite corps. The colonial authorities could not permit this institution to endure, so they simply abolished all such entities, with the practitioners themselves merging back into the ranks of the commoners. Likewise with priests; because the Spaniards aspired to christianize all of the natives, they could not allow native priests to continue to publicly espouse their creed and perform their rituals. The occupation was outlawed. Finally, long-distance trade in scarce commodities was too lucrative to be left to indigenous businessmen. Spanish traders simply forced them out of most such commerce through sharp competition, though native traders continued to proliferate, concentrating primarily on local or regional exchanges.

Mesoamerican peoples in particular retained their trading and marketing traditions. Nearly every community operated a regional market that met regularly on a weekly or monthly basis. They readily incorporated European-made

An indigenous map of the Mexican community of Cuzcatlan in 1580
(Barbara R. Mundy, *The Mapping of New Spain: Indigenous Cartography
and the Maps of the Relaciones Geografícas*, Chicago: University
of Chicago Press, 1996. Ministerio de Educación, Cultura y Deporte.
Archivo General de Indias.)

goods into such exchange systems. As in precontact times, women dominated
these marketplaces, not just as purchasers but also as operators of the many small
stands. Direction of these petty commercial enterprises commonly passed down
from mother to daughter. The greater presence of Spaniards and other hispanized individuals such as blacks and *mestizos* in the countryside in Mexico
than in greater Peru, coupled with this resilient heritage of trade in the former
area, largely explains the more widespread dissemination of hispanic products

and cultural styles in Mexico than in the Andes. Larger numbers of subsistence-oriented native communities and a far sharper cultural separation between the indigenous and the Hispanic populations characterized the Andean highlands.

Colonial officials eliminated the political pretensions of both the Inca and the Aztec royal lineages. But the Spaniards continued to honor the social status and property that pertained to this elevated class. Committed to the rightfulness of strict social hierarchies, Spaniards recognized the native royal families as "natural lords" (*señores naturales*) who were worthy of respect. A fair number of *conquistadores* and early settlers married into these families and benefitted from the rank and wealth attached to these lineages. Doña Isabel Montezuma, a daughter of Emperor Montezuma, married Cuauhtemoc, the last emperor of the Aztecs. After his death, she married three Spaniards in succession. Each of the first two gained control over her *encomienda* and lands, but died after only a few years. Her final marriage was to Juan Cano, who though one of the conquerors, had never received an *encomienda*. Their wedding in 1536, however, made him rich in lands and laborers, and their descendants continued to prosper, with members of the Cano y Montezuma lineage living in Mexico City, enjoying wealth and status, through the end of the colonial period. Several of these mixed Spanish-Indian lineages ultimately gained noble titles awarded by the Spanish crown. A few even relocated to Spain itself, where they were accepted into the more elevated ranks of society.

Just as the Spanish colonial system recognized the authority of ethnic and local rulers over their own peoples and commonly ruled through them (indirect rule), it also respected the properties claimed through these lineages (as distinguished from the lands that their people held in common). Colonial authorities likewise honored their claims to labor service from their own subjects. But they also held these *caciques* personally responsible for the delivery of tribute and labor service to the Spanish. Failure to provide the specified amounts could result in imprisonment or confiscation of the ruler's personal property to cover the shortfall.

As might be imagined, some *caciques* struggled mightily over time to protect their people as best they could from the demands of the colonial system. Yet others made deals with local colonists and authorities and benefitted personally as their subjects suffered from heightened demands. Over the decades, many rulers became increasingly acculturated to Spanish ways, and some even married with Spanish or *casta* women without threat to their political standing. Thus some families ruling over native districts were in fact biologically *mestizo,* and sometimes quite urban oriented. But they would never divorce themselves formally from their connections with their home province, for these ultimately provided them with their status and some share of their wealth.

Changes in Material Culture

The native peoples of Mesoamerica and the Andes quickly adopted certain aspects of European material culture into their own way of life, but without sacrificing their identity as Indians either in their own eyes or in that of the

Spaniards. With the incorporation of the Americas into the global economy for the first time, the native population could finally access goods from elsewhere in the world. With the passage of time, indigenous peoples have been increasingly incorporated into the larger market economy, although certainly not steadily and without resistance. Even in the precontact period, native peoples throughout the Americas engaged in commerce and exchanged goods over long distances.

The Indians found metal tools to be a vast improvement over their lithic devices. Few natives owned firearms, but this was not solely because of an outright ban by colonial authorities fearful of rebellions. It also resulted from their high cost and limited utility, there being little hunting for large animals. The indigenous people also adopted European clothes and weaves. Hence some articles of clothing and design patterns that in modern times are considered to be distinctively "Indian" were in fact adopted by them in the early colonial period.

The Spaniards introduced pastoralism to much of the New World, though, of course the Andes had an ancient tradition of herding camelids. Spaniards highly prized raising sheep and cattle. In the Americas, these large animals sometimes ruined the crops of nearby Indian villages, which had never had the need to erect fences. In addition, sheep sometimes stripped land of all of its grasses, engendering ecological catastrophes as weeds and bushes grew to replace them and as erosion ruined the land for agriculture.

Natives adopted smaller European food animals, particularly chickens but also pigs and goats, into their diet. These animals were inexpensive to acquire and quite easy to raise. But Mesoamerican and Andean Indians found only limited use for sheep, cattle, oxen, mules, or horses. These large animals had little immediate utility as food or draft animals in native life. Being intensively agricultural, natives in these two regions had little open land for grazing. They also made limited use of European plows, probably because under the communal system of land ownership their individual plots of land were small and dispersed. Natives also had no need to ship large amounts of bulk items over long distances by wagons or animal back. Though the Mesoamerican peoples especially were very market oriented, such transactions usually involved small amounts of merchandise easily transported by the persons themselves.

With the exception of the incorporation of the chicken, and to some extent the pig, into their spectrum of comestibles, the Indian diet hardly changed over the centuries. The very nutritious complex of maize, beans, and squash (with potatoes replacing maize in the higher elevations of the Andes) endured as the daily foods, though, of course, natives prepared them in a variety of ways. Native communities grew wheat only as a cash crop to be sold to the Spanish colonists. Even Indians who were raised in colonial cities and were hispanized in many ways often continued to prefer maize over wheat as their staple grain.

The Christianization of the Native Peoples

Several factors shaped patterns of conversion to Christianity among the sedentary agricultural peoples. First, they continued their traditional pattern of accepting into their pantheon the primary god of any power that conquered

A portrait of a native Andean noblewoman in the mid-colonial period
(Karen Spalding, Huarochiaí: An Andean Society Under Inca and Spanish Rule, Stanford: Stanford University Press, 1984, p. 232. Photo by Martin Chambi of original in the Cuzco Art Museum, courtesy of John Rowe.)

them. The native peoples expected efficacy from both their gods and their political leaders. Just as they would repudiate a monarch who could not protect them from defeat in war or from famine, so too they would turn away from a god who seemed to lack effective power over worldly and human processes. James Lockhart states:

> One can hardly speak of an indigenous inclination to disbelief in Christianity. For the people of preconquest Mesoamerica, victory was prima facie evidence of the strength of the victor's god. One expected a conqueror to impose his god in some fashion, without fully displacing one's own; the new god in any case always proved to be an agglomeration of attributes familiar from the local pantheon and hence easy to assimilate. Thus the Nahuas [native peoples of central Mexico] after the Spanish conquest needed less to be converted than to be instructed.[5]

Even native religious movements that rejected all things Spanish might unconsciously incorporate sacred Christian figures or doctrine. In the Andes, a mere thirty years after the conquest, a millenarian movement called Taki Onqoy spread over a broad region, especially in the highlands. It did not attempt an immediate violent response to the Spaniards; instead it maintained that these aliens would disappear from greater Peru if the natives rejected all foreign cultural elements and values. The leaders of the movement held that the Andean peoples had to return to their precontact ways and their traditional belief in their local gods (*huacas*). If they avoided the foreign religion, tools, foods, and people in their midst, all of these elements would disappear. This movement resulted in part from the great die-off from epidemics and from the heavy labor demands imposed by the Spanish. The Andean peoples felt that only a spiritual purification of their culture would eradicate those afflictions. But even this effort, which was dedicated toward avoiding all things non-native, had unconsciously taken on some Christian aspects, for certain elements of Catholicism had been already been accepted as powerful and benign. For example, some Taki Onqoy leaders assumed the names of the highly popular saints Mary and Mary Magdalene. Once conscious of the existence and scope of this religious movement, colonial officials began to round up its promoters—they exiled many of them from their home regions—and eliminated it as a threat within a very short time.

Second, despite the horrible die-off, in every major sedentary agricultural zone, the native population continued to be substantial, numbering in the tens to hundreds of thousands, while the number of Spanish priests working to convert them was small, hardly more than a few dozen at any time during the first half century after the conquest. Thus, the type of religious training the priests managed to give was rather rudimentary. They taught only basic prayers and the most important rituals and conveyed the centrality of the sacraments. Understanding the influence of the native nobility among the indigenous people, the Spanish clergy established various schools for the sons of notables, where the friars trained them more systematically in the faith, with the expectation that when they came to rule, they would keep their people true to Catholicism.

Third, the Spanish organized parishes according to existing indigenous city-state structures, just as they had with *encomiendas*. The priest assigned to an

A colonial native chronicle asserts that the precontact Andean peoples knew Christianity

As the native peoples began to absorb Christianity into their belief systems and to understand the advanced moral standing that the Europeans ascribed to Christian peoples, some among them began to argue that the indigenous societies had already been Christian some centuries before contact. They continued that the imposition of the Aztec or Inca empire—as the case may be—forced the local peoples to adopt newly pagan ways. Hence the Spaniards were restoring Christianity, not introducing it, and the natives deserved to be considered as equals of the Europeans, not as lesser subjects. This belief is clearly stated in the following passage from the Andean chronicler, Guaman Poma de Ayala, who in a voluminous report to the king in the early seventeenth century asserted that the elevated civilization of the local Indian peoples merited official respect and attendant reforms in colonial rule.

The first white people in the world were brought by God to this country. They were descended from those who survived the Flood in Noah's Ark. It is said that they were born in pairs, male and female, and therefore multiplied rapidly. These people were incapable of useful work. They could not make proper clothes, so they wore garments of leaves and straw. Not knowing how to build houses, they lived in caves and under rocks. They worshipped God with a constant outpouring of sound like the twitter of birds, . . . With the little understanding which they possessed they adored their Creator, and not idols or demons. They wandered like lost souls in a world which they did not understand. . . . The white people knew the institution of marriage and lived peacefully with one another. They learnt the skills of ploughing and sowing, in the simple way in which these had been practised by Adam and Eve. The gods of the white people were Viracocha and Pachacama [the names of traditional Andean gods] and their manner of worship was on bended knees, their hands joined and their faces turned upwards to the sky. . . . In their turn these first people were succeeded by the two castes: the great lords, who were the ancestors of our Incas, and the common people who were descended from bastards and multiplied rapidly in number. However barbarous they may have been, our ancestors had some glimmer of understanding of God. Even the mere saying of the name Pachacamac is a sign of faith and an important step forward. Christians have much to learn from our people's good way of life.

Source: Huamán Poma, *Letter to a King: A Peruvian Chief's Account of Life Under the Incas and Under Spanish Rule,* trans. by Christopher Dilke (New York: E. P. Dutton, 1978), pp. 24–25.

indigenous parish was centered in the headtown, where the main church was located. He based himself there, but once or twice a year, he rode circuit to visit outlying hamlets. The priest remained one or at most two weekends in each settlement, saying mass and hearing confession, and performing such important sacraments as baptism and marriage. Other than these visits, most Indians in rural areas did not come into contact with priests during the rest of the year.

In the absence of priests native officials called *fiscales* in Spanish administered church affairs—including control over local parish funds—and to some extent the supervision of proper ritual and moral conduct. These local men enjoyed stature that sometimes rivalled community political leaders. They effectively carried the rank and performed some of the duties characteristic of pre-contact indigenous priests.

Generally lacking the regular presence of clergy, native communities practiced a public religiosity that emphasized processions, displays, and festivals. Catholicism became intertwined with community and ethnic identity. Villages identified themselves with specific saints or sacred sites that they celebrated, usually according to an annual cycle. The community ceremoniously paraded the revered image through town. The parish priest for the region was always present to bless the event (it was also a perfect time to collect clerical fees), and the order of people and groups in the procession corresponded to their standing in local society.

The entire community, or at least some major group within it, sponsored the festival, promoting local identity. But while sponsorship and active participation in the event was limited to community members, people from throughout the region were invited to attend and to join in the more general festivities. Temporary stands sold food, drink, and local wares. Such fiestas often included music and dancing and sometimes gambling and races.

All of this public religiosity fostered an intense localism in religious celebration and identity. Communities promoted their own fiestas and complexes of beliefs against those of their neighbors. The parish church generally served as its central symbol. By at least the late seventeenth century, about a century and a half after the conquest, some locally composed histories of such communities in central Mexico no longer associated Catholicism and the construction of the local church with the arrival of the Spanish. Rather, the faith, its hierarchy of sacred figures, and the local church were all associated with ancient times—and with the very identity of the ethnic group. These histories presented the Aztecs as usurpers, and the Spanish, if noted at all, as restorers of the traditional true faith, not as its originators.

The Role and Popularity of Religious Sodalities

Indigenous communities avidly adopted religious brotherhoods, *cofradías*, common throughout Spain. (They were equally popular among the elites and lower classes in colonial cities.) Men, women, and children, usually together as family units, would join a sodality dedicated to the veneration of a particular saint, sacred symbol, or sacred site. This membership sharply distinguished native from Spanish practice, for in Spain *cofradías* characteristically restricted their membership to adult men. Over time, the indigenous pattern came to closely resemble the European. By at least the second half of the seventeenth century, Indian sodalities as well were typically exclusively masculine in composition.

Sodality members paid dues for the maintenance of the organization and the local chapel and for an annual public procession and festival, in which they carried a statue of the saint through the streets of the community. The brotherhood also commonly assured a proper funeral for its members in good standing.

These organizations controlled significant funds and had a hierarchy of offices. Public stature accrued to members who held the highest ranks and who even went into significant personal debt to sponsor the annual festivals. The willingness to sacrifice personal for group interests and the ability to carry out the organization and financing of such a large celebration indicated that the person was thoroughly trustworthy and able. Most importantly, he would protect the larger community against forces that might divide it or alienate some of its collectively held property. Thus, over time, the tendency developed for men who had held all of the major positions in a *cofradía* to be elected to ever higher local political positions as well. This practice is commonly referred to as "the civil–religious hierarchy," and persists in many areas of Latin America to the present day. A man who has attained all of these important positions is known as a *pasado,* and while he might appear to an outsider as a rather poor maize farmer, in his community he is revered, consulted on important decisions, and deserving of all honor.

The Cult of the Saints

Just as a community or a *cofradía* dedicated itself to a specific saint, so too individuals and households came to revere their own clusters of saints, whom they honored and called upon for protection and special intervention on their behalf. The cult of the saints became a central aspect of religious identification in rural communities, with some saints even viewed as the true owners of village lands. Villagers often asserted that they lived "to serve the saints." People viewed the saints as active spiritual agents, able to intervene in human affairs on behalf of those who offered them special devotion. Persons in need commonly made pledges to honor individual saints who answered their prayers to cure an illness or otherwise remedy a problem. Under such a spiritual patron-client contract, the beneficiary undertook a pilgrimage or built a shrine to extol the saint who had intervened on his behalf. James Lockhart describes the process by which the peoples of central Mexico adopted the Spanish belief in saints as follows:

> There is no doubt that a close parallel existed between the Spanish and preconquest Nahua religious systems. In Spain, the corporate aspects of local religion were expressed through images of saints with specialized supernatural powers, each image having its own attributes and being associated with a particular region, town, social group, or subdistrict. Among the Nahuas, a pantheon of specialized gods behaved in precisely

the same manner. A general principle of Spanish-Nahua interaction is that wherever the two cultures ran parallel, the Nahuas would soon adopt the relevant Spanish form without abandoning the essence of their own form. With the saints, the expected in due course happened.[6]

While Christianity duly modified to incorporate certain precontact beliefs and practices proliferated throughout Latin America, and replaced the earlier civilization-wide spectrum of gods and rituals, certain local-level beliefs in magic and individual and household gods persisted. These endured even though ecclesiastical administrations took repressive measures against indigenous religious celebrations. But even these were practiced in a furtive and private fashion, no longer celebrated publicly or as part of a group. Natives used them to promote individual or household interests or to avenge perceived slights and injuries within the community, rather than to express values intended to unite the larger society.

Language and Cultural Change in Mesoamerican Communities

In recent decades, scholars who have become adept in the major indigenous languages of Mesoamerica—Nahuatl, Mixtec, and Maya—have begun to analyze the vast corpus of documents composed by natives during the colonial period. Within a generation after Spanish settlement, the Indians of central Mexico, Oaxaca (an extensive complex of valleys in southcentral Mexico inhabited by Mixtec-speakers and other native-language groups), and the Yucatan Peninsula began to produce records in their own languages using the Spanish alphabet. Indigenous scribes composed testaments, land transactions and deeds, town council minutes, municipal histories, and the like. They typically did so autonomously, without intervention by Spanish officials or colonists, and thereby rendered valuable source material that depicts native concepts, perspectives, and institutions. These documents provide a much more intimate and reliable portrait of indigenous ways of life in Mesoamerica and the types and degrees of acculturation to European beliefs and practices they experienced over time than Spanish-language documents.

Indigenous-language documents demonstrate three stages of linguistic and cultural change in postconquest Mesoamerica. In the first stage, which lasted only thirty years or so, the indigenous languages witnessed no change at all, and expressed such new terms as sailing ships, horses, metal pots and tools, and firearms by new combinations of words within the native languages. The second stage, which lasted for about a century, is marked by the large-scale borrowing of Spanish nouns. Finally, in the third stage, which commences more than a century after systematic contact began, the language borrows other parts of speech— verbs, adverbs, prepositions, and conjunctions. This last stage reflects the growing number of bilingual Indians. Understandably, in areas where the ratio of colonists to natives was lower, cultural and linguistic change occurred more slowly.

Nor was all the linguistic change restricted to indigenous languages. Mexican Spanish incorporated hundreds of Nahuatl words into its vocabulary. Such well-known words as "chocolate" and "tomato" derive from Nahuatl.

The Character of Native Revolts

This fragmentation of the vast indigenous civilization zones in the early colonial period discussed in its different aspects in this chapter expressed itself even in the nature of revolts by the native peoples, for revolts occurred with some frequency. These uprisings, more common after about 1700, generally occurred at the community level, rarely expanding to encompass either an entire region or an ethnic group. Further, they did not aspire to overthrow Spanish colonial rule but rather to redress local grievances. Usually these complaints emerged in response to some change in government policies or to some unwelcomed initiative. These include attempts at a new community census or a survey of village boundaries.

Other unwanted steps involve efforts to collect new civil or ecclesiastical taxes or to force Indians to purchase goods. Another category of complaints consisted of efforts to protect community values and perogatives. Any attack on a village saint or sacred site (even if done by the local priest) constituted a threat to the community's identity, as did any effort to replace a local official or to restructure the community's standing relative to other political entities in the region.

Some examples drawn from eighteenth-century Mexico include the following causes: Tulancingo in 1756 rose up to protest a new labor draft imposed on its men; San Andrés revolted in 1762 against a search for illegal liquor on the eve of a community festival; Achiutla in 1785 protested a district official's harsh efforts to collect taxes; and in 1792 Amanalco mobilized against a priest attempting to take a census for tax purposes.

These local uprisings were almost always spontaneous and lacked central leadership. Little evidence of advance planning is apparent. Oftentimes women in the village center initiated the protest and then called their menfolk out of the fields to support them. Violence and generalized destruction were uncommon. Local participants targeted specific individuals and sites. Deaths rarely occurred, if for no other reason than the rioters wielded few firearms. Nor was the protest long sustained. Once the people had secured their immediate aims, they ceased to protest. Instead, they awaited the inevitable arrival of colonial officials sent to determine what had transpired and to negotiate an end to the revolt. Officials typically accomplished this easily, most often through an agreement to restore the previous situation. Likewise, the punishments meted out were few and measured; commonly a few people were whipped, fined, sentenced to a term in penal servitude, or sent into exile.

In contrast to the spontaneous, local revolts in Mesoamerica, several major uprisings did erupt in the Andes toward the end of the colonial period. The first was the Tupac Amaru revolt in 1780–1781 near the ancient Inca capital of Cuzco in highland Peru. A provincial *cacique* who was involved in the colonial economy as the owner of some mule teams and who was even married to a Spanish woman organized it. Frustrated in his personal social aspirations and by local Spanish officials who extracted labor and money from native subjects, this *cacique* changed his name from Condorcanqui to Tupac Amaru, the namesake of the last independent Inca emperor who had been captured and executed by the Spaniards in 1572. Beginning in November 1780, Tupac Amaru's force executed one of the Spanish officials, engaged a number of military units, and even besieged Cuzco. Tupac Amaru briefly controlled much of the highlands, especially in the south, but he experienced difficulty gaining the support of other *caciques*, who considered him a rival and questioned his pretensions for the Inca throne.

While the vast majority of Tupac Amaru's army was composed of indigenous people, its leadership came substantially from locally-born Spaniards and *castas* of the substantial middle sectors of society. These people also had their complaints against the colonial regime; they desired a fairer tax system, more dispassionate courts, and a more open economic system. So the leaders of the revolt always portrayed it as a reformist movement, seeking substantial change, but within the colonial system. They never declared for independence nor sought a race war of the native peoples against all others.

Spanish officials captured and executed most of the leaders in early 1781. New outbreaks of the movement erupted in other highland areas through 1783, when it was ultimately squelched. It was particularly long-lived and vicious in Upper Peru (modern Bolivia), where the movement took on far more of a race-war aspect. In early 1781, a resentful *cacique* named Tomás Catari led a revolt near the important silver-mining center of Potosí. A couple of months later, a nephew of Tupac Amaru named Andrés took over an entire province on the eastern shore of Lake Titicaca. When the provincial city of Sorata fell to his forces after a three-month siege, he killed all of the Spaniards. He then besieged the regional capital of La Paz, and was joined there by forces under another rebel who assumed the name Tupac Catari. Only the arrival of troops from Buenos Aires lifted the siege late that year. Tupac Catari was captured and executed.

The Impact of Eighteenth-Century Population Growth

A major factor that brought about change in Indian life starting in the early eighteenth century was a substantial increase in native population growth rates. The indigenous population in the sedentary agricultural regions reached its nadir in the mid-seventeenth century. It then began a gradual climb, which accelerated in the 1700s. But by then, roughly two centuries into the colonial period, the Spanish American world was quite dense with creoles (people of Spanish descent born in the Americas), *castas*, and blacks (most of whom were by then born in the Americas). Further, the colonial economy and society now extended well into the rural hinterland, as the market economy—oriented toward export to Europe and production for the growing colonial cities, steadily expanded. By this time, the countryside had become densely settled by rural estates, both large complexes commonly termed *haciendas* and less profitable family farms often called *ranchos.*

Given this setting, little land was available for the growing populations in native communities.   Now these villages faced possible subsistence crises— heightened demand for fixed resources—as they were scarcely able to improve the productivity of their lands.   Legal and sometimes armed conflicts with Spanish enterprises and with other native communities over boundaries, access to water, and other resources substantially increased. Numerous young people, unable to secure adequate livelihoods in the communities into which they had been born, migrated to *haciendas,* mining towns, or provincial centers, where most were relegated to a hard life as poorly paid, temporary laborers.

Nonetheless, indigenous villages retained their ethnic and cultural distinctiveness well past the end of the colonial period. Their members had successfully incorporated Spanish material culture—and also the demands of the colonial political and economic systems—into their existing cultural frameworks. Most native communities remained ethnically homogeneous. A common language, shared natural resources, cooperative labor patterns, market systems, local religious and civic beliefs and practices, community-sponsored festivals, frequent intermarriage, and indigenous local leadership all fostered an enduring distinctiveness. Finally, though resources certainly flowed from the community into the colonial government and church, they did so through accustomed channels and means, with the locality assembling them collectively and funnelling them through its own community leaders in a manner that had precedence from the prehispanic period.

Conclusion

In fundamental ways, the Spanish relied on traditional central Mexican and Andean indigenous institutional arrangements to govern and make use of the indigenous population. They retained the ethnic provinces, community structures, and structures of political authority. The governance of native communities, recruitment of draft laborers, payment of tribute, and rural parishes were all based on these structures.

The great die-off that resulted from the waves of imported epidemic diseases deepened the native population's degree of acculturation to European ways. The number of Indians in the two most heavily populated zones of the Americas plummeted by some 90–95 percent over the first 100–150 years after their initial encounters with Europeans. This profound shift in the population ratios between Indians and Spaniards meant that the latter's cultural patterns penetrated native communities more thoroughly.

Most acculturation transpired as part of informal interactions between individual colonists and natives, as the former moved increasingly into the countryside and recruited workers for their enterprises. The Indians incorporated European tools and implements, cloths and articles of clothing, and animals into their daily lives. They also converted in mass and without great travail to

Catholicism, because they adapted its beliefs and rituals to preexisting parallels. By the late sixteenth century, in Mexico and the Andes, most instances of Indians celebrating precontact religious ceremonies were discovered in peripheral areas, such as rugged mountains or arid reaches, where the native population was small and Spanish penetration was limited. Catholicism, as it emerged in native villages, stressed the cult of the saints, god-parenthood, religious sodalities, and public festivals. These served effectively to strengthen or ratify relationships within the group, to assert the community's distinctiveness and values, and to provide a means by which men could prove their abilities and dedication to the community and hence gain social and political stature.

Kevin Terraciano expresses some general principles underlying cultural change in the colonial world.

> In many ways, native concepts and forms of organization defined the extent and nature of interactions between the two groups and the types of adaptations on each side. The impact of externally imposed changes was moderated by what the two cultures had in common. Most successful introductions were based on existing native mechanisms or some preconquest precedent, so that Mesoamericans came to view many introductions as their own, or they recognized that an introduction corresponded to some familiar practice or concept.[7]

An enormous and unfortunate change for the indigenous peoples of Mexico and the Andes was the destruction of their larger civilization zones. For roughly two millennia before the Europeans arrived, each zone had shared ideas, products, and people throughout its reaches. But the Spanish conquest and colonization caused the fragmentation of these broad regions of shared civilization, although this was never the overt policy of colonial rulers. This disarticulation resulted from the breakup of the Aztec and Inca empires, but even more so from the disintegration of the earlier zones of indigenous trade and exchange of ideas. Some traditional ruling families retained more encompassing visions and associations abetted by their marriage patterns, property holdings, business operations, and interactions with colonial authorities. But overall the focus of native life and identity became the local municipality and its immediate hinterland to an extent never before known. Among the commoners, connections and shared values and identities with other communities hardly existed any more, as evidenced by the complaints posed in their petitions to colonial authorities and by the local nature of their revolts when they did mobilize against the colonial regime.

Select Bibliography

Adorno, Rolena. *Guaman Poma: Writing and Resistance in Colonial Peru.* Austin: University of Texas Press, 1986.

Andrien, Kenneth J. *Andean Worlds: Indigenous History, Culture and Consciousness Under Spanish Rule, 1532–1825.* Albuquerque: University of New Mexico Press, 2001.

Boone, Elizabeth Hill and Tom Cummins, eds. *Native Traditions in the Postconquest World.* Washington, DC:Dumbarton Oaks Research Library and Collection, 1998.

Chance, John K. *Conquest of the Sierra: Spaniards and Indians in Colonial Oaxaca.* Norman: University of Oklahoma Press, 1989.

Chance, John K. *Race and Class in Colonial Oaxaca.* Stanford: Stanford University Press, 1978.

Cline, S. L. *Colonial Culhuacan, 1580–1600: A Social History of an Aztec Town.* Albuquerque: University of New Mexico Press, 1986.

Cline, S. L., ed. *The Book of Tributes: Early Sixteenth-Century Nahuatl Censuses from Morelos.* Los Angeles: UCLA Latin American Center Publications, 1993.

Cook, Noble David. *Born to Die: Disease and New World Conquest, 1492–1650.* Cambridge, England: Cambridge University Press, 1998.

Cook, Noble David. *Demographic Collapse: Indian Peru, 1520–1620.* Cambridge, England: Cambridge University Press, 1981.

Gibson, Charles. *The Aztecs Under Spanish Rule: A History of the Indians of the Valley of Mexico, 1519–1810.* Stanford: Stanford University Press, 1964.

Gibson, Charles. *Tlaxcala in the Sixteenth Century.* Stanford: Stanford University Press, 1967 [1952].

Griffiths, Nicholas. *The Cross and the Serpent: Religious Repression and Resurgence in Colonial Peru.* Norman: University of Oklahoma Press, 1996.

Griffith, Nicholas and Fernando Cervantes, eds. *Spiritual Encounters: Interactions Between Christianity and Native Religions in Colonial America.* Lincoln: University of Nebraska Press, 1999.

Gruzinski, Serge. *The Conquest of Mexico: The Incorporation of Indian Societies into the Western World, 16th–18th Centuries.* Trans. by Eileen Corrigan. Cambridge, England: Polity Press, 1993.

Gruzinski, Serge. *Man-Gods in the Mexican Highlands: Indian Power and Colonial Society, 1520–1800.* Trans. by Eileen Corrigan. Stanford: Stanford University Press, 1989.

Haskett, Robert S. *Indigenous Rulers: An Ethnohistory of Town Government in Colonial Cuernavaca.* Albuquerque: University of New Mexico Press, 1991.

Kellogg, Susan and Matthew Restall, eds. *Dead Giveaways: Indigenous Testaments of Colonial Mesoamerica and the Andes.* Salt Lake City: University of Utah Press, 1998.

Larson, Brooke and Olivia Harris, eds. *Ethnicity, Markets, and Migration in the Andes: At the Crossroads of History and Anthropology.* Durham, NC: Duke University Press, 1995.

Lockhart, James. *The Nahuas After the Conquest: A Social and Cultural History of the Indians of Central Mexico, Sixteenth Through Eighteenth Centuries.* Stanford: Stanford University Press, 1992.

McCaa, Robert, "Spanish and Nahuatl Views on Smallpox and Demographic Catastrophe in Mexico," *Journal of Interdisciplinary History, 25*:3 (Winter 1995), pp. 397–431.

Schroeder, Susan. *Chimalpahin and the Kingdoms of Chalco.* Tucson: University of Arizona Press, 1991.

Spalding, Karen. *Huarochirí: An Andean Society Under Inca and Spanish Rule.* Stanford: Stanford University Press, 1984.

Spores, Ronald. *The Mixtecs in Ancient and Colonial Times.* Norman: University of Oklahoma Press, 1984.

Stern, Steve J. *Peru's Indian Peoples and the Challenge of Spanish Conquest: Huamanga to 1640.* Madison: University of Wisconsin Press, 1982.

Taylor, William B. *Drinking, Homicide, and Rebellion in Colonial Mexican Villages.* Stanford: Stanford University Press, 1979.

Terraciano, Kevin. *The Mixtecs of Colonial Oaxaca: Ñudzahui History, Sixteenth Through Eighteenth Centuries.* Stanford: Stanford University Press, 2001.

Wightman, Ann M. *Indigenous Migration and Social Change: The Forasteros of Cuzco, 1520–1720.* Durham, NC: Duke University Press, 1990.

Endnotes

1   Charles Gibson, *Tlaxcala in the Sixteenth Century* (Stanford: Stanford University Press, 1967 [1952]), p. 145.

2   Noble David Cook, *Demographic Collapse: Indian Peru, 1520–1620* (Cambridge, England: Cambridge University Press, 1981), p. 114.

3   John K. Chance, *Race and Class in Colonial Oaxaca* (Stanford: Stanford University Press, 1978), pp. 112–113.

4   Steve J. Stern, *Peru's Indian Peoples and the Challenge of Spanish Conquest: Huamanga to 1640* (Madison: University of Wisconsin Press, 1982), pp. 37–38.

5   James Lockhart, *The Nahuas After the Conquest: A Social and Cultural History of the Indians of Central Mexico, Sixteenth Through Eighteenth Centuries* (Stanford: Stanford University Press, 1992), p. 203.

6   Lockhart, *The Nahuas After the Conquest,* p. 243.

7   Kevin Terraciano, *The Mixtecs of Colonial Oaxaca* (Stanford: Stanford University Press, 2001), p. 360.

5

Native Response to Settlement in the East and Southwest in North America

Unlike the fully sedentary native societies of Latin America considered in the previous two chapters, the peoples of eastern North America were primarily semisedentary in their way of life, except for those in northern Canada, who were hunters and gatherers. Though the Spanish and the Portuguese established their regimes largely without challenges from other European powers, in most of Latin America, the French, Dutch, and English—and to some extent even the Spanish—vied openly against each other in the eastern half of North America. This competition among the colonizers enabled the indigenous peoples to play the Europeans off against each other.

European fishermen reached North America soon after the Spanish discovered the New World. The French, British, and even the Portuguese sent vessels into far northern waters, making contact with coastal societies. The French and British rather routinely dispatched fishing vessels to the Grand Banks. These fishermen commonly landed to dry their catches on shore, setting up temporary camps.

Spain in Eastern North America

In the southern part of North America, as in South America, the Spanish were the first Europeans to make a notable impact. Juan Ponce de León discovered Florida in 1513. He would die in an unsuccessful effort to colonize it in

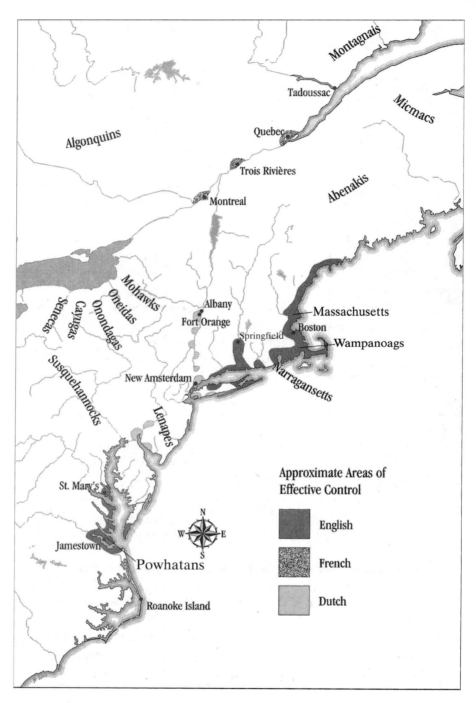

Major Indian peoples and European bases in Eastern North America in the mid-seventeenth century (*Daniel K. Richter,* Facing East from Indian Country: A Native History of Early America, *Cambridge, MA: Harvard University Press, 2001, p. 65. Copyright © 2001 by the President and Fellows of Harvard College. Reprinted by permisison.*)

1521. In 1526, Lucas Vázquez de Ayllón set sail from Hispaniola with six ships and 500 men for the coast of North America. After one failed landing, they established a modest base along the coast of South Carolina. But racked by disease and attacks from the natives (with Ayllón himself one of the casualties), the 150 survivors returned to Hispaniola before the year was out. A 1528 effort led by Pánfilo de Narváez to subdue west Florida quickly suffered major reversals and only a few survivors ever returned to Mexico. Between 1539 and 1543, an expedition headed by Hernando de Soto, one of the conquerors of Peru a few years earlier, journeyed through much of the southeast, even crossing the Mississippi River. But the expedition withdrew to Mexico after having suffered many deaths and having failed to find precious metals or large native populations that could be readily transformed into a subordinate labor force.

French Protestants (Huguenots) established a colony in northern Florida in 1564 as a challenge to Spanish domination of the area and a threat to Spanish shipping leaving the Gulf for the open Atlantic. Spain responded with an expedition of its own, destroying the French settlement, executing most of its members, and erecting a fortress, San Agustín, in 1565. Around this time, Spanish Jesuits established the mission of Santa Elena on the coast of South Carolina. In 1570 they even tried to install a mission in coastal Virginia, but natives attacked and destroyed it after only a few months. Some evidence indicates that a few Spanish survivors lived under the protection of Powhatan, the most powerful ruler in eastern Virginia, until about the founding of Jamestown in 1607.

By the 1580s, Spain had ceased efforts to colonize eastern North America north of Florida. Its explorers had found nothing in North America above northern Mexico to rival the resources and peoples it already controlled farther south. Spain did eventually establish very successful colonies in New Mexico and California.

During the first thirty years of the seventeenth century, France, the Netherlands, and England shifted their emphasis away from raids against the Spanish American empire to the erection of formal colonies of their own in North America. We cannot neatly separate these colonies in our examination, for they were almost continually interacting. They traded and pursued diplomatic relations with the local natives. Colonies engaging in military confrontations with each other characteristically saw Indian allies participating on both sides.

These early colonies emerged among native societies that had prior experience with Europeans. Sixteenth-century European fishing and coastal ventures had already made an impact on the indigenous populations. Considerable evidence indicates that diseases had begun to wrack major areas of coastal North America before Europeans erected any permanent settlements. Early colonists commented about abandoned villages and cornfields. Natives told of tremendous die-offs.

The indigenous peoples generally seem to have considered Europeans as persons of unusual capacity. They thought that Europeans had the ability to bring death—through unknown diseases—and that they possessed certain coveted technological advantages. The Indians very early began to trade for

European cloth goods and metalware, particularly copper pots to cut up into a variety of useful implements. They were also impressed by the killing power of the European firearms. But these attitudes did not challenge the natives' fundamental belief that their own culture was vastly superior to that of the newcomers. The Indians voluntarily adopted certain material advantages the foreigners possessed without transforming their established way of life.

The Spanish Impact on the American Southwest

The American southwest, composed of the modern states of Texas, New Mexico, Arizona, and California, contained three distinct types of native cultures in the sixteenth century. Nomadic hunting societies populated Texas, Arizona, and substantial parts of New Mexico. They inhabited vast areas, but remained rather small in population because of their near total lack of agriculture and the relative shortage of large animals and plants to provide nutrition. Some of the peoples in Texas, though, benefitted from hunting the large herds of buffalo that grazed in some parts of the region.

In the middle of this challenging environment, the upper reaches of the Río Grande River afforded sufficient water for the intensive cultivation of maize along a rather narrow strip of central New Mexico. The Pueblo Indians dwelled here, in widely separated, but substantially sized communities. The autonomous settlements of the Pueblos recognized no higher political authority and rarely cooperated with each other. The Pueblos even spoke five distinct languages. Their total population probably approached 60,000 in 1600.

The peoples in the southern two-thirds of California enjoyed a temperate climate, a fertile land that yielded abundant nuts, grains, berries, and animals, and an ocean and rivers that provided fish, sea mammals, and other marine life. This natural richness maintained an ample population, perhaps as many as 300,000 when the Spanish arrived, living in scattered, small communities with no need to practice agriculture. The California Indians belonged to six different major language groups and resided in bounded territories. Warfare seems to have been rare among them, unlike their nomadic counterparts in the deserts and plains in much of the rest of the American southwest.

The Spanish settlement of the American southwest proceeded directly from their movement into the rugged desert country of the Mexican north. This vast expanse extended for hundreds of miles. It contained dozens of distinct, mobile native groups that could move their encampments to evade Spanish expeditions. Through the use of ambush and bows and arrows, they inflicted substantial casualties on the intruders. If captured, these people did not become a compliant labor force. Rather they rose up or ran away unless transported to unfamiliar regions far to the south where they were isolated among the large numbers of sedentary Indians who inhabited central Mexico. But these desolate northern lands contained many of the richest silver deposits in Mexico, inevitably drawing the Spanish to found mining towns and camps scattered unevenly across the territory and to set up farms and ranches to provide grain and animals to these mining communities, and, eventually, to the towns in central Mexico. Colonial officials dispatched occasional expeditions far to the north. The most famous was the very large undertaking headed by Francisco Vázquez de Coronado between 1540 and 1542. Despite the inflated descriptions of the Pueblo towns reported back to the authorities by these ventures, no one ordered a colonizing expedition into this region until the very end of the sixteenth century.

Juan de Oñate had inherited a complex of silver mines in Zacatecas, the largest mining town in northern Mexico. (His wife, who had brought independent wealth into the marriage, was the great granddaughter of Montezuma and the granddaughter of Cortés.) In 1598, he commanded a colonizing expedition into the lands of the Pueblos, some 800 miles beyond the nearest Spanish settlement. His force consisted of about 130 men with their wives and children and Indian dependents, totaling roughly 500 people.

Initially, this colonizing effort resembled that of the Spanish among the Guaraní, described earlier. In both situations a small group of Spaniards settled in an isolated area among a relatively populous agricultural people who were regularly raided by nomadic peoples who surrounded them on all sides. But the relatively peaceful situation of the colonists intermixing with the Guaraní and adopting many of their cultural practices did not prevail in New Mexico, as this colony in the American southwest came to be called. Unfortunately, much more exploitation and antagonism soon resulted.

The Pueblos initially received the Spanish peacefully, probably because they did not expect them to remain. But the settlers started to seize food and clothing from the Pueblos and to rape and murder with impunity. Before the first year was out, the people of Acoma retaliated by killing 11 Spanish men. The colonists subdued this community, located atop a steep mesa, only after a difficult campaign. In victory, they killed some 500 men and 300 women and children, and took another 80 men and another 500 women and children captive. The Spanish sentenced all adult men to have one foot severed and all adolescents to 20 years of servitude. They turned the children over to Franciscan missionaries.

Many of the early colonists, disappointed by the lack of resources and the little available wealth, returned to Mexico. Few new settlers arrived to replace them. As late as 1680, the Spanish population of New Mexico totaled no more than 3,000. They founded Santa Fé as the capital of their province in 1610, but established no other settlements during the following 70 years. Instead, most colonists lived on scattered farms along the upper Río Grande River. Far to the south, but still along the river, the Spaniards established a very modest community at El Paso del Norte in 1659.

The Franciscans who accompanied the Oñate expedition moved into Pueblo communities and used native labor to build chapels and churches. Unlike the nomadic peoples of Texas, the Pueblos had long resided in permanent communities, so there was no need to gather them into settlements. The missionaries campaigned to eradicate the native religion, targeting *kachinas,* the small decorated divine figures and masks central to Pueblo beliefs, and *kivas,* underground chambers where Pueblo males gathered for religious rituals. They hanged some indigenous religious leaders as witches.

With minimal possibilities to accumulate wealth or conduct trade, the colonists profited primarily from demands for tribute and the exploitation of native labor. They routinely imposed heavy, unauthorized burdens on the native communities they controlled. In the mid-seventeenth century, individual Pueblo settlements rose up against these impositions every few years but none of these insurrections spread to other Pueblo communities. Realizing that the Indians routinely took children captive in raids against other tribes, the colonists bartered for these children, turning them into a permanent servant class.

The colonists also conducted their own raids against nomadic peoples, such as the Utes, Apaches, and Navahos, who lived within reach of the Pueblo communities. They took captives and sold them as slaves to Spanish mining enterprises to the south. Outraged, these nomadic societies retaliated against the Pueblos, their traditional enemies since before the arrival of the Spanish, and carried away food, horses, cattle, and children. The Pueblos abandoned several communities under this recurrent onslaught.

Epidemic diseases accompanied the colonists to New Mexico, decimating the Pueblo Indians. These diseases, combined with the atrocities carried out by the settlers, reduced the native population from perhaps 60,000 in 1600 to some 15,000 a century later.

Suffering such afflictions, the Pueblos turned back to their traditional beliefs, rejecting Christian ones imposed by the Franciscans. Native priests, most notably one named Popé from the village of San Ildefonso, journied to communities along the river to coordinate a rebellion whose goal was the complete elimination of Spaniards from Pueblo territory. The Pueblo Revolt of 1680, planned in secrecy and involving some two dozen independent communities whose members spoke at least five distinct languages, erupted in August and killed over 400 Spaniards and 21 Franciscan priests. At least 1,500 colonists fled to safety in El Paso, accompanied by several hundred Pueblos who remained true to their Christian faith. The rebels destroyed Spanish buildings and fields in their effort to eradicate all evidence of the colonists' former presence. News of the successful uprising spread throughout northern Mexico, inspiring other revolts against missions and Spanish settlements for some years.

With the Spaniards driven out, the unity among Pueblo communities proved unsupportable, and the settlements returned to their traditional autonomy and rivalry. In 1692, Diego de Vargas, a nobleman recently arrived from Spain to further his fortune, undertook to pacify New Mexico. He found that he could play the Pueblo communities against each other. A number of them negotiated peaceful surrenders, but others resisted the return of about 800 settlers. Vargas's force, supplemented by some Pueblos who allied with him, defeated them in combat. The Spanish had attained effective control over the province by 1694.

The new regime did not try to restore the repressive policies that had prevailed before the 1680 revolt. Instead, the Spaniards now permitted the Pueblo peoples to practice many of their religious rituals. Native communities no longer had to deliver assigned labor service to individual colonists. Spanish officials moderated tribute requirements. Colonial officials maintained closer ties to the native communities to ensure military cooperation against increasingly frequent raids by Apaches, Navajos, and Comanches.

The Spanish presence, even at a distance, transformed the cultures of the nomadic peoples of modern-day Texas, New Mexico, and Arizona. The introduction of European animals revolutionized their way of life. Horses appeared in the late sixteenth century, and the native peoples widely adopted them during the seventeenth century. The adoption of horses gave the nomadic peoples much greater mobility, speed, and military impact. Horses enabled them to vastly increase their hunting of the massive buffalo herds that populated the grassy plains. Hunting parties now followed herds over long distances and killed many more than they previously had. Also, the Navajos of New Mexico and Arizona converted to a pastoral way of life by massive adoption of sheepherding. Mutton became the basis of their diet, and the wool was woven into blankets.

With the horse, nomadic tribes could raid other Indian groups and Spanish settlements and ranches over much wider areas. Warfare came to center around hit-and-run attacks on horseback. Small parties would strike suddenly, seize goods and captives, and disappear before a community could organize its defense. Bands also attacked each other to capture horses. By the late seventeenth century, colonial officials responded to this increasingly common and effective mode of Indian warfare by setting up a chain of forts, called *presidios,* from southern Arizona to the western boundary of Texas. But these failed to have the desired effect, and the Apaches especially increased their raids in the eighteenth century.

In Texas, the Spanish enjoyed little success with founding permanent settlements. The few towns and outlying ranches were incessantly beleaguered by Indian attacks, particularly by the Mescaleros, who became sworn enemies of the Spanish virtually on their arrival in the region. The Comanches moved into the region from the plains to the north to hunt buffalo and to raid both Spanish communities and other native peoples. They enjoyed almost continual success over many years, because they had regular access to firearms supplied from French trading posts and small settlements scattered along the Mississippi River.

The Spanish did not establish any missions in Texas until the late 1750s. They finally did then only because of rumors of possible silver mines in the area. The Jesuits and Franciscans set up a few widely separated missions in Texas and westward into Arizona over the subsequent decades. (Because of political disputes and suspicions centered in Europe, the Spanish monarchy expelled the Jesuits from the country and all of its colonies in 1767. The Franciscans thereupon replaced them in the southwest.) Almost always, the authorities installed a *presidio* near each mission. The friars running the missions, usually no more than two at each one, counted on the soldiers for protection and to help round up Indians to place in their care. Presidio soldiers also pursued runaways from the mission system.

Although Spanish naval expeditions had reached California as early as 1542, Franciscan friars and accompanying military units did not enter the vast expanse north of the Baja California peninsula to set up missions until 1769. Even then, they only acted in response to pressure from colonial authorities who were concerned that other European powers might attempt to occupy the region if the Spanish did not act first. Over the next several decades, the Franciscans, initially under the direction of Father Eusebio Kino, constructed a chain of twenty-one missions that extended from San Diego to San Francisco. A small number of colonists also migrated to California, where they established ranches to supply meat and hides to the *presidios,* and increasingly to the ships of different nations that passed along the coast.

The Franciscans in California were rather aggressive, gathering numerous native bands into their missions and then attempting to convert them into practicing agriculturalists as well as Christians. They sought to transform indigenous marriage and family patterns, residences, social relations, and gender roles. Ultimately, they had less success than they anticipated because the missions became deathtraps for the native children born there. Squalid living conditions and periodic outbreaks of disease caused most of the deaths. Other mission Indians fled into the backcountry in an effort to escape the unhealthy climate and the priests' insistence that they renounce their cultures.

The French Arrival in Canada

In the mid-1530s, Jacques Cartier made two voyages to Canada, initially seeking a route to Asia. Both times local leaders proved eager to barter. On the second voyage, the headman of Stadacona, near present-day Quebec City, tried to prevent the French from proceeding farther up the river, because he wanted to monopolize trade between them and other native groups. But Cartier persisted and reached the rival village that would become Montreal. Upon his return to Stadacona, Cartier's relations with the local people had become sufficiently strained that the French constructed a moated fort guarded by cannon. James Axtell comments about how quickly Indian awe of the Europeans was replaced by concern about these very-human newcomers:

> As the initial honeymoon of contact gave way to conflict and the erup-
> tion of irreconcilable differences, naive preconceptions gave way to
> more realistic notions, at once more complex and less optimistic. In
> Indian eyes, the strangers in their midst devolved fairly quickly from
> beneficent "gods" dropped from "the heavens," to dangerously powerful
> "spirits" or shamans, and finally to all-too-human or even sub-human
> "enemies" who deserved to be killed before they did irreparable harm.[1]

Cartier determined to spend the winter of 1535–1536 in the fort, but he and his 110 men found themselves totally unprepared for the rigors of a Canadian winter. At least 25 Frenchmen died, and most of the remainder became quite ill, primarily from scurvy. Further casualties were avoided when the natives provided them a remedy made from tree bark. In 1541, another expedition tried to settle in Canada, but it too suffered many deaths during the winter and was soon abandoned. By now French authorities appreciated that Canada offered neither the immediately exploitable resources nor the advanced indigenous cultures that the Spanish had discovered. France took only slight interest in North America for over half a century. Instead, it made a couple of efforts to challenge Spanish and Portuguese preeminence in the tropical regions. But these endeavors resulted in complete failure.

By the first decade of the seventeenth century, a lively coastal trade in beaver furs had developed in North America. This once again drew French attention to the St. Lawrence River region. A trading base established near the mouth of the river did not survive a decade, but it recruited Samuel de Champlain as a member. Champlain laid the basis for early colonial New France. He founded a fort and trading base in 1608 that became Quebec City. Trading in furs with the natives remained the foundation of French Canada until it was lost to the English in the 1760s.

Few Frenchmen—and far fewer Frenchwomen—came to Canada in the early years. Their numbers did not exceed a hundred as late as the 1630s, and they remained heavily dependent on the indigenous people. The natives provided the furs that maintained the colony. French traders could not even supply themselves adequately with food. They remained dependent on comestibles either shipped from France or provided by the Indians. The natives prized the metal goods and firearms the French could supply, and the colonists in turn relied on such native devices as snowshoes and canoes to get around.

The traders had to learn local culture and languages to prosper in this setting. The resident French, by and large, were far more acculturated to native ways than the natives were to those of the French. Some of them settled down with native women (few, though, in formal marriages), not just for female companionship but for the closer integration into native society and its web of relationships that would strengthen their trading connections. The French had to fully honor native ritual and ceremonial prerogatives. No trader could just come into a community and begin to trade. He first had to engage in a lengthy round of greetings, rituals, and gift-giving with the most prominent men.

The Indians could not conceive of trade solely as an economic activity. Rather, it was bound up in political alliances, as Champlain found out only a year after founding Quebec. The nearby Algonquian people, longtime enemies of the Iroquois to the south, insisted that Champlain, bearing firearms, accompany them on a campaign against their foes. Champlain's few muskets had the desired effect. Their devastating impact disconcerted the Iroquois, who were routed and lost many captives to the Algonquians.

For the rest of the seventeenth century, the five tribes of the Iroquois, particularly the Mohawk, remained implacable enemies of the French. Only a couple of decades after this initial defeat, they developed their own fur trade, now with the Dutch settlers along the Hudson River. The Iroquois now had their own source of firearms and metal implements. Champlain cemented Canada's enduring preeminence in the fur trade, though, by developing strong ties with the Hurons, who resided around the Great Lakes and could obtain great numbers of prime pelts through trapping and by trade with peoples even farther to the west.

Bruce G. Trigger relates the political and ceremonial aspects of this trade between the French and the Hurons and notes how very structured it was and how strong was the Huron position.

Champlain's account of his 1609 voyage up the St. Lawrence

A year after founding the fortified trading base that would develop into Quebec City, Samuel de Champlain traveled upriver with a contingent of Montaignais and recorded their actions.

> Immediately each began, some to cut down trees, others to strip bark from the trees to cover their wigwams in which to take shelter, others to fell big trees for a barricade on the bank of the river round their wigwams. They know how to do this so quickly that after less than two hours' work, five hundred of their enemies would have had difficulty in driving them out, without losing many men. They do not barricade the river bank where their boats are drawn up, in order to embark in case of need. After their wigwams had been set up, according to their custom each time they camp, they sent three canoes with nine good men, to reconnoitre two or three leagues ahead, whether they could perceive anything; and afterwards they retired. All night long they rely upon the explorations of these scouts, and it is a very bad custom; for sometimes they are surprised in their sleep by their enemies, who club them before they have time to rise and defend themselves. . . . Besides when they go to war they divide their men into three troops, that is, one troop for hunting, scattered in various directions, another troop which forms the bulk of their men is always under arms, and the other troop of scouts to reconnoitre along the rivers and see whether there is any mark or sign to show where their enemies or their friends have gone. This they know by certain marks by which the chiefs of one nation designate those of another, notifying one another from time to time of any variation of these. In this way they recognise whether enemies or friends have passed that way. The hunters never hunt in advance of the main body, nor of the scouts, in order not to give alarm or to cause confusion, but only when these have retired and in a direction from which they do not expect the enemy. They go on in this way until they are within two or three days' march of their enemy, when they proceed stealthily by night, all in a body, except the scouts. In the day time they retire into the thick of the woods, where they rest without any straggling, or making a noise, or making a fire even for the purpose of cooking. And this they do so as not to be noticed, if by chance their enemy should pass that way.

Source: From "July to October, 1609. Champlain's voyage up the St. Lawrence and Richelieu rivers, and his return to France," in David B. Quinn, ed., *New American World*, Vol. IV (New York: Arno Press, 1979), p. 427.

Each summer, when the main party of Huron traders visited the French, an elaborate ceremony was performed to reaffirm the alliance between their two nations. Before meeting the French, the Hurons would paint their faces and put on their best clothes. During an initial round of speeches, feasts, and ceremonies, the Huron chiefs presented rich gifts of

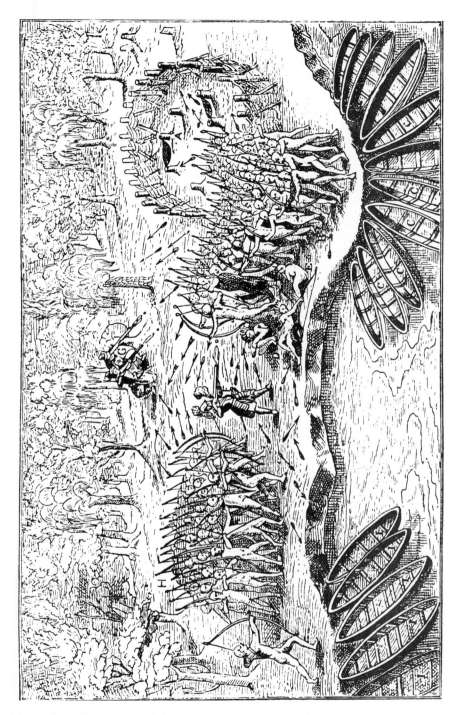

Samuel de Champlain fighting with Indian forces attacking the Iroquois stronghold of Ticonderoga *(Ernest and Johanna Lehner,* How They Saw the New World, *New York: Tudor Publishing Company, 1966, p. 92.)*

furs to the French administrators and asked them to see that the Huron traders obtained high-quality goods at reasonable prices. Then individual Hurons exchanged their furs with the French traders. More feasts and ceremonies followed and the French officials gave the Huron chiefs presents equal in value to those they had received and invited them to return to trade the following year. Unless major chiefs had performed this ceremony, the ordinary Hurons who accompanied them or who came later in the season to trade felt uncomfortable in their dealings with the French.[2]

The French Avoidance of Conflicts over Land and Authority

Unlike the English colonial experience, the French in Canada substantially avoided land disputes with the natives. The French never found an enterprise to rival the fur trade for profit, and they remained heavily dependent on the Indians for the delivery of pelts. This pattern persisted despite the existence of some French backwoodsmen, the famed *coureurs de bois*. Few settlers came to Canada, as opposed to traders, soldiers, and priests. These settlers established farms primarily along the St. Lawrence between Quebec and Montreal. This territory was uninhabited when the first colonists began to arrive in the early 1600s. As early as 1664 the government prohibited settlement farther inland than Montreal, and reasserted this policy early in the eighteenth century. Cornelius J. Jaenen states

> In New France there was no alienation of Amerindian lands. . . . There was no displacement of native population to make way for white European settlement; there was no advancing and threatening frontier of colonization. Instead, there were native peoples settled voluntarily within the French seigneurial tract in the Saint Lawrence valley on *réserves* administered by the missionary clergy, and there were also small islands of French settlement scattered at strategic commercial and military locations in the Amerindian hinterlands.[3]

Nor did the French assert direct judicial authority over the Indians in Canada. The local situation largely determined jurisdiction over criminal and civil disputes. Sometimes French authorities adjudicated conflicts between Frenchmen and natives and sometimes native ones did. No overarching colonial policy existed. Even natives who lived in French communities along the river were never subject to tribute, taxes, or labor or military service.

France certainly did assert its sovereignty in Canada against the pretensions of other European powers, and at the imperial level it maintained that all the native peoples of New France swore allegiance to the French monarch. But the French in the colony itself were in no position to insist on such recognition. The French remained dependent on the Indians for the economic health of the colony, and for military support. By as early as the mid-seventeenth century, the English in

North America substantially outnumbered the French, and the latter's continued control of Canada against the combined might of the English colonists and the English navy was inconceivable without staunch support from their native allies.

The Fur Trade and the Huron

For nearly thirty years before 1650, the highly profitable fur trade of Canada centered on the Huron, an ethnic group that numbered in the several tens of thousands and resided in the lands abutting the northern shores of Lake Ontario and Lake Erie. Each year a couple of hundred Hurons canoed to Montreal to exchange between 20,000 and 30,000 pelts, mostly beaver, for European goods, primarily copper pots, metal axes and knives, cloth, alcohol, and firearms. The Huron's control over substantial amounts of manufactured goods greatly enhanced their standing with neighboring peoples near the Great Lakes. Huron chiefs accrued greater authority because they could distribute more gifts among their own people and with others, which facilitated their diplomacy—a primary task for chiefs.

When the number of furbearing animals began to plummet in their own territory, the Hurons turned from actual production of pelts to trading for them with other peoples, mostly to their west. The Hurons exchanged manufactured goods obtained from the French for furs and then transported the furs to Montreal, where they were in turn exchanged for yet more European-made products.

The sustained contact the Huron, and also the Iroquois, maintained with Europeans hastened the arrival of epidemic disease. In the mid-1630s, several virgin-soil epidemics raged throughout the Northeast and killed off more than half of the population of these two major indigenous groups in less than two decades.

In 1615, the first French missionaries arrived in Canada. These few Recollets, never more than four in number, had utter contempt for native culture. They thought that before any conversion could take place, candidates had to learn French in order to understand Christian doctrine and also to become very Europeanized in their way of life. The Huron and other native cultures of the north were still intact and saw nothing attractive in what the Recollets preached. The rather indifferent efforts of these few missionaries over a decade yielded a total of perhaps 50 conversions, a number of them deathbed conversions by natives who possibly thought baptism constituted a healing ritual.

In the mid-1620s the Recollets were succeeded by Jesuits who came in greater numbers and with a very different approach to conversion and to indigenous culture. They sought to live individually or in pairs in native communities, learning the language and very much participating in indigenous life and culture. The Jesuits sought neither to Europeanize the natives in any systematic way nor to have them live in the midst of French settlers, whom the Jesuits themselves saw as poor examples of proper Christian life. Finally, the Jesuits appreciated that the Huron tolerated them, at least in the early years, because they feared losing their role in the fur trade if they did otherwise. The missionaries tried to ensure that their villages were favored in the trade and that any converts obtained a sure supply of European goods, especially firearms.

The Catholic emphasis on saints readily reconciled itself with indigenous pantheistic beliefs, while the practice of godparenthood appealed to the preexisting native emphasis on kinship and lineage. But the natives disdained Catholic priests for their strict celibacy, for they practiced rather free heterosexual relations themselves. It also inhibited the priests' connection to the kinship and marriage networks which underlay the natives' social world and relationships. Natives likewise looked down on the priests' intentional fasting, for they prized feasts and the massive consumption of food whenever such was possible. They also drew little comfort from the priests' acceptance of death for the baptized. The natives felt that the Jesuits should try to help the ailing to recover rather than to welcome death and the supposed salvation that followed. Many Indians sought baptism to ensure reuniting with other dead family members rather than for the reasons prescribed by Catholic theology.

The Jesuits wanted the Huron to believe that they possessed supernatural powers. They demonstrated their mastery of the European technology the natives so admired, the superiority of literacy over the indigenous oral culture, their ability to predict eclipses and other natural occurrences, and also the supremacy of their healing rituals compared to those of native shamans. Lacking effective political or military force over the native people, the Jesuits could do little else. Later, they did establish a fortified compound in Huron territory, complete with a hospital and separate living quarters for converts.

As religion permeated virtually all indigenous social and cultural practices and relationships, conversion to christianity required a native to abandon his or her community and its established ways and beliefs. Bruce Trigger notes some of the broad ramifications of conversion among the Hurons and other native peoples.

> Since public feasts and celebrations invariably involved traditional religious rituals, converts were not allowed to participate in them. In effect this meant that they ceased to be an integral part of their community's network of economic reciprocity and redistribution. They were also forbidden to contract ritual friendships with non- Christians and to supply goods that would satisfy the desires of the souls of sick people. To avoid involvement in native rituals, Christian warriors often refused to fight alongside traditionalists or to comply with decisions that were made on the basis of divinations.[4]

Great tension developed within Huron society, particularly as this divisiveness closely followed the devastating epidemics of the 1630s and growing hostility with the powerful Iroquois confederacy, who were supplied with firearms by Dutch fur traders at Fort Orange (later Albany). Huron chiefs and shamans increasingly opposed the Jesuits and their converts, but they could not take direct action against them because of their own dependence on the French.

Beginning in the 1640s and culminating in their complete victory in the early 1650s, the Iroquois undertook first to attack Huron trading expeditions and eventually to annihilate entire settlements. The reasons for these attacks are not completely clear. Some historians assert that the Iroquois had determined to usurp the Huron's profitable position as middlemen in the fur trade. Others note that the Iroquois did not manifest the clearest economic motives, but rather were conducting large-scale traditional "mourning wars" to avenge or replace their own deceased in war.

In fact, by 1654 the Iroquois had destroyed the Hurons (and their nearby allies) as an autonomous people and had driven them out of their extensive traditional territory. A small group of Hurons fled to the west, where they formed a new cultural identity. The Iroquois had killed thousands and adopted a large number into Iroquois society. As a substantial fraction of these were Christians, the Iroquois now had to deal with the same cultural divisiveness afflicting the Hurons previously. Finally, some Hurons were brought into French territory near to Montreal, where they lived under the direction of Jesuit priests and remained staunchly loyal to the French cause.

This warfare, made more deadly by the use of firearms by both sides, illustrates the dramatic change in the nature of combat among indigenous societies in the wake of European colonization. Before European contact, Indian warfare in Eastern North America involved large contingents fighting each other in open country away from settlements. Though these forces had previously made heavy use of arrow fire, these missiles moved so slowly through the air that they could sometimes be avoided. Even arrows that struck flesh often lacked the velocity and sharp points to cause serious injuries. Thus relatively few deaths seem to have occurred. The natives grieved tremendously over the demise of any kin or tribal members. Such fatalities themselves demanded condolence raids—retaliatory warfare to capture an opponent who was then slowly tortured to death, or adopted into the kin group as a replacement for the member who had died. Patrick M. Malone characterizes precontact Indian warfare in the Northeast as follows:

> Feuds between kin groups and intertribal or interband wars of varying
> scale and intensity were common. Combat was usually on a small scale,
> however, with ambushes and raids on villages much more frequent than
> actual battles. Indians did undertake prolonged sieges of fortified posi-
> tions on occasion and would sometimes meet in open fields for battles
> or skirmishes involving large numbers of warriors. In all these forms of
> warfare, relatively few participants were ever killed.[5]

But the massive introduction of muskets greatly increased the killing power of Indian forces. As a consequence, warfare was quickly modified to stress small-unit operations based around stealth and ambush, with the intent as much to minimize one's own casualties as to inflict injury. But the spread of firearms also permitted the complete eradication of enemy settlements despite substantial fortifications, as demonstrated by the Iroquois devastation of all Huron villages in the above-mentioned campaign.

French Warfare against the Iroquois

The French engaged in warfare against the Iroquois from the time that they mounted their first settlements in Canada. They initially acted on behalf of Algonquian allies who were traditional enemies of the confederacy, and then to protect the fur trade from Iroquois incursions. But with the Iroquois annihilation of the Huron, the French stood quite alone against this growing native power and its European supporters, first the Dutch and, after 1664, their replacements—the English. With just a small population of settlers in Canada, France felt compelled to introduce regular military troops into the colony to counter the rising threat of the Iroquois and the vastly larger English settler population. In 1665, a regiment of over a thousand men marched south against Mohawk villages. Despite considerable ineptitude that resulted in heavy losses, this contingent destroyed several settlements and substantial food supplies. This campaign caused all five tribes in the Iroquois confederation to send delegations to Quebec to negotiate a peace, which lasted for nearly twenty years. This period of tranquility enabled the French to consolidate their once-threatened preeminence in the fur trade. Despite periodic efforts by the English, New France maintained its control over this profitable trade until it was conquered by England in 1760 in the French and Indian War.

The Iroquois, however, were not permanently opposed to the French. They repeatedly made overtures to the Jesuits, and at times even let them establish missions in their midst. In 1656, the Onondagas accepted a mission of seven priests and fifty French workmen in their territory. By 1668, all five Iroquois tribes had missionaries among them. They viewed the Jesuits as useful diplomatic agents to French colonial officials. Most Iroquois were not attracted to the religious message the Jesuits communicated. As relations with the French deteriorated, the missionaries were gradually recalled, the last leaving in 1686.

By the 1680s, England and France were engaged in a bitter international rivalry that would last through the end of the colonial period, including actual warfare between the two countries roughly every twenty years. The Iroquois at this time were once again so closely affiliated with the English that the French mounted a campaign against an Iroquois people, this time the Seneca, the westernmost of the five tribes. The force of 2,000 men, including a number of native allies, destroyed the major Seneca settlement in 1687, but failed to defeat the Seneca warriors themselves. The Iroquois were temporarily cowed, but just 2 years later an Iroquois army of about 1,500 men attacked the heartland of French settlement along the St. Lawrence river. It killed over 100 colonists and destroyed some 50 farms. By 1690, the French were once again able to launch attacks, and though these proved not terribly effective, the Iroquois nonetheless bore the brunt of them. Contingents of French settlers and native allies ambushed parties of Iroquois along trails and at river crossings, withdrawing quickly after fierce firefights. This style of warfare was so effective that the Iroquois could supply the English in Albany with far fewer beaver pelts, while the French fur trade remained unaffected.

By the end of the decade, continuous warfare had reduced the Iroquois fighting strength by about half. With the latest war between the French and the

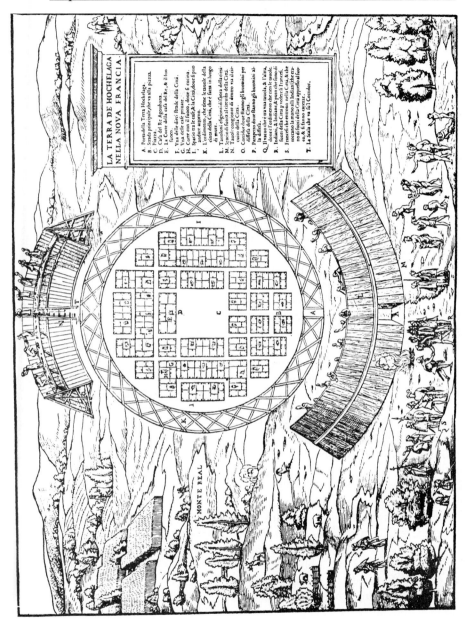

A depiction of the Iroquois town of Hochelaga *(Ernest and Johanna Lehner,* How They Saw the New World, *New York: Tudor Publishing Company, 1966, p. 80.)*

English winding down, in 1701 the Iroquois agreed to separate treaties with both colonial governments, promising that the Iroquois would remain neutral in any future warfare between the two colonies. Such a policy was effective as long as neither of the two European powers had the capacity to eliminate the other. France and England also had to view potential Iroquois armed support for one side as decisive in any such struggle. Thus for sixty years the Iroquois remained substantially out of the several colonial wars, while both the French and the English provided them with ample supplies and dispatched diplomatic envoys to their settlements to ensure their continued neutrality.

French Settlement along the St. Lawrence in the Eighteenth Century

As late as 1680, the population of French Canada numbered only some 10,000 persons, including roughly 3,500 soldiers and probably only 1,100 females. Very few French emigrated to the colony in the eighteenth century, so despite a healthy positive natural growth rate New France contained barely 70,000 people in 1760, while British North America held some 1,500,000 at the same time. The farms scattered along the St. Lawrence between Quebec and Montreal were quite productive, but their harvests primarily fed the colony; little was exported. Canada remained economically dependent on the fur trade, which spread ever farther into the western expanse. Quite regularly every spring perhaps 1,000 men abandoned their farms and crafts in the east to trap in the forested western expanses around or even beyond the Great Lakes.

The French were able to hold onto Canada despite several lengthy wars with the British because of the active military support they received from their Indian allies. As early as the 1670s some Mohawks, members of the Iroquois Confederation, converted to Catholicism and moved from eastern New York to Canada. They had been heavily influenced by Catholic Hurons they had earlier adopted. For over twenty years these Mohawk converts held back from participation in French war campaigns against the English and the Iroquois Confederation, but finally in 1693 they actually joined an expedition against the other Iroquois tribes in New York.

Many displaced Indians from throughout the northeastern part of North America settled in reserves the French established along the St. Lawrence River basin. Jesuits operated these rather autonomous reserves, and most of their inhabitants converted to Catholicism, at least formally. But they did not dramatically alter their culture or economy to any great extent. Reserve Indians remained under the rule of their own chiefs and tribal councils and commonly lived in matrilineal-organized longhouses. They likewise retained traditional gender roles, with women devoting themselves to agriculture and men to hunting, diplomacy, and warfare. They also retained their native languages, and relatively few could speak French even as a second language. These peoples staunchly supported the French in their warfare against the English.

Few French women resided even in this more densely settled eastern region. Because of this small number, only a minority of male colonists married

A Micmac comments about French and Indian cultures

About 1677, a Recollet missionary who was fluent in the Micmac language related the following comment by a Micmac elder to some French settlers in coastal Canada. It reflects remarks made by many natives about the relative attractions of indigenous and European culture.

my brother, hast though as much ingenuity and cleverness as the Indians, who carry their houses and their wigwams with them so that they may lodge wheresoever they please, independently of any seignior whatsoever? Thou art not as bold nor as stout as we, because when thou goest on a voyage thou canst not carry upon thy shoulders thy buildings and thy edifices. Therefore it is necessary that thou preparest as many lodgings as thou makest changes of residence, or else thou lodgest in a hired houses which does not belong to thee. As for us, we find ourselves secure from all these inconveniences, and we can always say, more truly than thou, that we are at home everywhere, because we set up our wigwams with ease wheresoever we go and without asking permission of anybody. Thou reproachest us, very inappropriately, that our country is a little hell in contrast with France, which thou comparest to a terrestrial paradise, inasmuch as it yields thee, so thou sayest, every kind of provision in abundance. Thou sayest of us also that we are the most miserable and most unhappy of all men, living without religion, without manners, without honour, without social order, and, in a word, without any rules, like the beasts in our woods and our forests, lacking bread, wine, and a thousand other comforts which thou has in superfluity in Europe. Well, my brother, if thou dost not yet know the real feelings which our Indians have towards thy country and towards all thy nation, it is proper that I inform thee at once. I beg thee now to believe that, all miserable as we seem in thine eyes, we consider ourselves nevertheless much happier than thou in this, that we are very content with the little that we have; and believe also once and for all, I pray, that thou deceivest thyself grealy if thou thinkest to persuade us that thy country is better than ours. For if France, as thou sayest, is a little terrestrial paradise, art thou sensible to leave it? And why abandon wives, children, relatives, and friends? Why risk thy life and thy property every year, and why venture thyself with such risk, in any season whatsoever, to the storms and tempests of the sea in order to come to a strange and barbarous country which thou considerest the poorest and least fortunate of the world? Besides, since we are wholly convinced of the contrary, we scarcely take the trouble to go to France, because we fear, with good reason, lest we find little satisfaction there, seeing, in our own experience, that those who are natives thereof leave it every year in order to enrich themselves on our shores.

Source: Crestien LeClerq, "A Micmac Responds to the French, ca. 1677," in Colin G. Calloway, ed., *The World Turned Upside Down: Indian Voices from Early America* (Boston: Bedford Books, 1994), pp. 50–51.

Europeans. Many cohabited with Indian women, though few of these arrange-ments were formalized by church ceremonies. But, in contrast to Latin America, a culturally distinct mixed-race category emerged only very gradually in Canada, for the vast majority of mixed offspring were raised by their mothers within the Indian world and were fully accepted into these tribes regardless of their biologi-cal makeup. The longstanding indigenous practice of adopting people from other ethnicities certainly facilitated this acceptance of people of mixed race, termed *métis* in French.

Nonetheless, the French, including the French colonial government, dis-played a much more tolerant attitude toward race mixture and cultural absorp-tion of native peoples than did their counterparts elsewhere in North America. In the late seventeenth century, fearful that the English might overrun lightly populated Canada, the French government more actively encouraged Indians to live among the colonists to facilitate acculturation. Louis XIV, for example, pledged a substantial gift to any native woman who wed a colonist. Understandably, though, given the resilience of indigenous cultures, few Indian women contracted marriages with French men and few Indians entered fully into the French colonial world.

The Canadian West and the Mississippi River Valley in the Eighteenth Century

In the latter half of the seventeenth century, the period after their devasta-tion of the Hurons and up to their peace treaty with the French in 1701, the Iroquois raided successfully along the Ohio River Valley and into the territory of the western Great Lakes from Lake Ontario to the southern shore of Lake Superior. They sought to expand their participation in the fur trade and to dom-inate the native peoples in that region. Their repeated military victories created great disarray and disruption. Numerous peoples and villages were forced to re-locate. Fragments of different tribes joined together in new villages.

Despite this devastation, the fur trade continued to flow quite reliably to the east, and most of it stayed in French hands, despite the efforts of the Iroquois and their English allies. After the British capture of New Netherlands in 1664, the Iroquois found themselves increasingly subordinated to their ally's imperial ambitions. Once the 1701 treaty between the French and the weakened Iroquois removed the latter as a threat to the Great Lakes region, the peoples there re-turned to a more traditional way of life emphasizing agriculture and fishing over fur trapping.

The French presence in this territory included a scattering of Jesuit mis-sions established at important native settlements, several lightly manned forts at important passes, and roughly 1,000 trappers. These *coureurs de bois* set out each spring from Montreal to transport furs already gathered by these western peo-ples, or sometimes to travel up to 1,000 miles, perhaps to Lake Winnipeg or even to the base of the Rocky Mountains, to run their own strings of traps. All of these Frenchmen depended on understandings, alliances, and mutuality of interest with the different tribes that they moved among. The expansion of the English trading system into the region by the second decade of the eighteenth century weakened the French bargaining position with these Algonquian-speaking western peoples.

Given their tenuous situation, the French had to accept native authority over many aspects of life. The French recognized the necessity to reconcile sexual liaisons to native expectations and to settle instances of loss of life in ways agreeable to indigenous custom. The fur trade itself depended on an extensive system of alliances of support and friendship that the tribes expected of the French, as well as extensive gift-giving to native leaders. The French also mediated disputes between the native peoples themselves. Richard White notes the primary aspects of this enduring accord.

> From its inception, then, the alliance was not simply the natural result of poor and shattered peoples' seeking to share French wealth and power but, rather, an initially precarious construction whose maintenance seemed as essential to Canadian as to Algonquian survival. The alliance endured not because of some mystical affinity between Frenchmen and Indians, nor because Algonquians had been reduced to dependency on the French, but rather because two peoples created an elaborate network of economic, political, cultural, and social ties to meet the demands of a particular historical situation. These ties knit the refugee centers to each other and each center to the French. Central to this whole process was the mediation of conflicts both between the French and their various allies and among the allies themselves.[6]

This French-Algonquian alliance persisted through the extended warfare between the French and English in the 1750s. With the English conquest of Canada in 1760, this alliance of course ended. Western Indians found themselves bereft of European assistance as they faced English colonists, who showed little interest in the fur trade, instead seeking to take over native lands as their rapid population growth drove the agricultural frontier ever westward.

The benign race relations in French Canada were largely dictated by population and gender ratios and by French economic and military dependence on a number of indigenous peoples. The French in North America were no more inherently accommodating to native needs than were the other European colonizing nations, as demonstrated by the contemporary French colony in the southern Mississippi River Valley.

In 1682 the explorer Robert La Salle was the first Frenchman to venture into the lower Mississippi Valley. The rather advanced and heavily populated native societies there had experienced only intermittent exposure to Europeans before 1713, when the French situated a small trading base along the river. At the beginning of the 1720s, the French raised a substantial fortified settlement on the river in the territory of the Natchez people. The settlement included soldiers, women, and black slaves. The intent was to erect an agricultural colony. The French did not pursue trade or military alliances with the Natchez, as they were already cultivating such relationships with the nearby Choctaw.

Before long, escalating tensions and misunderstandings resulted in conflict. The Natchez killed five traders who had mistreated them, the French responded by executing local chiefs. Then in 1722, the French commander burned down three Natchez villages. In 1729, the French demanded land from the Natchez without compensation. The natives responded with a military assault, seizing a fort, killing several hundred French, and capturing many others. In 1731, the French in turn invaded Natchez territory supported by cannon and Choctaw allies. They killed over a thousand Natchez, burned some captives at the stake, and sold several hundred captives into slavery in the French West Indies. The surviving Natchez dispersed and were adopted as individuals or small groups by other native peoples of the southeast. The upshot was the disappearance of a complete ethnic group. This rapid elimination of a local people that Europeans determined to be useless was a practice likewise utilized by both the Dutch and the English.

The Dutch in New Netherland

When the Dutch became interested in North America in the early seventeenth century, they had recently emerged as the preeminent commercial power of Europe. They would maintain the position until the second half of the century, when the British navy defeated them in a series of wars. Dutch settlement along the Hudson River lasted a mere 50 years, and the colonists numbered no more than 10,000 when the English conquered the colony in 1664. Nonetheless, this Dutch settlement substantially shaped the course of European-Indian relations in early colonial North America because it offered the native peoples a commercial and political alternative to the French. Early on, the Dutch also sought to establish bases along the Connecticut and Delaware Rivers, but soon withdrew them in favor of the Hudson River Valley and the islands of Manhattan and Long Island.

In 1609, Henry Hudson sailed up the river that now bears his name, under the auspices of the Dutch East India Company. Five years later the Company established a small trading base, Fort Nassau, well up the river. A flood in 1617 caused its abandonment. It was replaced by intermittent trade between European vendors on horseback and the natives. Similar to the French in Canada, the initial impulse of the Dutch was to trade for furs rather than to settle and cultivate the area. Not until 1624 did the Dutch establish an agricultural colony, New Amsterdam, on Manhattan Island. A delegation travelled up the Hudson that same year and founded Fort Orange near the former site of Fort Nassau. As Fort Orange and, after the 1664 English takeover, as Albany, it thrived as a major fur trading center in North America. The history of Dutch relations with the native peoples of New Netherland is readily bifurcated between the trading region in the north centered at Fort Orange and the agricultural settlements in the south around New Amsterdam.

The Dutch Fur Trade at Fort Orange

In the first decade or so of fur trading with Indians, the Dutch dealt mainly with the Mahicans, who lived along the Hudson River. But by 1625, these people had trapped the beaver population to exhaustion in their region. The Dutch then traded with the Mohawks, the easternmost of the Iroquois peoples who were longstanding enemies of the Mahicans. The Mohawks then destroyed the weakened Mahicans over the course of three wars, eliminating them as an autonomous people.

For the next 40 years, the Dutch at Fort Orange served as the primary trading partners of the Iroquois, who supplied over 10,000 pelts a year. The Dutch provided the Iroquois with metalware, cloth, and enough muskets that they soon became the best armed native group in North America. This trade in turn enabled the Iroquois to undertake wars of aggression against native peoples to their north and west. These neighboring peoples could not just shut down trade with the Iroquois, however, because through the Dutch they had become the primary suppliers of wampum to peoples of the interior. Wampum, strings of assembled white shells found along the shores of Long Island, had become vital to personal adornment and religious rituals among the peoples of the larger region. It likewise constituted a standard measure of value in trade. But the Dutch also supplied the indigenous people with considerable alcohol, which over decades fueled social disintegration within kin groups and tribes.

Unlike the French, the Dutch dispatched few traders into Indian territory. Instead, they were quite content to sit back in Fort Orange and await the delivery of pelts by the Indians. Further, while the French had a rather active interest in converting Indians to Catholicism, with the Jesuits establishing a series of missions well within native territory, the Dutch, being staunch Calvinists, viewed the natives as being beyond the pale of Christianity and did not seek to missionize among them.

The Dutch at Fort Orange, similar to the French in Canada, were unable to assert legal authority over the local Indians and had to participate in the elaborate rituals and political alliances that invariably accompanied trade in the native world. However, little miscegenation between the Dutch and native peoples seems to have taken place. Considerable distrust and some level of tension characterized Indian–Dutch dealings around Fort Orange, but Allen W. Trelease comments

> There was little more trust or affection between the Dutch and Indians around Fort Orange than there was at New Amsterdam. Animals were killed, thefts were reported, and mutual suspicion at times ran rampant, yet neither side ever resorted to war. Peace was maintained because both sides had everything to lose and nothing to gain by hostilities.[7]

When the English seized New Netherland in 1664 and renamed Fort Orange as Albany, it hardly affected the structure of trade. The Iroquois continued to supply substantial numbers of furs to Dutch traders still based there. They in turn shipped them downriver to New York City (the former New Amsterdam). Only there did the trade shift from its pre-1664 pattern, as the pelts were now sent on to England instead of the Netherlands. Such remained the pattern through the rest of the seventeenth century. It changed during the eighteenth century, for Albany lost most of its former importance in the fur trade, as the Iroquois could no longer secure the previous number of pelts from interior tribes.

Dutch Settlement Around New Amsterdam and Its Impact on the Native Peoples

The trajectory of relations between the Dutch and the native peoples around New Amsterdam, and particularly along the northern coast of Long Island, differed greatly from that found at Fort Orange. The colonists of New Amsterdam had no interest in trade with the Indians and viewed them as a military threat. Dutch families predominated in this area, as women commonly accompanied their husbands to the colony; few Dutch men cohabited with Indian women.

The Dutch did accept the concept of native ownership of the land and did not erect settlements or farms until they had purchased the land from tribal leaders. In 1626, the governor of New Netherland, Peter Minuit, consolidated the failing outlying Dutch settlements by purchasing Manhattan Island from its native residents. In 1661, the Dutch established the first significant upriver settlement, Schenectady, with the purchase of land not far from Fort Orange. Fort Orange, just a fortified trading post, did not incorporate adjacent lands.

European settlement expanded around New Amsterdam, especially along the northern shore of Long Island. Far from all of the new arrivals were Dutch. Some were French Huguenots, and others were Puritans who migrated or were driven to territory not under Puritan jurisdiction by the rather strict and sometimes arbitrary rule of the New England magistrates.

As the number of farms expanded and they came to dominate some areas, tensions increased between the settlers and the natives. Many disputes involved the damage that domestic animals caused to native fields of corn. The Indians sometimes responded by killing the animals. This only exacerbated matters and brought the crucial issue of jurisdiction to the fore. The numerous settlers, considering the local indigenous peoples to be a hindrance to their full, effective use of the land, sought to drive them out or at least make them conform to Dutch practices and law. And, of course, once Indians became subject to Dutch law, they were rarely able to prevail, and colonists could use court proceedings as an instrument against them.

The Dutch West Indies Company operated the colony of New Netherland as a business venture; it pressured the governors on the scene to keep costs low and returns high. In 1639, the colony expended considerable money on fortifications and the maintenance of soldiers. Governor Krieft determined to recover these costs by levying a tax on the Indians near Manhattan to be paid in furs, corn, or wampum. His success in this collection is unknown, but the next year a serious conflict began with local Indians.

The early 1640s were a time of warfare around New Amsterdam. By 1643, bands of Dutch had begun to raid native settlements, slaughtering men, women, and children and driving away any survivors not taken as slaves. Nearly simultaneously, indigenous peoples along the borders of the colony began to attack. But warfare ceased once the annual planting season began and the natives became preoccupied with cultivating crops. The fall brought a new wave of warfare, with attacks by both sides. Numerous noncombatants were cut down. Conflict continued intermittently until late summer of 1645 when the parties signed a peace treaty. Perhaps a thousand Indians had been killed over the previous five years. The number of settlers had declined also, but more from migration away from the war zone than from fatalities. The Dutch, however, could be resupplied in men and equipment from Europe, while the indigenous population had only its own diminishing resources.

Epidemic diseases had also decimated the native peoples around New Amsterdam. Combined with the warfare of the early 1640s, epidemic disease caused the native presence in the region to decline precipitously in New Netherland's final two decades. The natives found it hard to retain their independence; they needed the Dutch to protect them from their traditional enemies. By the end of Dutch rule, the indigenous population around New Amsterdam barely reached a few thousand people, some of them working as dependents on Dutch farms.

Conclusion

The French, English, and Dutch did not take Eastern North America away from the Spanish. Rather, the Spanish had arrived at the Atlantic coast first and found that it did not reward their serious attention, given the precious metals, rich agricultural lands, and vast native populations they already controlled in Mexico and Peru. They did, however, colonize the American southwest; however, they did this only later in the colonial period and with relatively few colonists. New Mexico developed into a significant province, courtesy of the settlers' exploitation of the Pueblo communities. Texas and California, on the other hand, contained few colonists, and these depended largely on the missions that were installed in both places.

The Pueblos responded in 1680 with one of the most successful native revolts against Spanish rule. Although the Spaniards recolonized New Mexico some twelve years later, they did not reinstitute many of their previous impositions on the native population. The introduction of horses and sheep transformed the ways of life of local peoples elsewhere in the southwest.

The French, Dutch, and English were slow to settle in eastern North America, for the resources and the semisedentary peoples of that region did not initially promise great wealth. France and England first established bases along this coast intending to raid Spanish treasure fleets leaving the Caribbean for the open ocean.

Eventually the French and the Dutch turned their attention to the resources of the continent itself. Their colonization patterns shared important similarities. Both economies relied heavily on the fur trade; farming was very secondary. Both depended on native allies to provide pelts and thus had strong reasons to remain on good terms with the indigenous peoples. Considerable biculturation occurred along the frontiers in these situations, as colonists incorporated aspects of indigenous culture into their way of life. Where trade with the Indians was important, both the French and the Dutch respected native political authority and land ownership. In areas where trade was inconsequential, however, neither colonial power hesitated to eradicate local peoples. Rather few immigrants settled in either colony. Their populations remained quite small until the end. They depended heavily on their native allies for military defense and for attacks against other fur-trading peoples.

But the French and Dutch differed in several important ways as well. The French were far more inclined to mate with native women than were the Dutch. They also ventured great distances away from their trading bases, unlike the Dutch. Finally, while the Dutch showed little interest in religious conversion of the natives, the French, through their Jesuit missionaries, pursued it avidly.

While some tribes were eventually destroyed by some combination of epidemic disease and more deadly warfare, most native cultures proved very resilient—and considerably flexible—before the unprecedented and unrelenting impact of the European colonies and their economic and religious pressures. Tribal chiefs routinely allied their peoples with one or the other European colony in order to use it for their own interests and against traditional enemies. They likewise required colonial authorities and traders to respect and honor native customs, including gift-giving, conducting rituals, and engaging in lengthy speeches at the start of negotiation sessions.

Ethnic identity and pride endured. The rate of adoptions probably increased notably because of the demographic disruption and decline that resulted. Religious conversion also proved divisive within native communities. Many had to split up, unable to resolve their internal conflicts. Eventually, a degree of reconciliation and religious synthesis took place among some of these peoples, or at least a recognition emerged that ethnic identity transcended particular religious beliefs.

Both colonies affected native peoples whom they never contacted directly, or at most glancingly. Epidemic disease radiated out from their settlements and trading posts, affecting indigenous populations well into the interior and causing them to rise or fall in power relative to their neighbors. Also, the European goods available to tribes who controlled the fur trade encouraged them to pursue aggressive policies against peoples quite removed from actual Dutch and French outposts. The metal weapons and firearms provided them by their European allies, of course, dramatically enhanced their military might. European influence, then, shaped native culture and history in areas far removed from any colonial settlement.

Select Bibliography

Anderson, Gary Clayton. *The Indian Southwest, 1580–1830: Ethnogenesis and Reinvention.* Norman: University of Oklahoma Press, 1999.

Axtell, James. *The Invasion Within: The Contest of Cultures in Colonial North America.* New York: Oxford University Press, 1985.

Dennis, Matthew. *Cultivating a Landscape of Peace: Iroquois-European Encounters in Seventeenth-Century America.* Ithaca: Cornell University Press, 1993.

Dickason, Olive Patricia. *Canada's First Nations: A History of Founding Peoples from Earliest Times.* Norman: University of Oklahoma Press, 1992.

Eccles, W. J. *The Canadian Frontier, 1534–1760.* Rev. ed. Albuquerque: University of New Mexico Press, 1983.

Gutiérrez, Ramón A. *When Jesus Came, the Corn Mothers Went Away: Marriage, Sexuality, and Power in New Mexico, 1500–1846.* Stanford: Stanford University Press, 1991.

Jaenen, Cornelius J. "Characteristics of French Amerindian Contact in New France," in David B. Quinn et al. *Essays on the History of North American Discovery and Exploration.* The Walter Prescott Webb Memorial Lectures n. 21. College Station: Texas A & M Press, 1988, pp. 79–101.

Jaenen, Cornelius J. *Friend and Foe: Aspects of French-Amerindian Cultural Contact in the Sixteenth and Seventeenth Centuries.* New York: Columbia University Press, 1976.

Knaut, Andrew L. *The Pueblo Revolt of 1680: Conquest and Persistence in Seventeenth-Century New Mexico.* Norman: University of Oklahoma Press, 1995.

Milanich, Jerald T. *Florida Indians and the Invasion from Europe.* Gainesville: University Press of Florida, 1995.

Morrison, Kenneth A. *The Embattled Northeast: The Elusive Ideal of Alliance of Abenaki-Euroamerican Relations.* Berkeley: University of California Press, 1984.

Nash, Gary B. *Red, White, and Black: The Peoples of Early America.* 3rd ed. Englewood Cliffs, NJ: Prentice-Hall, 1992.

Richter, Daniel K. *The Ordeal of the Longhouse: The Peoples of the Iroquois League in the Era of European Colonization.* Chapel Hill: University of North Carolina Press, 1992.

Rink, Oliver A. *Holland on the Hudson: An Economic and Social History of Dutch New York.* Ithaca: Cornell University Press, 1986.

Snow, Dean R. *The Iroquois.* Cambridge, MA: Blackwell, 1994.

Trelease, Allen W. *Indian Affairs in Colonial New York: The Seventeenth Century.* Ithaca: Cornell University Press, 1960.

Trigger, Bruce G. *The Children of Aateantsic: A History of the Huron People to 1660.* 2 vols. Montreal: McGill-Queen's University Press, 1976.

Trigger, Bruce G. *Natives and Newcomers: Canada's "Heroic Age" Reconsidered.* Montreal: McGill-Queen's University Press, 1985.

Usner, Jr., Daniel H. *Indians, Settlers, and Slaves in a Frontier Exchange Economy: The Lower Mississippi Valley Before 1783.* Chapel Hill: University of North Carolina Press, 1992.

Weber, David J. *The Spanish Frontier in North America.* New Haven: Yale University Press, 1992.

White Richard. *The Middle Ground: Indians, Empires, and Republics in the Great Lakes Region, 1650–1815.* Cambridge, England: Cambridge University Press, 1991.

Endnotes

1   James Axtell, "Imagining the Other: First Encounters in North America," in idem, *Beyond 1492: Encounters in Colonial North America,* (New York: Oxford University Press, 1992), p. 73.

2   Bruce G. Trigger, *Natives and Newcomers: Canada's "Heroic Age" Reconsidered* (Kingston: McGill-Queen's University Press, 1985), p. 186.

3   Cornelius J. Jaenen, "Characteristics of French-Amerindian Contact in New France," in David B. Quinn et al., *Essays on the History of North American Discovery and Exploration,* The Walter Prescott Webb Memorial Lectures, no. 21 (College Station: Texas A & M Press, 1988), pp. 89–90.

4   Trigger, *Natives and Newcomers,* p. 256.

5   Patrick M. Malone, *The Skulking Way of War: Technology and Tactics Among the New England Indians* (Baltimore: The Johns Hopkins University Press, 1993), p. 9.

6   Richard White, *The Middle Ground: Indians, Empires, and Republics in the Great Lakes Region, 1650-1815* (Cambridge, England: Cambridge University Press, 1991), p. 33.

7   Allen W. Trelease, *Indian Affairs in Colonial New York: The Seventeenth Century* (Ithaca: Cornell University Press, 1960), p. 115.

6

The British and the Indians of Eastern North America

The English first became active in North America at about the same time as the Dutch, around 1600. Like the Dutch, their activities in this region were just one aspect of a much larger expansion throughout many parts of the globe. This growing involvement in Africa, South Asia, the Spice Islands, and East Asia meant that neither country devoted much attention to the small number of colonists in North America. Both the English and the Dutch initially hoped to repeat the Spanish success in discovering mineral wealth and numerous Indian laborers. Their attitudes toward the native peoples of the Americas largely paralleled those of the Spanish. In addition, the leaders of some early English colonies planned to capture Spanish treasure ships as they departed the Caribbean.

The English had already subjugated and colonized foreign lands. In the second half of the sixteenth century, English expeditions overran Catholic Ireland, a society the largely Protestant English regarded as primitive and hardly a part of European civilization. Nicholas P. Canny, a historian of this English campaign against Ireland, notes

> Certain traits of the Gaelic way of life, notably the practice of transhumance, were accepted as evidence that the Irish were barbarians, and the English thus satisfied themselves that they were dealing with a culturally inferior people who had to be subdued by extralegal methods.[1]

Early English Undertakings in North America

England's initial efforts in the New World focused on an unlikely gold mining scheme on Baffin Island, situated above Hudson's Bay in the far north. Between 1578 and 1583, Sir Humphrey Gilbert sold shares of land there, but the English never successfully established a colony there despite attempts by two expeditions.

The next serious attempt was undertaken by Gilbert's half-brother, Sir Walter Ralegh. He planned the colonization of Roanoke Island by some one hundred men in 1585–1586, thinking that this base would prosper through some combination of raids against Spanish shipping and the discovery of precious metals. As I remark about the Roanoke colony in another publication,

> The initial attempt in 1585 involved seven ships carrying about six hundred men, of whom just over a hundred settled at Roanoke. The others engaged themselves in privateering raids in the south. The first colonists were predominantly veterans of military service in Ireland and on the continent of Europe. They built a fort for protection against a possible Spanish attack and, living off the supplies brought by ship, settled down for some months to see what sort of naval venture might develop. The colony was run largely as a military camp, though the men were allowed to search for gold as individuals.[2]

The venture encountered immediate problems, and when an English relief expedition arrived at the island in 1590—England having had no contact with the small colony for three years—it found the settlement completely deserted. No one has offered a convincing explanation of what happened to the colony.

Jamestown and English Settlement in the Chesapeake

Venturous English investors continued searching for a way to profit from their claims in North America. The next undertaking, the 1607 settlement of Jamestown, constituted a larger and somewhat better financed undertaking than Roanoke, but the aims of both efforts were similar, including the expectation of raiding Spanish shipping. In his study of early Virginia, Edmund S. Morgan comments

> It seems clear that some of the investors in the Virginia Company expected to use an American colony as a base from which to continue their depredations, far from the king's watchful eye. But the company could not officially engage in such exploits or even condone them, nor could it serve as a cover for schemes to subvert the Spanish empire. Probably the majority of investors looked toward legitimate profits. They invested their money in hopes of finding precious metals or minerals, of discovering valuable plants for dyestuffs and medicines, and

perhaps of opening a northwest passage to the Pacific. But they were prepared to settle for less spectacular goods like glass, iron, furs, potash, pitch, and tar, things that England needed and mostly had to import from other countries.[3]

The hundreds of English who came to Jamestown in its early years settled in territory controlled by Powhatan, a newly powerful chief. He had earlier subordinated some 30 surrounding tribes into a rudimentary empire of perhaps 10,000–20,000 people spread across all of coastal lowland Virginia. Each of the tribes retained its own chief, but as paramount chief, Powhatan enjoyed authority over all of them. He displayed no fear of the colony. Shortly after Jamestown's founding, 200 of Powhatan's warriors attempted to burn it down and only cannon fire from the English ships drove them back. From then on, the colonists went around armed, expecting attack at any time.

The Powhatan Indians may have refrained from a concerted military attack because they expected the colony to fail on its own. The English proved incapable of growing enough food to supply themselves in the early years of the settlement. The English routinely traded with the Powhatan for their ample agricultural surpluses. The Powhatans negotiated hard terms and sometimes refused to deal. The colonists responded with armed forays to collect grain. But given the colonists' abiding weakness, such an approach was only occasionally successful. In the early years some settlers fled from Jamestown to live with the Indians. The colonial authorities considered this behavior to be so injurious to their sense of cultural superiority that they passed a law invoking the death penalty for any apprehended English runaways.

Both sides in this unstable relationship tried to use the other as an ally. The English sought food and other forms of material assistance from the Indians. Powhatan, on the other hand, sought to recruit the English against his enemies and to incorporate them into his confederation. The Indians did not stand in awe of the English nor did they see them as utterly alien. They knew that they were foreign, but found their behavior and values to be understandable. They never viewed them as a threatening category of humans to be avoided. They had no reason to think in such terms. They had long witnessed such peoples sailing along the coast.

Despite sporadic episodes of violence, the English frequently visited native villages, enjoying their hospitality, praising the great feasts to which they were welcomed, and noting the lively discourse and conversations that characterized such occasions—as best they could be comprehended through the few translators available. In 1608, the English staged a ceremony in which Powhatan was to receive a crown offered by the British monarch. The colonists viewed this as a ritual display of subordination, but Powhatan, understanding their intention, refused to kneel to receive the crown. When it was finally placed on his head, he made the event into an exchange between equals by presenting his mantle in turn to the presiding English official.

After nearly a decade of failure and a couple of instances of near abandonment of the colony, Jamestown gained a stronger footing in the mid-1610s, when

A depiction of the Indian community of Pomeiock *(Ernest and Johanna Lehner,* How They Saw the New World, *New York: Tudor Publishing Company, 1966, p. 83.)*

new immigrants arrived and the settlement finally discovered a cash crop. In 1610, Jamestown contained barely 60 survivors of the more than 900 people who had come during the first 3 years. Even though some 1,200 additional people arrived in 1610–1611, as late as 1616, the unimpressive colony included a mere 650 Englishmen. A major reason for the incessant population decrease is that no

An encounter between Powhatan and Captain John Smith

For a couple of years after its founding, Jamestown was under the command of Captain John Smith, a soldier of long and diverse experience in European wars. In this passage Smith describes the hard bargaining that transpired when he led a small English contingent into Powhatan's encampment seeking food and the remarks that Powhatan directed at him about the continuing state of tension between the English and his people.

Quartering in the next houses we found, we sent to Powhatan for provision, who sent us plentie of bread, Turkies, and Venison. The next day having feasted us after his oridinarie manner, he began to aske, when we would bee gon, faining hee sent not for us, neither had hee any corne, and his people much lesse, yet for 40 swords he would procure us 40 bushels. The President [Smith] Shewing him the men there present, that brought him the message and conditions, asked him how it chaunced he became so forgetful, thereat the king concluded the matter with a merry laughter, asking for our commodities, but none he liked without gunnes and swords, valuing a basket of corne more pretious then a basket of copper, saying he could eate his corne, but not his copper. . . . Wherewith each seeming well contented; Powhatan began to expostulate the difference betwixt peace and war after this manner. Captain Smith you may understand, that I, having seene the death of all my people thrice, and not one living of those 3 generations, but my selfe, I know the difference of peace and warre, better than any in my Countrie. But now I am old, and ere long must die, my brethren, namesly Opichapam, Opechankanough, and Kekataugh, my two sisters, and their two daughters, are distinctly each others successours, I wish their experiences no lesse then mine, and your love to them, no lesse then mine to you; but this brute from Nansamund that you are come to destroy my Countrie, so much affrighteth all my people, as they dare not visit you; what will it availe you, to take that perforce, you may quietly have with love, or to destroy them that provide your food? what can you get by war, when we can hide our provision and flie to the woodes, whereby you must famish by wronging us your friends; and whie are you thus jealous of our loves, see us unarmed, and both doe, and are willing still to feed you with that you cannot get but by our labours? think you I am not so simple not to knowe, it is better to eate good meate, lie well, and sleepe quitely with my women and children, laugh and be merrie with you, have copper, hatchets, or what I want, being your friend; then bee forced to flie from al, to lie cold in the woods, feed upon acorns, roots, and such trash, and be so hunted by you, that I can neither rest, eat, nor sleepe; but my tired men must watch, and if a twig but breake, everie one crie there comes Captaine Smith, then must I flie I knowe not whether, and thus with miserable feare end my life; leaving my pleasures to such youths as you, which through your rash unadvisednesse, may quickly as miserably ende, for want that you never know how to find? Let this therefore assure you of our loves and everie yeare our friendly trade shall furnish you with corne, and now also if you would come in friendly manner to see us, and not thus with your gunnes and swords, as to invade your foes.

Source: Captain John Smith, "The Generall Historie of Virginia, New-England, and the Summer Islaes," in Philip L. Barbour, ed. *The Complete Works of Captain John Smith (1580–1631)*, Vol. II, with a foreword by Thad W. Tate. (Chapel Hill: University of North Carolina Press, 1986), pp. 194, 195–196. Copyright © 1986 by the University of North Carolina Press. Used by permission of the publisher.

Englishwomen arrived before 1619. What saved and transformed Jamestown was the cultivation of tobacco, a native crop that proved phenomenally popular in England. Jamestown shipped its first crop to the home country in 1617.

Native peoples throughout the Americas commonly smoked tobacco. They had been doing so for nearly two thousand years. In North America the preferred means to smoke tobacco was through stone pipes. The Indians followed elaborate protocols that involved smoking through these pipes, termed *calumets,* to seal peace treaties or trade agreements.

The rapid population growth of the colony after the discovery of tobacco as a marketable crop and the subsequent demand for cultivable land placed unprecedented pressures on the native societies. They could no longer entertain notions that the colony might eventually fade away or that the settlers would remain substantially dependent on trade with them. Instead, competition over limited land resources increased. In 1618, in the midst of these developments, Powhatan died and was succeeded by his brother Opechancanough, an experienced leader who advocated a more aggressive policy toward the English. Around this time a few natives became laborers on colonists' lands, probably to gain greater access to European-made goods. They acculturated to a considerable extent and identified with the English, even to the point of warning them about expected Indian raids.

In 1622, the Powhatans launched a large-scale attack against Jamestown, seeking to destroy the colony once and for all. Though the natives succeeded in slaying fully one-third of the settlers, the English gradually turned the tide, utilizing their disciplined fighting formations and concentrated firepower. Opechancanough may have refrained from follow-up attacks, expecting the English to behave like natives typically did—withdrawing permanently after suffering a bad military defeat. But the colonists instead took the offensive, attacking indigenous communities and slaughtering their inhabitants. The English took over much of the best land in the Tidewater. The weakened and chastized Powhatans withdrew into the interior, though raids and reprisals surged back and forth for several years. The Powhatans' local rivals gave military assistance to the English, sending supplies, intelligence, scouts, and warriors. The result was a rapid increase in the colonists' military power and political influence over nearby tribes

The 1622 war destroyed any regard the colonists held toward the Indians. They no longer traded with them, as they could now grow sufficient food on their own. They now regarded the natives as savages and obstacles to further English expansion. The English pursued complete separation of the peoples. The colonists insisted that the few Indians who lived among them be christianized and acculturated. But they refused to accept even these converts fully into white society, retaining instead an abiding suspicion and prejudice against them.

With the Powhatans steadily losing strength, especially with their declining population before the growing numbers of colonists, Opechancanough in 1644 determined to attempt one more attack against the English. After slaying some 400 English and throwing the colony into considerable disarray, Opechancanough again refrained from following up on a successful offensive. The

English quickly reorganized aided by the social discipline and strict hierarchy that they maintained. They then undertook a concerted attack into Powhatan territory, meeting little organized resistance and easily invading the head village. They sold the captives into servitude, already an established practice in the British colonies. The Powhatans had to flee yet farther into the backcountry, thereby opening up additional prime farmland to the colonists. In 1646, the English captured and imprisoned the aged Opechancanough. Shortly thereafter, only loosely guarded, he was shot down by a colonist.

With his death, the Powhatan confederation completely dissolved, and individual communities went their own way. From then on the surviving native peoples of the region lived within isolated pockets of land—virtual reservations—surrounded by the colonists' agricultural estates. A 1646 treaty between Virginia's governor and the English-imposed "emperor" of the Powhatans—for the English still wanted the local natives to have a single spokesman—stated that the chief held his dominions as a vassal of the English monarch and was not free to dispose of them as he wished. Further, the English could pick his successor. No Indian was allowed onto colonial lands except to deliver a message, and even then he had to wear special clothing. The Indians had to return any "negroes and guns," while the English could keep all native war prisoners as laborers. Any of these who fled into Indian territory had to be returned. Individual Englishmen were enjoined from going into native reserves, an effort to avoid provocations. Finally, any native child aged twelve and under was free to live among the colonists, to be acculturated, christianized, and transformed into a useful worker (in the English view).

In 1676 land hunger led to another war. This one witnessed a direct assault by rebellious colonists on the remaining independent tribes in central Virginia and also against a colonial administration that sought to protect Indian lands in order to avoid costly wars. Termed Bacon's Rebellion after the leader of the movement, it began when several members of the Doeg tribe on the Virginia frontier raided the estate of a man with whom they had a money dispute and killed a workman. Local colonists, however, did not retaliate against the perpetrators but rather against a community of friendly Indians, seemingly because they coveted their land. (A growing number of colonists had completed their indentures as plantation workers but lacked the funds to acquire their own estates.) This attack precipitated a wider uprising. Nathaniel Bacon, Jr. organized a vigilante group of landless colonists who conducted raids against communities of largely unarmed, friendly Indians who were already tributaries of the Virginia colony, killing large numbers of them.

In due course, Bacon turned against the colonial government in Williamsburg and intimidated it into letting his men have their way. Helen C. Rountree relates

> The General Assembly that met in June reflected the feelings of the vigilante element of the colony: laws were passed declaring all Indians who deserted their towns or harbored hostile Indians to be enemies, and any Indians captured in "war" were to be slaves. All trade with Indians was

prohibited; "friendly" Indians were to hunt with bows and arrows only; land deserted by any of them was to be sold to pay the expenses of a general Indian war.[4]

Bacon's forces attacked Indians throughout the colony, most of whom were members of weakened groups now dependent on the English. Bacon's death from disease late in 1676 precipitated divisions within the revolt, and the previous colonial government once again took control. It moved to end the war and to return prisoners. The following year the English authorities imposed a treaty on the surviving indigenous societies. It was somewhat modified in its final version in 1680.

In it, the Indian leaders acknowledged that they were subjects of the English monarch and that they held their reservations as a patent from him. To reduce the possibilities of conflict, the treaty stated that no English should live within three miles of a native settlement. The Indians could bring cases of alleged ill treatment to the governor of Virginia. The governor would also regulate trade with the natives. Subject Indians were to assist the English in campaigns against foreign Indians. Indians who were servants of English masters were to be employed on the same terms as their English counterparts. In sum, the remaining native peoples of Virginia had come under the jurisdiction of the colony.

Virginia's Indians retained their ethnic distinctiveness for the remainder of the colonial period, many of them living on the ascribed reservations. They routinely entered English-controlled territory to work and trade. Over time, increasing numbers of them remained in this sphere, where they labored for English masters and purchased goods and otherwise accommodated themselves. But they were never offered full membership in colonial society.

Puritan Settlement in New England and the Rapid Transformation of the Local Peoples

The colonization of New England, which began in 1620, was preceded by roughly a century of episodic contact between fishermen and the coastal peoples. This prolonged and generally benign period of limited English–Indian interaction had three major effects on the native societies in that region. First, Indians quickly learned that Europeans possessed no superhuman abilities and that they were rivals of each other. Second, Indians came to appreciate the cloth goods and metal tools that the visitors displayed in great abundance. Third, the Indians were devastated by Old World epidemic diseases well before the first English settlements were founded.

The worst of these waves of epidemic disease occurred just before the founding of the first English settlement. It struck southern New England in 1616–1618 and may have been either a single epidemic or several in succession. The outbreaks caused tremendous human devastation. The coastal population declined to perhaps 15 percent of its previous number, leaving many villages and their surrounding agricultural lands deserted.

The Pilgrims in 1620 landed in an area already devastated by disease. Considerable unoccupied land was therefore available. Further, the remnant peoples of the region welcomed the Pilgrims as possible political and military allies against traditional enemies in the interior who had been less affected by the epidemics. Despite their weakness, the natives insisted on being treated as sovereign peoples and expected the customary political ritual and gift-giving that characterized native diplomatic dealings. They were extremely dismayed to learn that the Europeans sought political preeminence rather than reciprocity.

The Pilgrims also encountered Squanto, a Wampanoag, who had been kidnapped by an English ship captain six years earlier and had spent the intervening period in Spain and England and on several voyages to the New England coast. On his most recent return, he had found everyone in his community dead from disease. He welcomed the Pilgrims and gave them invaluable aid in dealing with the various local peoples and in adjusting to the soil and the climate of New England. He died a natural death just two years after the Pilgrims' arrival.

The much more numerous Puritans began to arrive in New England in 1630. They organized themselves into highly structured and unified towns based on family subsistence farms. The Puritans came to the New World largely in family units, unlike the French in Canada or the English in the Chesapeake. With their emphasis on small-scale agricultural production, they had little use for Indian trade or even for the natives as a subservient labor force. Further, the Puritan religion focused on seeking God's few elect. Hence the colonists initially manifested little interest in the conversion of the indigenous peoples. Puritan writers stressed the alienness of the Indians and their perceived backwardness. Many described the local peoples as hunters and gatherers, even while the Puritans accepted a share of their agricultural harvests to avoid abject starvation. They termed them nomadic, even though they visited their permanent settlements.

The Puritans refused to recognize native rights to the land or their judicial authority. From the earliest years, the Puritans consistently sought to have all Indian issues settled in their courts. After some years, the Puritans finally decided to purchase lands from the Indians because other settlements in the region might be able to claim title if they did not.

Francis Jennings explains the structural inequality underlying the exchanges between Indians and colonists in early New England.

> There was a fundamental disparity in the exchanges between Europeans and Indians. After the Europeans had been taught how to make and use canoes, moccasins, buckskin clothing, and backwoods shelters, they could dispense with further Indian guidance. When Indians granted or sold lands, the territory became European forever. In return the Indians received trade goods but not the means or skills of making and repairing such goods themselves. Becoming addicted to European products, the Indians soon lost their own neolithic skills through disuse; bowmakers found no apprentices where hunters and warriors knew the advantages of guns, and an artisan gap of a single generation can wipe out a craft in an illiterate society. In the trade that thus came to dominate

their economy, the Indians had no choice but to supply the commodities demanded by the Europeans. Apart from personal and military services, the Indians' only commodities of value were food, peltry, and lands.[5]

In 1636–1637, the Pequots, the most powerful tribe in southern New England, fell before a Puritan military campaign prosecuted to seize their lands in eastern Connecticut. The Pequots had sought an alliance with the Narragansetts, located to their east, to jointly resist Puritan aggression. But the Narragansetts sided with the colonists, seemingly because they had prospered from trade with them and had not themselves lost any lands.

European military tradition stressed "total war," which focused on the killing of one's opponents rather than their capture. Noncombatants might be slain with impunity, crops destroyed, and towns razed. But the practice of war among the Eastern Woodlands Indians was much more moderate and controlled. Patrick M. Malone describes some of its characteristics.

> Feuds between kin groups and intertribal or interband wars of varying scale and intensity were common. Combat was usually on a small scale, however, with ambushes and raids on villages much more frequent than actual battles. . . . In all these forms of warfare, relatively few participants were ever killed.[6]

When warned of a possible attack, *sachems* (tribal leaders) would relocate their communities into easily defensible locations or scatter their followers into small, highly mobile bands. Most commonly, warfare involved relatively small numbers of warriors trying to ambush their opponents, often in wooded areas. The two forces disengaged when either side suffered a few casualties or captives. The losing side was permitted to withdraw without hindrance, as it acknowledged by its retreat that the victors held the field and that the campaign was over.

In the early part of the Pequot War, neither contestant enjoyed much of an advantage. Then in the spring of 1637, a Puritan expedition with many Narragansett allies surrounded a Pequot community along the Mystic River that contained mostly women and children. The main Pequot fighting force was campaigning elsewhere. The Puritans set the wooden structures on fire, and those who did not die in the flames were shot down as they fled. The Puritans were so caught up in the slaughter that they also wounded some twenty of their Narragansett supporters. An English commander reported that the Narragansetts were horrified by English tactics and the many casualties that they caused; it was so unlike warfare that they knew. The English sold the few Pequots taken captive to other tribes or to British colonies in the West Indies. Most surviving bands of Pequot warriors now fell easily to the English, and some of them were also sold into slavery. The Pequot headman and his band fled into Mohawk territory in New Amsterdam to seek adoption into the tribe. They were refused and then slain by the Mohawks, who had entered into a lucrative deal with the English. Also, the Mohawks' trade along the coast stood to benefit from the

Pequots' destruction. A 1638 treaty between the Puritans and local tribes declared the Pequots extinguished.

The Puritans took only modest steps to convert native groups to Christianity, and their missionaries only worked among peoples who had lost their autonomy and were already within the boundaries of colonial settlement. These few ministers—the most noted of whom was John Eliot, the so-called "Apostle to the Indians"—could not envision religious conversion without an accompanying total cultural conversion to the English way of life. Puritan ministers gathered the Indians into "praying towns" separate from both Indian and Puritan communities. Each nuclear family resided in a separate house. The husband became the agriculturalist and the head of the household and the wife devoted herself to domestic tasks, a radical transformation of gender roles. All members were expected to wear European-style clothing and to cut their hair in the English fashion. They were totally subject to Puritan law and ministers and were denied indigenous leaders with independent authority.

Neal Salisbury describes the larger process.

> By the time Eliot began preaching to a group of Indians, the group had typically passed through the earlier stages of English domination: it had been devastated by epidemics; it had sold or otherwise lost much of its land under the incessant pressure of English immigration; it had become economically dependent on the English; and it had submitted to the political authority of the colonial government.[7]

These praying towns suffered from the animosity of neighboring Puritan communities, which typically coveted their lands and feared that the residents had not attained a sufficient level of "civilization" and peacefulness. The missionaries argued in rebuttal that these Indians could serve as allies of the Puritans against independent tribes on the other side of the frontier. When Mohawks raided into Massachusetts in the 1660s, the English supped the praying Indians with guns and ammunition.

In the Puritan view, true conversion required profound religious knowledge and culminated in a "conversion experience," authenticated by Puritans of proven devotion. For the Indians, of course, this expectation required complete repudiation of their original cultural identity. But the colonists would not accept those natives who converted fully to Puritanism into their midst as equals. They prohibited them from residing outside of their designated communities and from mingling freely with the English. The English employed them only as occasional manual laborers and required them to return to their own communities once their tasks were completed.

The Puritans placed tremendous land pressure on the remaining independent peoples of eastern Massachusetts in the early 1670s, and threatened their independence and cultural integrity. They responded by planning a coordinated uprising in 1675–1676. Called King Philip's War, it was led by Metacom, the *sachem* of the Wampanoags (known to the Puritans as King Philip). In this war, a few praying Indians sided with Metacom, causing the Puritans to distrust all of them. The Puritans removed those converted Indians professing loyalty from their towns and placed them on an isolated island without adequate supplies. Eventually some served in the colonial militia, particularly as scouts, aiding in the defeat of Metacom.

The Wampanoags under the leadership of Massasoit, Metacom's father, had originally allied themselves with the newly arrived Pilgrims. Metacom succeeded to chief of the tribe in 1662, upon the death of his older brother. Under great pressure from the colonists to make concessions, he sold pieces of tribal lands over the next decade in an effort to retain influence with important officials. But these authorities increasingly interfered in native politics. At a 1671 meeting convened in Plymouth at the colonists' insistence, Metacom was required at gunpoint to surrender his people's muskets and to sign a retroactive agreement placing himself under the rule of Plymouth's governor.

After this event, Metacom began to plan an uprising, including the recruitment of other tribes in southeastern New England, particularly the Nipmucks and the Narragansetts. The latter no longer benefitted from the alliance they had developed with the colonists for the Pequot War of a generation earlier. Full-fledged warfare erupted when an Indian informant to the colonists was found murdered and gunfire broke out between Wampanoags and settlers at Swansea over damage possibly caused by settler-owned livestock.

Young Wampanoags and Puritans were both eager for war in the early weeks of King Philip's War. When the initial Wampanoag strategy of hit-and-run raids on colonial towns severely damaged the colony, other tribes joined the campaign. The Narragansetts allied with Metacom, but other tribes sided with the Puritans. Warfare became endemic along the frontier. The Mohawk decision to aid the colonists may have decided the outcome of the war. The Mohawks refused shelter to beleaguered tribes and attacked other peoples along the frontier, providing great military assistance to the Puritans. The killing of Metacom in combat in mid-1676 ended the war. Several thousand Puritans had been killed, and perhaps double that number of Indians. The Puritans sold native captives, including Metacom's wife and son, as slaves in the West Indies. Indians had raided 52 of some 90 Puritan towns and had destroyed a dozen of them. It took the colonists about 40 years to again expand westward to the point they had reached on the eve of this war.

With the elimination of the last autonomous native peoples in southern New England, the position of the praying Indians deteriorated notably. Neal Salisbury remarks

> Under terms of a 1677 law, those Indians who had not been killed, sold into slavery, or driven northward as a result of the war were physically restricted to one of the four remaining praying towns. The towns were no longer havens for those making conscious commitments to Christianity; they were reservations for an entire native population, now reduced, mostly as servants and tenant farmers, to a state of complete dependency on the English. Onto the lands formerly occupied by the Indians, both friendly and hostile, moved an onslaught of English settlers.[8]

In the hundred years between the end of King Philip's War and the outbreak of the American War for Independence, the Indians residing in eastern Massachusetts retained a degree of cultural distinctiveness, but suffered disdain from the rapidly increasing number of colonists. Few of them, even those living in the remaining Indian towns, could make a living working their own lands. Many labored on colonists' farms or as manual workers in Puritan towns. These Indian laborers increasingly merged into the growing permanent lower class in established eastern New England cities. Other natives worked as crew members on whaling ships. In these settings they interacted infrequently with other Indians and married fellow natives even more rarely. Their cultural distinctiveness barely survived, perhaps enduring as much by the colonists' continued refusal to assimilate even these peaceful, detribalized Indians as by the strength of their traditional practices and beliefs.

In Indian towns, many converts remained devoted to the Puritan faith, but fewer colonial ministers chose to serve them. Most ministers in Indian towns were themselves natives, often the descendants of *sachems*. Late in the colonial period cultural cohesion and land retention plummeted dramatically in these few remaining native communities. Daniel R. Mandell, who has studied these societies, states:

> Between the end of the Seven Years War and the conclusion of the American Revolution, many Indian groups in eastern Massachusetts disintegrated. Members of enclaves that had sold land to white settlers found themselves a shrinking, marginalized minority, pursued by poverty, illness, and homelessness. Some moved to neighborhoods within the growing cities. Others left to join the few native villages that retained substantial communal resources. These enclaves increasingly served as sanctuaries where natives could often ignore or transcend the handicaps imposed by Anglo-American culture. In the wake of the colonial wars, an increasing percentage of Indians within and without the refuges were the "mixt posterity" of intermarriages, as many widows and young women found African American husbands.[9]

The Iroquois in the Eighteenth Century

In the last third of the seventeenth century, the five tribes of the Iroquois confederation found themselves badly divided and suffering substantial losses from their participation in wars between the French and the English and against other native groups over control of the fur trade. But the Iroquois reversed their fortunes, becoming prosperous and avoiding most warfare during the first half of the eighteenth century, through the elaboration of what has been termed the "play-off system."

More than a century before Europeans reached the Americas, the five Iroquois tribes—the Mohawk, Oneida, Onondaga, Cayuga, and Seneca—had joined together in the Iroquois Confederacy, a political compact to act in concert

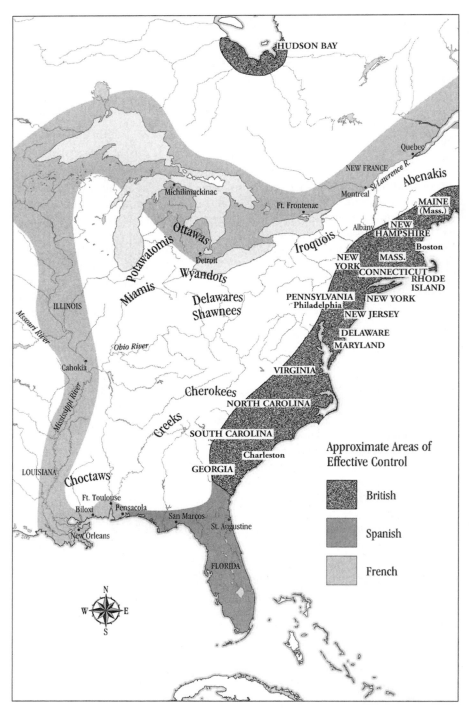

European colonies and important Indian peoples in Eastern North America in the mid-eighteenth century *(Daniel K. Richter,* Facing East from Indian Country: A Native History of Early America, *Cambridge, MA: Harvard University Press, 2001, p. 165. Copyright © 2001 by the President and Fellows of Harvard College.)*

in war and peace and in trade agreements. This accord greatly strengthened the Iroquois tribes by requiring diplomatic rather than military solutions in cases of disagreements between them. The constituent tribes each sent a designated number of chiefs to the Grand Council, which was empowered to negotiate with foreign peoples and to adjudicate disputes within the Confederacy. Great efforts were taken to achieve a consensus if at all possible to avoid dissension within the Confederacy and its possible dissolution. No other North American Indian alliance achieved a similar level of cooperation or permanence, which left the Iroquois with unrivaled power among the Eastern Woodlands peoples.

In 1701, the Iroquois entered into treaties with the French, their enemy during the previous century, and the English, who were their primary trading partners. The first agreement assured the French of Iroquois neutrality in any conflict between the two European powers in North America. The Iroquois conceded the English their hunting grounds in the west to demonstrate that they still desired a close relationship with them. The upshot of this successful two-pronged diplomatic initiative was that both European countries competed against each other over the next fifty years to ensure that the Iroquois did not side with their opponent in the event of war. Both understood that an Iroquois alliance with their opponent would determine the outcome of any war. Both therefore supplied wagonloads of goods to Iroquois towns to maintain their neutrality. The Iroquois profited greatly while avoiding actual combat.

The first half of the eighteenth century was a time of peace, growth, territorial stability, and prosperity for the Iroquois. They remained central players in the fur trade and obtained abundant supplies of European manufactured goods through trade linked to the play-off system. Their power was such that the English colonists avoided encroaching on Iroquois lands for fear of reprisal raids and of pushing them into the French camp. The Iroquois assimilated the remnant populations of devastated coastal peoples, thereby replacing their own declining numbers.

The assimilation of substantial numbers of Tuscarora people from the Carolinas as the sixth tribe of the Iroquois in 1722 perhaps highlighted this era of success. Though once a powerful people who spoke a language similar to that of the Iroquois, for some years the Tuscarora had been victimized by neighboring peoples in league with Virginia and Carolina traders. Their children had been sold into slavery and their lands became substantially diminished. As early as 1710, the Tuscarora negotiated with both the Iroquois Confederacy and the colony of Pennsylvania about coming under the protection of one of them in the north. But they reached no agreement. The Tuscarora then affiliated themselves with nearby lesser, but similarly aggrieved, tribes, and in 1711 attacked North Carolina colonists, killing well over 100 in the first wave of assaults. The settlers reorganized, however, and began a systematic, devastating campaign against Tuscarora towns. In a horrible defeat in early 1713, several hundred Tuscarora were burned to death defending a fortified community, another couple of hundred were captured and slaughtered. The colonists took away the remainder, about 400—mostly women and children—and sold them into slavery in the Caribbean.

Perhaps 2,000 Tuscarora subsequently abandoned their territory to drift northward to seek absorption by the now-sympathetic Iroquois. The Iroquois voted to accept them into the Confederacy, though seemingly not as full equals to the original five tribes. The Iroquois admitted them despite the protestations of high-level colonial officials. Over the next couple of decades, the Tuscarora militated with the other Iroquois to limit their ties to the English.

By the 1740s, strains had begun to develop in the Iroquois play-off system, as the member tribes, and even component villages, frequently pursued their independent interests, and as the English and French placed new pressures on the Iroquois in an effort to get more favorable agreements. The play-off system was still fundamentally operative when the French and Indian War broke out in the second half of the 1750s, but by then, Iroquois unity could not be maintained, and many joined the French. The combined strength of the French and Iroquois inflicted major defeats on the English in central New York and required some English settlements to withdraw to the east. But after several years, French fortunes declined, and the Iroquois backed away from their staunch support of them.

An adoption ceremony among the Seneca

The peoples of North America commonly adopted some of the captives taken in warfare to replenish their own numbers. Some of these captives included English men and women. The weakest and wounded captives would be quickly killed in order not to slow down the march back to the war party's tribal territory. Many survivors were eventually redeemed. But some never were, and a few made the choice to remain with the natives even when presented with the opportunity to return to their home communities. Mary Jemison was captured by the Seneca in 1758, when she was about fifteen, and spent the rest of her life living with them in western New York. She married a member of the tribe and raised a family. She was so contented that she refused an opportunity to return to white society. Her autobiography was published in 1824.

It is the custom of the Indians, when one of their number is slain or taken prisoner in battle, to give to the nearest relative to the dead or absent, a prisoner, if they have chanced to take one, and if not, to give him a scalp of an enemy. On the return of the Indians from conquest, which is always announced by peculiar shoutings, demonstrations of joy, and the exhibition of some trophy of victory, the mourners come forward and make their claims. If they receive a prisoner, it is at their option either to satiate their vengeance by taking his life in the most cruel manner they can conceive of; or, to receive and adopt him into the family, in the place of him whom they have lost. . . . It was my happy lot to be accepted for adoption; and at the time of the ceremony I was received by the two squaws, to supply the place of their brother in the family; and I was ever considered and treated by them as a real sister, the same as though I had been born of their mother.

Source: "Mary Jemison. A Narrative of Her Life, 1824," in Colin G. Calloway, ed., *The World Turned Upside Down: Indian Voices from Early America* (Boston: Bedford Books, 1994), pp. 74, 75.

The takeover of New France by the English in the Treaty of Paris in 1763 gravely hurt the Iroquois. They could no longer practice a play-off system, for only a single colonial power remained in North America. Nor would the English deliver loads of goods to ensure their friendship. Further, the war had caused the English to establish forts throughout New York, the Ohio River Valley, and up to Lake Michigan; these military bases remained even after the treaty was signed. In response, in 1761 some Iroquois tried to instigate a war against the English at Detroit and other western forts. They then supported Pontiac's Rebellion in 1763, for it sought to drive the English out of the Ohio territory. Despite some notable military successes by the Seneca and other tribes, the English prevailed. Subsequently, however, the Colonial authorities exacted few reprisals and generally protected Iroquois lands against the colonists' demands.

Pontiac was an Ottawa leader in the Great Lakes region who became noted for his anti-English rhetoric at intertribal councils after 1760, the year that the British occupied Canada. He was increasingly influenced by Neolin, known as the Delaware Prophet, who preached Indian renewal and brotherhood. Neolin called for a return to the old ways that prevailed before European colonization. He also sought greater cooperation among tribes against their common enemies. This appeal threatened the status of tribal chiefs, many of whom opposed his movement. In 1763, Pontiac led an attack on the British garrison at Detroit that turned into a prolonged siege. Some French Canadians participated in the venture. Pontiac expected that regular French military units would soon join him, but none remained in North America.

Pontiac coordinated other attacks throughout the Ohio River Valley, but these largely failed and an English relief column reached Detroit and lifted the siege. Despite this failure, Pontiac still remained a powerful leader, and he traveled widely in the region preaching intertribal cooperation and the end to tribal rivalries. Pontiac believed that he led an effective alliance of Ohio River and Great Lakes peoples who esteemed him above their tribal leaders. But his imperious attitude alienated many, and he soon lost much of his support. In 1769, a member of the Peoria chiefdom lineage shot Pontiac dead in the village of Cahokia, ending his attempt to create a union of tribes.

The Iroquois staunchly supported the English crown against the patriots in the American Revolution. Joseph Brant was perhaps the most notable Loyalist leader among the Iroquois. The stepson of a *sachem,* he became well connected to British colonial authorities in New York when his sister became the mistress of the Superintendent of Indian Affairs, Sir William Johnson. Brant even studied English at a school in Connecticut. When Sir William was succeeded by his nephew Guy as Superintendent of Indian Affairs, Brant served as his interpreter and aide. In a visit to London in 1775–1776, Brant was received by King George III. Upon his return, he began to argue that the Iroquois should abandon their policy of neutrality in disputes between the colonists and the British. Brant foresaw that a victory by the revolutionaries would leave his people destitute of supporters against the land-hungry settlers.

Brant assembled a combined Iroquois-Loyalist force that enjoyed military success against the Americans in New York and Ohio for five years. But the war

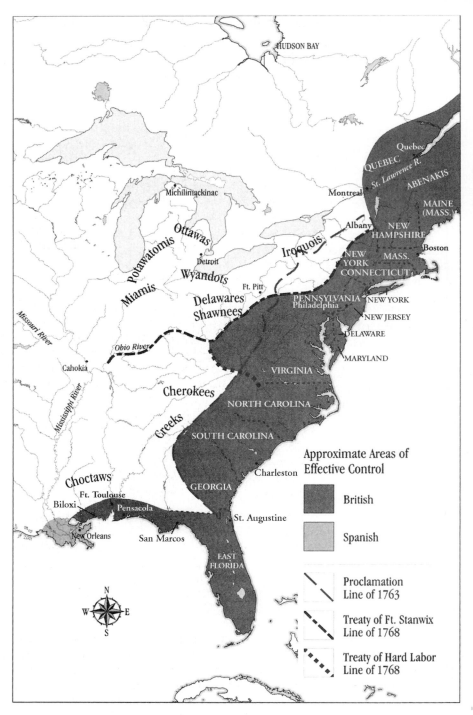

Approximate Areas of Effective Control

British

Spanish

Proclamation Line of 1763

Treaty of Ft. Stanwix Line of 1768

Treaty of Hard Labor Line of 1768

Eastern North America after the French and Indian War *(Daniel K. Richter,* Facing East from Indian Country: A Native History of Early America, *Cambridge, MA: Harvard University Press, 2001, p. 212. Copyright © 2001 by the President and Fellows of Harvard College.)*

divided the Iroquois Confederacy, despite Brant's unrelenting efforts to keep all its tribes on the British side. The Americans also destroyed numerous Iroquois settlements.

With England's defeat, Iroquois concerns were not addressed in the Treaty of Paris, which recognized American independence in 1783. Instead, the British ceded all lands south of the Great Lakes to the Americans and did not insist that native rights be recognized. The Iroquois were soon forced onto reservations, and their former lands were opened up to eager settlers, who now had government protection. The Iroquois had to abandon pretensions to sovereignty over large parts of the Ohio Territory. Many Iroquois preferred to live in British Canada. Brant and his followers were allotted a substantial, fertile tract of land in Ontario. Brant himself spurred the creation of an intertribal alliance that laid claim to much of the old Ohio Territory. But American officials successfully exploited abiding divisions within the newly formed confederation and secured their claims to the lands in question by a treaty in 1789. Brant lived out his life in comfort and distinction in British Canada. He enjoyed a largely European style of living, although he was unrelentingly proud of his Indian heritage and practiced traditional ceremonies until his death in 1807.

The Carolinas in the Eighteenth Century

The southern half of eastern North America, roughly the territory south of the Chesapeake Bay and east of the Mississippi, generally contained soils more suitable for agriculture than did the region to the north. Further, evidence suggests that the peoples of the southeast were influenced by the sophisticated cultures of Mesoamerica in the centuries before European contact and often had denser populations than those in the north. The Southeast peoples sometimes developed more elaborate hierarchies than those in the north, with chiefs enjoying authority over all the communities in an area, and maintained large-scale central temple sites as part of their religious worship.

English colonization of the Carolinas began late in the seventeenth century, a good half-century after the founding of Jamestown. Settlers in this new region maintained a long-term rivalry with the better-established colony of Virginia. The early colonists had little need for extensive landholdings and traded extensively with the coastal societies. These tribes initially welcomed the settlers' assistance in warfare against their traditional enemies in the interior, particularly against the Westos, who had obtained numerous firearms through trade with the Virginians.

A profitable fur trade soon developed between Carolina traders and the local tribes. But unlike in the north, the commodity was not beaver pelts, but deerskins. The Carolinas contained vast herds of deer, and the natives were expert at hunting them. However, whereas the deer had previously been pursued for meat and hides to satisfy local needs, they now produced an export item that could be exchanged for the cloth, metal goods, and firearms desired by the indigenous people. In the period 1699–1715, the Carolinas exported an average of 54,000 deerskins a year, and the number generally increased over the next 30 years or so, reaching more than 150,000 skins in peak years.

But a far more nefarious commerce developed nearly simultaneously with this one: an Indian slave trade. Encouraged by the colonists, the more powerful tribes raided the villages of their weaker neighbors to obtain captives to trade in colonial towns for imported goods. Once in the hands of Europeans, most of the Indians were shipped to the West Indies to work on sugar plantations. Others were dispatched to New England and New York, but some remained in colonial Carolina communities. In 1708, the Carolinas contained about 5,300 white settlers, 2,900 African slaves, and 1,400 Indian slaves.

As these raids became more extensive early in the seventeenth century, the Carolina colonists targeted the natives gathered at Spanish missions in northern Florida. Gary B. Nash describes the extent of these attacks:

> In 1704, a Carolina Indian trader, Thomas Moore, led about 1,000
> Creek warriors and fifty of his countrymen into Apalachee territory.
> Other raids in the next six years left the Spanish mission system, initiat-
> ed in 1573, in a shambles. Some 10,000 to 12,000 Timucas, Guales, and
> Apalachees were caught in the net of English slavery.[10]

The Yamasees had served as important British allies in the campaign against the Tuscaroras. But just two years after this victory, the Yamasees organized the largest native rebellion in the Carolinas. It was caused by the colonists' ever-increasing demands. The colonists encroached on Yamasee lands and sought to restrict them to reservations at the same time that they depended on their support in warfare and slave raiding. Perhaps even more pernicious were the policies of the Indian traders who dealt with the Yamasees. They supplied great amounts of alcohol to the hunters and thereby burdened them with large debts. A 1711 report noted that the Yamasees owed perhaps 100,000 skins—fully 5 years of hunting—to the traders. These dealers even debauched Yamasee women while their mates hunted in the interior. They subsequently began to seize Yamasee women and children to sell into slavery to cover these debts.

In April 1715, the Yamasees and their Creek allies coordinated a carefully planned attack on some British settlements. Eventually, perhaps 15 tribes numbering over 30,000 people participated. But just as the movement began, the English colonists persuaded the powerful Cherokee tribe to switch sides, largely because of its heavy dependence on English trade goods. Desperately needing men and equipment to counter the intense native onslaught, the Carolina colonists recruited fighters among their own black slaves. They also sought support from Virginia and supplies from New England. Before the war ended in 1716, the colonists suffered over 400 deaths and very heavy material losses. The Creeks moved far to the west to escape the reach of the English, establishing new trading connections with the French and the Spanish. The surviving Yamasees migrated to the safety of Spanish Florida.

These early eighteenth-century wars in the Carolinas, combined with the Indian slave trade that had shipped some thousands of slaves out of the region to the profit of Charleston traders, opened up extensive tracts of quality agricultural land to the colonists. By the early eighteenth century, South Carolina was importing large numbers of black slaves for its thriving agricultural plantation economy.   Within a couple of decades the black population of the colony outnumbered the white, while the vast majority of the native population had been killed.   The few native survivors had fled into the hinterland or lived on small, isolated reservations.

James H. Merrell describes those who remained within the boundaries of the colony:

> Those who chose to remain with colonists embarked on a long, slow
> slide into obscurity. Many joined like-minded groups and for a time
> maintained a collective identity. Pedees in the lowcountry, for example,
> divided in half, some living with Winyaws beyond the Santee River, the
> rest closer to Charleston with some stray Natchez from Louisiana and a
> few Cape Fears. With "kings" and "war captains," each of these enclaves
> could boast some semblance of a political organization. Well before the
> end of the century, however, kings and captains were gone, Pedee, Cape
> Fear, and other names were replaced by the nondescript terms
> Settlement Indians or "Parched-corn Indians," and virtually all had bro-
> ken down into their constituent parts, the extended family.[11]

The Native Peoples West of the Appalachians until the American Revolution

Until well after the American Revolution, autonomous and quite intact native peoples inhabited the land west of the Appalachian Mountains. These societies had not been insulated from the activities and influence of the colonists, but they had learned from witnessing the experience of the coastal peoples, who had been substantially destroyed by the end of the first third of the eighteenth century.

These interior societies appreciated the advantages of European-made goods. They regularly traded for them, and no leader argued for his people to purge themselves of Western material influence. Tribes far removed from the coast who perhaps never encountered a European participated avidly in the fur trade to obtain European manufactured goods. They sometimes waged war against each other to gain privileged access to them. The Indians quickly appreciated that metal pots, tools and weapons, woven cloth, and firearms improved their way of life. Further, these items did so generally by making such ordinary tasks as cooking, hunting, warfare, and keeping oneself warm and dry—and nicely adorned—more efficient, without transforming the indigenous peoples' culture and identity. Indians appropriated European goods and gave them their own meaning.

Until the end of the French and Indian War in 1763, the peoples of the Ohio River and Mississippi River Valleys benefitted from their ability to trade with the French, who were few in number, overwhelmingly dependent on continued Indian domination of the fur trade, and not in the least interested in the acquisition of land for agriculture. The fur trade continued to flourish and provided considerable wealth to some interior societies. And despite occasional conflicts, no single tribe threatened to dominate this commerce.

The devastation of incessant warfare on the Chickasaws in the 1750s

The Chickasaws were a small tribe located in northern Mississippi who sided resolutely with the English of the Carolinas against the onslaught of the French and their Indian allies in the eighteenth century. In this plea for assistance from 1756, the headmen of the Chickasaws report to the governor of South Carolina the degree of damage they have received over the previous several years.

> Therefore we beg of you, our best Friends, to send back our People that are living in other Nations in order to enable us to keep our Lands from the French and their Indians. We hope you will think on us in our Poverty as we have not had the Liberty of Hunting these 3 Years but have had enough to do to defend our Lands and prevent our Women and Children from becoming Slaves to the French. Our Traders that come here are not willing to trust us Gun Powder and Bulletts to hunt and defend ourselves from our Enemies, neither are we able to buy from them. Many of our Women are without Flaps, and many of our young Men without Guns which renders them uncapable of making any Defence against such a powerful Enemy. . . . We look upon your Enemies as ours and your Friends as our Friends. The Day shall never come while Sun shines and Water runs that we will join any other Nation but the English. We hope you will stil take Pity on us and give us a Supply of Powder and Bullets and Guns etc. to enable us to outlive our Enemies and revive a dying Friend. We have had no less than four Armies against us this Winter and have lost 20 of our Warriours and many of our Wives and Children carried of alive, our Towns sett on Fire in the Night and burnt down, many of our Houses etc. destroyed our Blankets etc.

Source: "Chickasaw Headmen, Speech to the Governor of South Carolina, April 5, 1756," in Colin G. Calloway, ed., *The World Turned Upside Down: Indian Voices from Early America* (Boston: Bedford Books, 1994), p. 129

The size and cultural integrity of these peoples were substantially affected by two roughly concurrent processes: the onslaught of epidemic diseases and the adoption of remnant societies migrating from the east. That relatively few Europeans traveled regularly west of the Appalachians helped to limit disease outbreaks. But by the first third of the eighteenth century, population decline in this region had become substantial. However, the surviving fragments of coastal peoples, far more decimated by disease and warfare, began to move into this territory around this same period and were incorporated into the existing tribes. Some evidence exists that entirely new ethnic groups emerged in this century, a phenomenon noted at other times and places in the Americas.

Eventually cultural change beyond the incorporation of European material culture became evident among these interior peoples, largely in response to the unremitting pressure from the colonists. The political hierarchy in these societies became more rigid. Before the arrival of Europeans, chiefs served primarily as spokesmen for their tribes and had little effective political authority. Instead, they sought to persuade their people to their way of thinking, using the respect they had garnered over decades. Further, chiefs were promoted from the male rank-and-file; the position was not inherited from one's father. But the Europeans always wanted to deal with a single leader. In addition, practicing primogeniture themselves, they expected the sons of chiefs to succeed to their fathers' posts. Over time, native societies in constant contact with British colonial society tended to have permanent leaders.

Colin G. Calloway elaborates on this phenomenon:

> As traditional bases of power weakened, European agents and traders cultivated client chiefs, giving them medals and gifts to buy and bolster their support. Chiefs always had acted as redistribution agents, maintaining influence not by accumulating wealth but by giving it away, thereby earning respect and creating reciprocal obligations. The gifts client chiefs gave now came from European backers and represented their sole source of influence; without allies to supply them they often fell from power.[12]

Something similar occurred to the position of war chief. Previously, warriors selected a leader for each campaign. Now permanent war chiefs began to appear, ready to respond to the larger military challenges posed by combat against other native peoples and, of course, the colonists' standing militias.

Women seem to have lost some of their influence and effective power in native societies as well. Trade, warfare, and diplomacy—all traditional male activities in indigenous culture—became more prominent. Further, agriculture—predominantly the purview of females—lost its earlier preeminence, as the people came to rely substantially on commercial hunting and trade with the colonists and as heightened mobility became required of individual communities. One must also acknowledge the impact of Christian teachings on some native peoples, even those that remained politically autonomous, with their emphasis on the "proper" economic and domestic roles of men and women, as understood by the Europeans as integral to truly civilized and Christian peoples.

Until at least the American Revolution, the major interior peoples remained sufficiently powerful to negotiate several key issues with settlers and traders: land ownership; sex; and violence. Native groups permitted certain small groups of colonists—often no more than one or two—to establish farms within tribal territories. These farmers commonly worked out specific agreements with the natives, offering political advice and providing goods and information. They married native women with some frequency, producing mixed-blood offspring who typically identified strongly with their mother's culture, but who likewise knew the languages and oftentimes the ways of their father's people. Numerous chiefs emerged from this mixed-race category in the late eighteenth century, bearing the English and Scottish surnames of their fathers.

J. Wright Leitch, Jr. remarks about this development among the peoples of the Southeast.

> Fostering a mixed-blood progeny, white parents might live and die in the Indian country or eventually return to white society. In any case their offspring customarily remained among the Indians. As a result, in the eighteenth century "Indian" chiefs had such names as McDonald,

Perryman, Colbert, Brown, Price, McGillivray, McIntosh, and Galphin, and in 1800, at least according to available documents, it was almost impossible to find a pure-blooded chief of any consequence.[13]

The native peoples continued to insist that their traditional procedures and values be invoked in cases of violence between their members and Europeans, many of which had developed as offshoots of commercial dealings. Native peoples avoided ceding judicial authority to the colonies. Instead, representatives from both cultures negotiated the procedures and standards required to settle the infraction. Both sides also wanted to limit the frequency of violence attendant to commerce in this zone.

Conclusion

The numerous tribes along the Atlantic coast of North America were undaunted by the establishment of the English colonies. They often felt in a dominant position for at least several decades, as the colonists depended on them for food and sometimes for military assistance. The leaders of these coastal peoples often sought to affiliate with the English in order to use them in their own political and military designs. Certain tribes translated their crucial role in the fur trade, of such great importance to the colonial economy for so many years, into a powerful negotiating position. British commercial and political agents reluctantly recognized native sovereignty and accommodated themselves to traditional practices of gift-giving and ritual to maintain good relations. The colonists did not undertake campaigns to exterminate or drive away local tribes until trade with them had declined in importance and repeated epidemics had decimated them.

Instead, the native societies responded to the English presence in very creative, self-interested ways. They made unprecedented use of their customary practices of migration over long distances and cultural adoption by other tribes to endure as resilient and distinctive entities. They engaged in far greater and more extensive long-distance trade of commodities than had ever been the case previously. Even peoples far from the immediate frontier participated in the much expanded fur trade. Even when no colonist had ever entered their settlements, tribes in the interior suffered from the diseases Europeans had brought with them to the Americas and depended on the manufactured goods.

Population ratios worked severely against native interests, particularly by the beginning of the eighteenth century. While the number of Indians continued to shrink, that of colonists rose dramatically. The population of British North America doubled roughly each 25 years, increasing by fully 400 percent between 1700 and 1750.

Finally, certain prescient Indian spokesmen began to question the utility of the extremely decentralized nature of native society, where even tribal identity had only tenuous claims on mobilizing peoples whose primary loyalty was to their lineages and communities. They called for a broader concept of identity and cooperation among the native peoples of eastern North America. Several spiritual leaders inspired movements that stressed a broader Indian identity over the worship of local deities. These visionaries were still far from promoting a shared racial identity among the Indians that differentiated them as a category from the Europeans and Africans who already populated so much of the Americas. But deep-seated rivalries and loyalties were not readily overcome, particularly in the face of competition among *sachems* and contrary actions by the colonists who well understood that any such development would be against their own interests.

Select Bibliography

Axtell, James. *Beyond 1492: Encounters in Colonial North America.* New York: Oxford University Press, 1992.

Calloway, Colin G. *The American Revolution in Indian Country: Crisis and Diversity in Native American Communities.* Cambridge, England: Cambridge University Press, 1995.

Calloway, Colin G. *New Worlds for All: Indians, Europeans, and the Remaking of Early America.* Baltimore: The Johns Hopkins University Press, 1997.

Calloway, Colin G. *The Western Abenakis of Vermont, 1600–1800: War, Migration, and the Survival of an Indian People.* Norman: University of Oklahoma Press, 1990

Cayton, Andrew R. L. and Frederika J. Teute, eds. *Contact Points: American Frontiers from the Mohawk Valley to the Mississippi, 1750–1830.* Chapel Hill: University of North Carolina Press, 1998.

Chaplin, Joyce E. *Subject Matter: Technology, the Body, and Science on the Anglo-American Frontier, 1500–1676.* Cambridge, MA: Harvard University Press, 2001.

Crane, Verner W. *The Southern Frontier, 1670–1732.* Ann Arbor: University of Michigan Press, 1964.

Daunton, Martin and Rick Halpern, eds. *Empire and Others: British Encounters with Indigenous Peoples, 1600–1850.* Philadelphia: University of Pennsylvania Press, 1999.

Dowd, Gregory Evans. *A Spirited Resistance: The North American Indian Struggle for Unity, 1745–1815.* Baltimore: The Johns Hopkins University Press, 1992.

Galloway, Patricia. *Choctaw Genesis, 1500–1700.* Lincoln: University of Nebraska Press, 1995.

Gleach, Frederic W. *Powhatan's World and Colonial Virginia.* Lincoln: University of Nebraska Press, 1997.

Jennings, Francis. *The Invasion of America: Indians, Colonialism, and the Cant of Conquest.* Chapel Hill: University of North Carolina Press, 1975.

Kupperman, Karen Ordahl. *Indians and English: Facing Off in Early America.* Ithaca: Cornell University Press, 2000.

Kupperman, Karen Ordahl. *Roanoke: The Abandoned Colony.* Totowa, NJ: Rowman & Littlefield, 1984.

Leach, Douglas E. *Flintlock and Tomahawk: New England in King Philip's War.* New York: W.W. Norton & Co., 1966.

Lepore, Jill. *The Name of War: King Philip's War and the Origins of American Identity.* New York: Alfred A. Knopf, 1998.

Malone, Patrick M. *The Skulking Way of War: Technology and Tactics Among the New England Indians.* Baltimore: The Johns Hopkins University Press, 1993.

Mancall, Peter C. and James H. Merrell, eds. *American Encounters: Natives and Newcomers from European Contact to Indian Removal.* New York: Routledge, 2000.

Mandell, Daniel R. *Behind the Frontier: Indians in Eighteenth-Century Eastern Massachusetts.* Lincoln: University of Nebraska Press, 1996.

Martin, Joel W. *Sacred Revolt: The Muskogees' Struggle for a New World.* Boston: Beacon Press, 1991.

Merrell, James H. *Into the American Woods: Negotiators on the Pennsylvania Frontier.* New York: W.W. Norton & Co., 1999.

Merrell, James H. *The Indians' New World: Catawbas and Their Neighbors from European Contact through the Era of Removal.* Chapel Hill: University of North Carolina Press, 1989.

Morgan, Edmund S. *American Slavery, American Freedom: The Ordeal of Colonial Virginia.* New York: W. W. Norton & Company, 1975.

Oberg, Michael Leroy. *Dominion and Civility: English Imperialism and Native America, 1585–1685.* Ithaca, NY: Cornell University Press, 1999.

Plane, Ann Marie. *Colonial Intimacies: Indian Marriage in Early New England.* Ithaca, New York: Cornell University Press, 2000.

Richter, Daniel K. *Facing East from Indian Country: A Native History of Early America.* Cambridge, MA: Harvard University Press, 2001.

Richter, Daniel K. *The Ordeal of the Longhouse: The Peoples of the Iroquois League in the Era of European Colonization.* Chapel Hill: University of North Carolina Press, 1992.

Rountree, Helen C. *Pocahontas's People: The Powhatan Indian of Virginia Through Four Centuries.* Norman: University of Oklahoma Press, 1990.

Salisbury, Neal. *Manitou and Providence: Indians, Europeans, and the Making of New England, 1500–1643.* New York: Oxford University Press, 1982.

Starkey, Armstrong. *European and Native American Warfare, 1675–1815.* Norman: University of Oklahoma Press, 1998.

Trigger, Bruce G. and Wilcomb E. Washburn, eds. *The Cambridge History of the Native Peoples of the Americas: Volume I North America, Part 1.* Cambridge, England: Cambridge University Press, 1996.

Vaughan, Alden T. *New England Frontier: Puritans and Indians, 1620–1675.* Boston: Little, Brown and Co., 1965.

Wallace, Anthony F. C. *The Death and Rebirth of the Senaca.* New York: Alfred A. Knopf, 1970.

White, Richard. *The Middle Ground: Indians, Empires, and Republics in the Great Lakes Region, 1650–1815.* Cambridge, England: Cambridge University Press, 1991.

Wright, Jr., J. Leitch. *The Only Land They Knew: The Tragic Story of the American Indians in the Old South.* New York: The Free Press, 1981.

Endnotes

1   Nicholas P. Canny, "The Ideology of English Colonization: From Ireland to America," *William and Mary Quarterly,* 3rd series, *30*:4 (October 1973, p. 595.

2   John E. Kicza, "Dealing with Foreigners: A Comparative Essay Regarding Initial Expectations and Interactions between Native Societies and the English in North America and the Spanish in Mexico," *Colonial Latin American Historical Review, 3*:4 (Fall 1994), pp. 386–387.

3   Edmund S. Morgan, *American Slavery, American Freedom: The Ordeal of Colonial Virginia* (New York: W. W. Norton & Co., 1975), p. 45.

4   Helen C. Rountree, *Pocahantas's People: The Powhatan Indians of Virginia Through Four Centuries* (Norman: University of Oklahoma Press, 1990), pp. 97–98.

5   Francis Jennings, *The Invasion of America: Indians, Colonialism, and the Cant of Conquest* (New York: W.W. Norton & Co., 1975), pp. 40–41.

6   Patrick M. Malone, *The Skulking Way of War: Technology and Tactics Among the New England Indians* (Baltimore: The Johns Hopkins University Press, 1993), p. 9.

7   Neal Salisbury, "Red Puritans: The `Praying Indians' of Massachusetts Bay and John Eliot," *William and Mary Quarterly*, 3rd series, *31*:1 (Jan. 1974), p. 35.

8   *Ibid.*, p. 54.

9   Daniel R. Mandell, *Behind the Frontier: Indians in Eighteenth-Century Eastern Massachusetts* (Lincoln: University of Nebraska Press, 1996), pp. 164–165.

10 Gary B. Nash, *Red, White, and Black: The Peoples of Early America*, 3rd ed. (Englewood Cliffs: Prentice-Hall, 1992), p. 133.

11 James H. Merrell, *The Indians' New World: Catawbas and Their Neighbors from European Contact through the Era of Removal* (Chapel Hill: University of North Carolina Press, 1989), p. 106.

12 Colin G. Calloway, *The American Revolution in Indian Country: Crisis and Diversity in Native American Communities* (Cambridge, England: Cambridge University Press, 1995), p. 7.

13 J. Leitch Wright, Jr., *The Only Land They Knew: The Tragic Story of the American Indians of the old South* (New York: The Free Press, 1981), p. 235.

7

Spanish and Portuguese Interactions with Tribal Peoples

$\mathbf{H}$istorical and popular literature commonly identify the Spanish American empire with the conquest and colonization of the fully sedentary, state-organized societies of Mexico and Peru: the Aztec and Inca empires. But the Spanish also encountered native peoples to the north and south of Mesoamerica, and throughout South America outside of the Andean zone, who were not densely populated, permanently settled agriculturalists. Some practiced substantial agriculture, but on lands whose limited fertility required periodic movement from one location to another within a certain region (that is, swidden or slash-and-burn agriculture) while others did not cultivate the land at all, living instead by hunting and gathering. The Portuguese encountered such semi-sedentary and hunter-gather societies in what would become Brazil.

In certain ways, greater variety marked the interactions between the Iberians (a term that refers to the Spanish and the Portuguese collectively) and these tribal and band-organized societies than those between the Iberians and the full-time agriculturalists. Some tribes in highland Colombia were substantially dependent on agriculture, had gathered adjacent tribes into confederations, and had nearly organized permanent states. Others relied only moderately on cultivation of the land and possessed only occasional loyalties to any structures beyond the community. Others, in inhospitable zones, practiced no agriculture at all and lived in hunting-and-gathering bands. These nonsedentary peoples resided in a diversity of environments, each of them at least somewhat daunting, including deserts, mountains, extensive plains, and tropical lowlands. The challenging natural settings and the resolute armed resistance of the local peoples meant that colonial ventures rarely thrived in these settings.

Migration and an Enduring Frontier among the Maya of the Yucatan Peninsula

In the 1540s, an expedition led by the Montejo family finally secured control over the northwestern corner of the Yucatan Peninsula. But even then, few Spaniards were attracted there. Despite having sent expeditions into many parts of the Yucatan over the preceding four decades, the Spanish had discovered no lucrative resources. The scattered native villages were difficult to subjugate and their people resisted mandatory labor service. For nearly two centuries the colonial economy remained so rudimentary that it depended primarily on cattle-ranching, not a particularly rewarding undertaking with the limited markets for hides and meat in the peninsula or for export, but requiring little manpower. Those Spaniards in the Yucatan with native laborers typically controlled only a few dozen to around a hundred. These men called themselves *encomenderos,* trying to emulate the privileged early colonists of Mexico and Peru who enjoyed exclusive access to the rotary draft labor service of large numbers of residents of native communities. But in fact these Mayan workers more resembled permanent retainers, living in the household compound of the master or in small hamlets on the periphery of his properties.

While the number of colonists gradually rose and the territory they effectively occupied increased over the decades, ethnic relations in the Yucatan were shaped by a substantial frontier zone until the end of the nineteenth century. Some tens of thousands of Mayas continued to live in autonomous communities, largely clustered in the eastern part of the peninsula near the modern nation of Belize. The colonists lacked the manpower and resources to subdue these independent people across the harsh terrain. Instead, they occasionally mustered slaving raids, venturing deep into native territory and gathering prisoners. These captives were then resettled in the Spanish zone as forced labor. Many escaped back across the frontier within a few years. Less common, but far from unknown, were raids by groups of independent Mayas into the Spanish-controlled region.

Small groups of Franciscan friars also journeyed deep into the countryside to try to convert the inhabitants to Christianity and to place them in a subordinated status under Spanish magistrates. In the process, several Franciscans were slain. Others received a serious hearing from the Maya but were ultimately rejected. A few remained in these communities for some years, and aspects of Christian belief crossed the frontier to be incorporated into the worldview of these still-independent Mayas. These included belief in the Virgin Mary, the cult of the saints, and the ritual of mass.

Trade between the two zones, though technically illicit, was common and largely unregulated. The autonomous Mayas harvested cacao, honey, and wax to exchange for coastal salt and European manufactured items—even for Christian figurines.

Mayas in both the colonized and the autonomous regions easily adjusted to conditions on the other side of their shared frontier, for both groups still shared important cultural characteristics. Nancy M. Farriss describes these commonalities as follows:

> Because of the steady communication across the frontiers, they possessed a single cultural system with gradations of Spanish influence, which neither permeated the culture of the conquered Maya thoroughly nor left the unconquered Maya totally untouched.[1]

While the extensive unincorporated area beyond the frontier reminded the colonists of their tenuous existence and substantial failure, and also constituted some level of actual physical threat, it also afforded the hope of sanctuary to thousands of workers who could flee their masters to cross the boundary to freedom.

The ongoing possibility of flight, and the longstanding Mayan tradition of accommodating invaders in the expectation that they would eventually depart or acculturate to local ways, inclined the Maya not to revolt against the Spanish. Those few uprisings that did occur were very much local affairs involving individual communities rather than entire provinces. It is notable that no major Maya revolt developed until 1848, when a recent rapid expansion of plantations finally threatened to eliminate the autonomous Mayan zone.

Muted Transformations among the Pacified Maya

The peninsula's lack of marketable commodities kept numbers of both Spaniards and forced native workers low. The labor impositions placed on the indigenous people did not even require them to travel long distances or to stay away for long periods. The laborers were often recruited by their own community leaders and remained under their direction for the duration of their labor service. The colonists did not pursue massive transformation of the Mayan culture.

The Spanish had little direct interaction with rural Mayas. Few colonists ventured into native communities, and the little Spanish-Maya contact that did occur was generally brief and circumscribed. Further, all economic and juridical transactions were commonly channelled through local leaders and thus affected the commoners only slightly. As a consequence, few Mayas spoke Spanish even at the end of the colonial period, and many important aspects of traditional culture had been preserved.

Epidemics, aggravated by periodic famines caused by extended dry periods, took a toll of the indigenous population. The first notable demographic decline occurred in the second half of the sixteenth century, the population falling from about 240,000 in 1550 to perhaps 170,000 at the end of the century. After some degree of recovery in the early seventeenth century, an even greater loss occurred in the decade or so that followed 1648. Epidemics of yellow fever and smallpox decimated the population, to be followed just a few years later by a horrendous drought. This wave of disasters seems to have cut the native population by a third to a half, reducing the number of Mayas living under colonial supervision to somewhere around 130,000. They still vastly outnumbered the colonists, who totalled only a few thousand. Despite the ravages of disease and crop losses in nearly every decade in the eighteenth century, the number of Mayas at the end of the colonial period approximated 290,000.

In the late sixteenth century, the Spanish imposed *congregación* on the dispersed Mayan communities, as they had done in central Mexico and the Andean region, requiring that inhabitants cluster in larger, central towns. But once the consolidation took place, colonial officials ceased monitoring Mayan compliance, and the people rather quickly moved back to their original villages. Further, new, distinct, small communities—many with fewer than 50 people—continued to spring up in outlying areas until the end of the colonial period.

Few priests were attracted to the Yucatan, and those who came often preferred to reside in one of the several colonial cities rather than to learn the difficult Mayan languages and work in the small farming hamlets that dotted the countryside. The natives received only cursory training in the new religion and were largely left alone to practice their faith, provided that they did not hold large-scale pagan celebrations or openly denounce Christianity.

The outstanding exception to this negligent attitude toward Christianization of the Mayas was the 1562 inquisition undertaken by the first bishop of the Yucatan, the Franciscan Diego de Landa. Although the Spanish only had a firm control of the northwest corner of the peninsula and few priests had worked among the Mayas, Landa reacted zealously when he discovered that supposed converts were hiding idols and still practicing human sacrifice. Some 4,500 Indians were brought before the Franciscans over the next 3 months, and many were tortured to confess. Around 160 died as a result. Landa also prosecuted some local Spaniards who protested his treatment of the Indians. Royal officials soon removed him from his position and ordered his return to Spain. His successor released those Mayas still incarcerated and ended the investigation.

Mayan material culture was transformed much less than that of the peoples of central Mexico. Mayans certainly adopted chickens and pigs, but apparently not as broadly as in the fully sedentary zones. The rudimentary economy of the Yucatan likewise created less demand for metal tools and other manufactured implements. The Mayas were even slower to adopt European cloth goods, and fewer Spanish terms passed into the Mayan language.

Mayan communities of the Yucatan lowlands engaged in long-distance trade when the Spanish arrived, but historians are not certain to what extent. (It was far different in the ecologically more diverse and resource-rich Highland Maya zone, largely contained in Guatemala. There regional trade thrived, and continues to prosper to the present.) Whatever the volume, it was certainly curtailed soon after the coming of the Spanish, and the indigenous communities consequently became even more subsistence oriented than before. The decline in trade appears to have damaged the wealth and stature of the already-weak Maya nobility. They had benefitted disproportionately from trade, and now had fewer valued goods to enjoy and to distribute among their favorites. Many regional networks broke down, heightening the localism of Maya communities. While a degree of loyalty to the ethnic province persisted, most group identification focused on the village. Few Maya leaders were able to reliably claim authority over more than their immediate locality.

The Spanish expected these communities to establish town councils (*cabildos*) in the European fashion. The Maya accomplished this with little disruption, members of established leading families of the village generally assuming the posts of councilmen and circulating the position of mayor among themselves. The hereditary ruling elites of these autonomous, though small, municipalities continued to perform much the same functions as in precolonial times: controlling access to land, adjudicating boundaries, assembling and directing labor gangs, and collecting tribute payments. Little or no competition for local political positions occurred.

Maya communities retained corporate ownership of the land, with the fields assigned to individual households worked by gangs of related men. The extended family through the male line also constituted the primary residential unit. Households were organized into compounds headed by the senior male in any lineage. When women married, they moved into the compounds of their husbands' family. Some private lands existed that could be inherited only through the male line. The nobility owned certain lands and seem to have retained some claim on rotary draft labor from their commoners, translating this privileged access to land and labor—however moderate—into somewhat greater wealth. This they utilized to finance larger houses and periodic feasts.

Religious brotherhoods (*cofradías*) and the cult of the saints constituted the primary means through which the Mayas practiced Christianity. The region retained something of the character of a mission zone, with friars residing in widely scattered missions, and individual parish priests responsible for numerous rural hamlets. Similar to central Mexico, these priests commonly resided in a headtown and rode circuit, visiting their outlying settlements perhaps several times a year to perform mass and administer the sacraments, but here the presence of Spanish clergy was even more superficial. In all other regards, native communities oversaw their own religious devotions. They gradually incorporated Christian beliefs into a Maya religious context rather than come into direct conflict with them. Many religious symbols were clearly Christian in origin, but the Mayas embued them with their own meaning, heavily influenced by their customary religious beliefs.

The religious brotherhoods came to possess considerable wealth within these isolated farming societies, often in the form of cattle herds. The brotherhoods became important community institutions in their own right. Their leaders sometimes held social status equal to that of the town councillors. In fact, by the eighteenth century local communities elected *cofradía* leaders as political officers with considerable frequency.

The Portuguese and the Peoples of Brazil

The Portuguese initially devoted much less attention to their American colony of Brazil than the Spanish did to their holdings. With the simultaneous emergence of their extremely lucrative trade with Asia, Brazil remained a peripheral part of the empire for more than fifty years after its discovery in 1500. But in the 1550s they had to repel France's strong interest in taking Brazil away from them at about the same time that the sugar industry started to develop in the colony.

When the Portuguese arrived, most of coastal Brazil south of the Amazon River basin and extending well into the interior was inhabited by a variety of ethnically distinct peoples who spoke forms of the Tupí language and practiced semisedentary agriculture. Instead of maize, they cultivated the primary crop of lowland South America, manioc. Its flour could be made into a reasonably nutritious bread, especially when supplemented with the flesh of the abundant wild animals and fishes in that part of the continent.

These peoples resided in villages of 400 to 800 people, organized into extended lineage groups, each occupying a distinct longhouse. Characteristic of many semisedentary peoples, women dominated the cultivation of crops, with the men assisting primarily in the cutting down of trees to open up fields. Males devoted most of their time to hunting, diplomacy, and incessant warfare organized around the taking capture of enemies to be sacrificed for ritual cannibalism.

During the first thirty years of contact, the Portuguese did not establish permanent settlements or agricultural enterprises. Instead, they conducted barter with the Tupí at coastal trading posts, exchanging cloth, trinkets, and axes and other metalware for manioc and especially dyewood logs, which became Brazil's first significant export to Europe. This form of intercultural exchange hardly disrupted the indigenous culture, for it required only occasional physical labor from the men and involved work—tree cutting—they already performed.

But beginning in the 1530s, the Portuguese undertook some settlement of the land, establishing communities and cultivating land. In this new setting, the colonists placed much greater demands on the indigenous population. They demanded foodstuffs from the natives and forced them to labor in colonists' fields. But the Indians hardly needed the additional manufactured goods they were given in payment until they wore out the cloths and metal tools they had previously obtained. The European concept of accumulation of goods was foreign and undesirable to these people who sought to possess only items they actually used. Further, while tree cutting had imposed just intermittent efforts from Tupí men and had been a customary activity, the agricultural labor the Portuguese now expected of them was grueling and unrelenting. Moreover, in Tupí culture such work was a female activity, and engaging in it for the colonists left precious little time for the customary male activities that gave them status in their own societies. Finally, laboring in agriculture for the colonists required that the Indians leave their own communities to live permanently among the Portuguese.

The Portuguese responded to the natives' refusal to provide full-time labor with coercive measures. As the colonists established sugar plantations along the

A Brazilian Indian family *(Ernest and Johanna Lehner,* How They Saw the New World, *New York: Tudor Publishing Company, 1966, p. 108.)*

northeastern coast, they sent expeditions into the interior to enslave Indians. Other natives were acquired as slaves from rival Indian peoples who had captured them. The colonists justified these purchases by claiming to be ransoming

---

Jean de Léry's description of civil order among the Tupí

In the 1550s, the French mounted a settlement in Brazil that challenged the Portuguese monopoly over the area. Though the French colony lasted hardly half a decade, several of its participants wrote useful accounts. Easily the best is by Jean de Léry, who spent some of his time living among the natives. In this passage he describes their civil society.

As for the civil order of our savages, it is an incredible thing—a thing that cannot be said without shame to those who have both divine and human laws—how a people guided solely by their nature, even corrupted as it is, can live and deal with each other in such peace and tranquillity. . . . Nevertheless, if it happens that some of them quarrel (which occurs so rarely that during almost a year I was with them I only saw them fight with each other twice), by no means do the others try to separate them or make peace; . . . However, if anyone is wounded by his neighbor, and if he who struck the blow is apprehended, he will receive a similar blow in the same part of his body by the kinsmen of the one injured. If the wounds of the latter prove to be mortal, or if he is killed on the spot, the relatives of the dead man will take the life of the killer in the same way. . . . In a given village of five or six hundred people, while several families may live in the same house, nevertheless each has its own place, and the husband keeps his wife and children separate; however, there is nothing to keep you from seeing down the full length of these buildings, which are usually more than sixty feet long.

Source: Jean de Léry, *History of a Voyage to the Land of Brazil, Otherwise Called America,* trans. by Janet Whatley (Berkeley: University of California Press, 1990), pp. 158, 159. Copyright © 1990 The Regents of the University of California. Reprinted by permission.

---

captives who were otherwise destined to be sacrificed. But these "redeemed" captives typically ended up as slaves as well. In fact, the use of enslaved natives as the labor force characterized the early period of Brazilian plantation slavery, roughly 1540–1600. As yet, the Portuguese imported few black slaves from Africa.

But the natives of Brazil were not that numerous, and they proved as susceptible to Old World epidemic diseases as did their counterparts elsewhere in the Americas, dying in great numbers. Many of them ran away to the frontier to find refuge, and retrieving them was difficult and time consuming. Several instances of collective violence are also recorded. The largest one occurred in the Northeast in 1567 and resulted in the killing of some plantation owners. To quell this widespread uprising, the authorities turned to natives who lived in Jesuit-run villages (*aldeias*) near the frontier to round up the rebels. With so many difficulties transforming the native population into a substantial, subservient labor force, the colonists turned to the Atlantic slave trade as an alternative.

One form of resistance that developed among these laborers even attracted runaway black slaves—a religiously inspired insurgency called *santidade* combined elements of Christianity and traditional indigenous beliefs. First documented in the 1550s, it persisted in the plantation zone until the 1620s. *Santidade* blended customary local faith in the existence of an earthly paradise

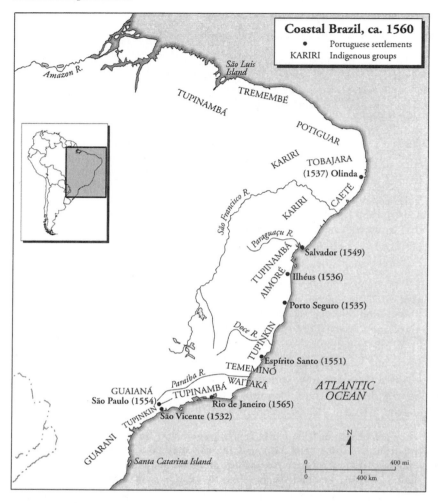

Native peoples and Portuguese settlements of coastal Brazil, c. 1560
*(John M. Monteiro, "The Crises and Transformation of Invaded Societies:
Coastal Brazil in the Sixteenth Century," in Frank Salomon and Stuart B.
Schwartz, eds.* The Cambridge History of the Native Peoples of the Americas,
volume III, South America, part I, New York: Cambridge University
Press, 1999, p. 976. *Reprinted with the permission of Cambridge
University Press.)*

with symbols from Catholicism. The cult centered on idols composed of gourds
or stone that practitioners thought to have spiritual power. As Stuart B. Schwartz
describes these idols,

> They endowed their followers with strength against the whites, and their
> victories would bring the millennium of Tupinambá paradise. The hoes

would go to the fields by themselves, and arrows would speed through the forest in search of game while the hunters rested in the village. The aged would be young again, all could have many wives, and all enemies would be destroyed or captured and eaten.[2]

The leaders of the movement were all former slaves, and at least one had been raised by the Jesuits. They called themselves "bishops" and "popes." One group of *santidade* followers erected an idol called Mary and prayed with a rosary. The cult ultimately preached violent resistance, and early in the 1560s, its followers began to attack sugar mills and rural estates. But before the decade was out, Portuguese retaliation combined with a wave of epidemic disease to weaken the movement. It survived on the outskirts of colonial settlement until at least the end of the first quarter of the seventeenth century, with members sometimes raiding Portuguese communities.

Jesuit-controlled villages, *aldeias*, formed in the hinterland around the colonial settlements and plantations in the second half of the sixteenth century. By 1600, the Jesuits claimed that 50,000 Indians lived in these *aldeias*. There, the priests not only taught the natives Christian doctrine but also sought to transform their culture. They insisted on individual households instead of extended families, European attire and appearance, and especially a gender-based division of labor in which men cultivated the fields and women took care of domestic tasks. While the Jesuits argued that they protected the Indians from the depredations of plantation owners, they in fact did not seek to preserve any major aspect of native culture. Rather, the Jesuits sought to transform the Indians into a European-style peasantry.

The Jesuits also argued that the residents of their *aldeias* would be available to work in the colonial economy system, but as hired wage laborers rather than as dependent workers. But the natives refused to become a peasantry, living by growing crops to supply cane-growing plantations. *Aldeias* endured only in the hinterland, justified by the military assistance their members provided, with declining populations except for new groups of natives brought in from the frontier. Brazilian plantation owners shifted massively to black slavery at the beginning of the seventeenth century. On average they imported well over 5,000 slaves from Africa each year over that century. With little further need for Indian laborers in that industry, the surviving native populations—and Jesuit *aldeias*—were located farther in the interior, well away from the thriving agricultural zone. By 1700 no Tupí communities survived along the entire coastal strip of Brazil.

Spanish Settlement among the Guaraní of Greater Paraguay

In 1535, an expedition of some 1,500 people departed Spain to found a colony in the Río de la Plata, at the time believed to be the probable site of major silver deposits. They named their settlement Buenos Aires. Yet the colonists not only found no precious metals in this zone of endless plains, they also founded their settlement in an unhealthy location surrounded by nomadic peoples who quickly besieged the town. The position of the settlers rapidly became untenable,

---

Alvar Núñez Cabeza de Vaca's description of the Guaycurú, an enemy tribe of the Guaraní

Cabeza de Vaca, a veteran of the Indies who had survived eight years among the Indians of the American South, was appointed governor of the new colony of Paraguay after his return to Spain. After traveling across country from the coast of Brazil, he was deposed by a disgruntled faction among the colonists after just a couple of years and returned to Spain as a prisoner. But he wrote a very useful commentary about his time in the colony. In this passage, he describes the nomadic Guaycurú, a people who regularly raided into the territory of the Guaraní, the agriculture-practicing allies of the Spanish.

> The riparian chiefs, and those inhabiting the vicinity of the Paraguai, near the town of the Ascension [Asunción], vassals of His Majesty, came and presented themselves before the governor, and complained of a tribe of Indians that dwelt near their borders. These Indians are great warriors, and valiant men, who live on venison, butter, honey, fish, and wild boar, eating nothing besides, neither they nor their wives and children. They go daily to the chase for it is their only occupation. . . . They are much feared by all the other tribes. They never remain more than two days in one place, but quickly remove their houses, made of matting, to distances of one or two leagues when they are in pursuit of game. . . . The chiefs of the Indians complained to the governor that the Guaycurús had dispossessed them of their land, and killed their fathers, brothers and relatives, and since they were vassals of His Majesty, they claimed protection and restitution of their property.

Source: "The Commentaries of Alvar Núñez Cabeza de Vaca," in Luis L. Domínguez, ed., *The Conquest of the River Plate (1535–1555)* by The Hakluyt Society. Published by the Hakluyt Society. (New York: Burt Franklin, nd), pp. 135, 136. Reprinted by permission of David Higham Associates.

---

for they lacked food and suffered numerous casualties from arrows and disease. After a couple of years, the survivors, some 350 in number, fled up the Paraná River and established the community of Asunción in the land of the Guaraní people, an offshoot of the Brazilian Tupí.

The Guaraní numbered some hundreds of thousands of people organized into villages and practicing slash-and-burn agriculture. They were located in the midst of nomadic plains peoples who incessantly raided into their territory, killing, looting, and taking captives. Hence the Guaraní were inclined to accept the Spanish presence and the additional military strength they represented. Soon, combined Spanish-Guaraní contingents, comprising a formidable force, responded to intrusions from the nomads.

The Guaraní began to integrate the Spaniards into their society as head-men. Few other Spaniards migrated to this unpromising land after the arrival of the initial group, so these colonists accepted Guaraní offers of women and positions in their local culture. Women dominated the cultivation of land, and lineage was traditionally measured through the female line. Further, family compounds were organized around the senior females of the various descent groups. These women of standing could assemble their male relatives to provide labor or to form war parties. Hence an individual Spaniard incorporated as many of these women into his household as he could to obtain greater access to native labor.

Unlike colonial native labor delivery systems in the fully sedentary zones of central Mexico and the Andean zone, where the two parties remained quite removed from each other and worked through intermediaries, close interaction among the colonists and their native dependents characterized this society. The entire cluster of women, their relatives, and servants over time became close personal dependents of individual colonists and delivered personal service to them. No mines or export agricultural products existed to promote a more systematic utilization of native labor.

The colonists and Guaraní of colonial Paraguay both experienced dramatic cultural transformation. Within a couple of generations, most Spaniards—even those in the local upper class—were biologically mixed. But the elite continued to call its members "Spaniards," and reserved the term *"mestizo"* for members of the middling and lower groups of society. Virtually all people in Paraguayan colonial society, even the elite, were bilingual and incorporated Guaraní foods and customs into their way of life. Paraguayan family structure was more native than Spanish in character.

But Spanish values and material culture gradually worked their way into this culture as well. Population decline struck the Guaraní as it did all other native groups, and the Spanish and *mestizo* portions of the population in central Paraguay gradually increased. The colonists eventually demanded labor service from peoples in more outlying areas, and increasing numbers of these natives came to live permanently in the central Paraguayan orbit.

Jesuit missions represent another important sphere of Spanish-Guaraní interaction. Beginning in 1607, the Jesuits opened missions well to the east of central Paraguay, quite far from the area already colonized. Eventually they erected some 30 missions, inhabited by something over 100,000 natives. Over the roughly 150 years that they lasted, these missions were notably successful, creating a substantial settled, ordered, and Christianized population. Soon the colonists coveted this congregated labor force, and an ongoing state of tension arose between them and the Jesuits, who wished to maintain their monopoly over these converts. The two groups barely avoided violent conflict several times in the colonial period.

The Portuguese colonists of the city of São Paulo in southern Brazil proved an even greater threat. Lacking any natural resources, the economy of this rather isolated community gravitated around alliances with nearby indigenous peoples. Beginning in the 1580s, groups of Paulistas (people from São Paulo) replete with native allies and dependents ventured deep into the continent in expeditions that might last two or three years. These *bandeirantes* (so-called because they were organized into semi-military companies around banners, *bandeiras*) sought out precious metals and other resources in this vast backcountry. They commonly returned with captured Indians placed in shackles, many of whom they sold to the northern sugar-raising zone of Brazil as slaves.

Around 1609, the Paulistas reached the Spanish Jesuit missions and began to seize their alcolytes. The Jesuits, though desperate, could do little for some thirty years, during which time thousands of their people were taken away. Finally, in 1639, the Spanish colonial administration authorized the Jesuits to arm their converts. This measure, combined with the abandonment of the most distant missions, curtailed most successful slave raiding.

Despite this development, the Jesuit missions of Paraguay did not last until the end of the colonial period. In 1767, the Spanish crown expelled the Jesuits from Spain and its territories because it feared the order's power and its perceived animosity to royal policies. Though these missions were handed over to the Franciscan order, they did not long thrive. Within forty years they held only half the population they once did, as many natives departed to work in the colonial economy.

The Formidable Araucanians of Southern Chile

The semisedentary Araucanian peoples of central and southern Chile cultivated maize, raised llamas, practiced metallurgy, and were otherwise influenced by the high cultures of the Andean zone to their north. The southernmost Araucanians lived in dispersed settlements with little effective connection to each other. These villages were organized into quite autonomous lineages (which themselves tended to fragment) and lacked even headmen. As with many other semisedentary peoples, the women dominated agriculture and the men hunted and conducted diplomacy and warfare.

In 1541 a Spanish expedition organized in Peru under the command of Pedro de Valdivia subdued the Indians of central Chile and established the city of Santiago in a fertile valley. Seven months later, the Indians of the region rose up and burned down the city. But the Spaniards drove them off and rebuilt their capital. Over the next twelve years, Valdivia led campaigns farther south, establishing towns and forts along the way. But in late 1553, Lautaro, an Araucanian chief who had worked as Valdivia's groom, and thus had learned the tendencies and weaknesses of the Spaniards in combat, ambushed and slew a Spanish force of fifty men led by Valdivia. Lautaro had similar success against other colonial detachments and drove the surviving settlers completely out of the south, even forcing them to abandon the city of Concepción. In 1557, Lautaro advanced on Santiago, but was killed in battle. Other chiefs took over leadership of the movement.

An epidemic of smallpox in 1561–1563 weakened the Araucanians, but they continued their resistance. Over the next quarter-century, however, the colonists, supported by reinforcements and subsidies from Peru, recaptured much of the area they had lost in the south. But they could only establish a tentative presence south of the Bío-Bío River.

In 1598, the Araucanians rose up, razing virtually all Spanish holdings south of the river, which for the rest of the colonial period constituted a true frontier. The Spanish reacted in their customary fashion, launching expeditions into Araucanian country that sought to destroy their villages. These failed against the staunch resistance and superior mobility of the natives. The colonial authorities then established a string of forts along the river to protect central Chile. These forts also periodically dispatched slaving raids into Araucanian country, selling any captives far to the north.

As previously noted, the Araucanians responded creatively and largely kept the Spanish military on the defensive. They adopted Spanish horses and developed a mounted force of bowmen who rode double on horseback. The Araucanians also constructed a sixteen-foot pike, which proved to be deadly against charges by Spanish cavalry. Renegades from colonial society even taught them how to make gunpowder for the firearms they captured from Spaniards. The Araucanians abandoned their tradition of mass attacks against their enemy, for that ran the risk of too many casualties against the well-armed Spanish and turned instead to guerrilla tactics. The continual state of war promoted the emergence of strong, permanent war chiefs and the beginnings of a true political confederation among the Araucanians. Finally, the Araucanians even adopted the cultivation of the Spanish crop, wheat, over their traditional maize, because its shorter growing season made their communities less vulnerable to Spanish scorched-earth policies.

This Araucanian alliance was so successful that by the eighteenth century they had expanded across the Andes from southern Chile to raid on the Argentina pampas. They commonly rustled cattle and drove them back to Chile to trade for Spanish-crafted goods. This pattern outlasted the colonial period, and the Araucanians on both sides of the Andes were not finally defeated until the final quarter of the nineteenth century, when both the Argentina and Chilean national militaries conquered them through the use of repeating rifles, barbed wire, and telegraph lines. This similarity to the late nineteenth-century defeat of the plains Indians in the western United States carried through to the final disposition of captives taken; the national governments compelled them to reside in government-run reservations.

Limited Spanish Success against the Nomadic Peoples of the Mexican Desert North

A vast desert, marked by steep mountain ranges and occasional limited river valleys, makes up the northern third or so of modern Mexico. The sedentary, densely populated, and culturally sophisticated societies of central Mexico stopped at its southern boundary. After their conquest of the Aztec empire in the early 1520s, the Spaniards sent several expeditions into this arid vastness. One ventured as far as the modern state of Kansas before turning back. This landscape—and peoples—in normal circumstances the Spanish colonists would just avoid. But beginning in the late 1540s, the discovery of silver mines scattered throughout this vastness transferred it into the major source of wealth in Mexico. These silver deposits attracted considerable settlement and investment, and the Spaniards created roads to ship silver south to central Mexico and necessary supplies north to the various mining camps.

Araucanian weaponry and tactics against the Spanish

By the early seventeenth century, the Spaniards in Chile were greatly frustrated about their lack of military success against the Araucanians, who firmly controlled the southern third or more of the colony after having risen up roughly a half century earlier. Many Spanish participants and observers issued recommendations to the government. One of the most incisive commentaries about the nature of Araucanian warfare is recorded in the following selection from the 1614 report by Alonso González de la Nájera, a professional soldier who served in Chile:

> The arms used by the Indian infantry consist only of pikes, arrows, and clubs. Each uses whatever arm is more to his liking and in which he is most skilled. The pikes are very straight and polished; and though they are not as strong as ours made of the ash tree, they are longer and lighter, . . . They also have iron in them that is made of pieces of Spanish swords with grounded points. . . . The bows they use are much shorter and more reinforced than those used by the Indians in the provinces of Cuyo, Tucuman, Paraguay, Brazil, and other areas. . . . These offensive arms are the ones that are commonly used among all the foot soldiers, since those who use the *macanas* [clubs] are relatively few. . . . Returning to the subject of the stratagems and practices of the Indians, with the control and advantages they have over our people in their cunning, I would say that they unfailingly know at all time where they can find (the Spaniards) to attack them, while they, on the other hand, are completely secure from being found, because our people have their homes, towns, ranches, and farmhouses in the open and in the same place, whereas theirs are hidden and movable, since their long punishment has taught them to reduce their troops to the size suitable for the business and need, as closely as their experience can tell them. . . . but at present they are completely safe and free from losing any battles, because they have come to be such good soldiers that even when they find themselves controlling the countryside because of (our) inferiority in cavalry, they do not fight with our men when victory is doubtful, as I said, but only when their advantage is completely clear and obvious. . . . Thus it may be noted with how much more skill these few Indians have learned how to defend their land from the much larger number of Spaniards who were present before, which is a notable example of the great importance of good order and discipline in war.

Source: "1614. González de la Nájera on Indian organization and tactics," trans. by the editors, in John H. Parry and Robert G. Keith, eds., *New Iberian World*, Vol. V (New York: Times Books, 1984), pp. 396, 397, 398. Reprinted by permission of Edward J. Joyce, trustee.

The nomadic peoples of northern Mexico, who prized Spanish cloth and metalware, soon attacked the well-equipped, but rather poorly defended, mining towns and wagon trains. All of these native bands, as diverse as they were, fought with bows and arrows and a strategy of ambushes. When facing a superior force, war parties did not hesitate to break off an engagement and flee in all directions, later to reassemble. Spanish mounted expeditions proved tiresomely ineffective, for the native fighters just evaded them until they turned back from exhaustion, and then harassed them with skirmishes. These nomadic bands also increasingly incorporated the horse into their way of life and warfare, which enhanced their threat to Spanish mines and wagon trains.

The first attacks began in 1550–1551. The Zacatecos killed an expedition of Tarascans, native allies of the Spaniards, and escaped with all of the merchandise they were transporting. Around the same time, the Guachichiles killed a herdsman and seized his animals. Soon afterwards they attacked a wagon train, killing nine men and absconding with a load of clothing. That same year they killed a Spanish merchant and forty Indian porters, again escaping with all the clothing. In 1551, the Guamares raided a ranch, slaying most of the residents and driving off most of the livestock.

Like the Araucanians of Chile, the nomadic peoples of northern Mexico came to appreciate the advantages of cooperation and formed temporary alliances for mutual support and to mount larger attacks. Strong leaders sometimes appeared. Not unusually these leaders had some previous experience among the colonists, knowledge that they then used against the Spanish.

The imperial authorities responded with two approaches. First, they established colonies of native allies from central Mexico in the north, both to share in the fighting and to provide logistical support to Spanish units. These communities largely retained their distinctive way of life—including their indigenous languages—until the end of the colonial period. Second, they based forts near settlements and along important roads and populated them with a paid, permanent soldiery. These soldiers were so poorly maintained that they sometimes undertook raids even during times of peace to capture slaves to sell away from the area, an abuse known in southern Chile as well.

Despite these measures, these nomadic bands were still creating havoc in the mining zones of northern Mexico at the end of the sixteenth century. Finally, the colonial authorities attempted a different approach that proved more successful. They offered raiding groups a stipulated amount of supplies annually from the government if they would settle down in one place and accept missionaries. A number of groups, under duress from the ravages of constant warfare and epidemic disease, accepted the Spanish terms. With time, the "Indian frontier" moved farther northward and into the mountains, but unsubjugated peoples continued to exist—and sometimes to raid—in northern Mexico until the end of the colonial period.

Missions in Spanish and Portuguese America

Missions developed in regions of Spanish and Portuguese America that contained semisedentary and nonsedentary native peoples. Their goals were to inculcate Christianity, a sedentary agricultural way of life, and European values

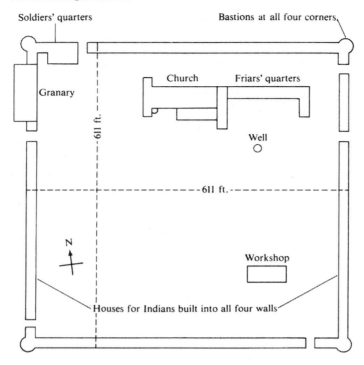

A Plan of a mission in San Antonio, Texas *(James Lockhart and Stuart B. Schwartz,* Early Latin America: A History of Colonial Spanish America and Brazil, *New York: Cambridge University Press, 1983, p. 295.* From *The Alamo Chain of Missions* Marion A. Habig. © 1968 by Franciscan Herald Press. Reprinted by permission.)

among these peoples. Such missions sprung up wherever a frontier situation long prevailed and where a rudimentary economy could attract only a few colonists. Thus, besides the Paraguayan missions among the Guaraní, both the Spanish and the Portuguese established strings of these institutions within the drainage basin of the Amazon River. But the most famous chain of missions was that located in northern Mexico, extending from Texas through Arizona and up the coast of California all the way to San Francisco.

The Guaraní missions were understandably the most successful, for these people had the densest populations. Their culture was already somewhat similar to the European, with its substantial reliance on agriculture and its residential and political organization into extended households and villages. A far greater challenge faced the missionaries among the raiding hunting-and-gathering peoples in the vast desert zone of northern Mexico.

By the time that Jesuits began to set up missions in this region in the late 1500s, warfare between the native tribes and the colonists had prevailed for several decades. Missions did not emerge as an alternative to official government policy toward these peoples, but rather as a new aspect of it. Colonial officials encouraged hostile native societies to forego the incessant warfare against the colonists in favor of a peaceful settled existence in which government agents would provide each tribe that entered a mission with a certain amount of supplies annually. Many depleted peoples who were under relentless pressure because of the continual state of war chose this option. Intact, autonomous peoples under strong leadership rarely did.

These missions were structured like large municipalities and were autonomous unto themselves. The resident missionaries had complete control over all aspects of life and existence. They required mission residents to live according to the norms of European culture as much as they could, expecting the men to labor in the fields and at crafts and the women to tend to domestic chores. Mission Indians had to wear their clothing and hair according to European styles. The personal independence and role in making decisions previously enjoyed by members of nomadic bands was replaced by a code of discipline enforced by strict missionaries. The priests likewise closely monitored expression of sexuality. Men and women often lived in separate barracks that were locked at night.

Understandably, in these conditions rather few children were born, and given the rampant epidemic disease and the unhealthy conditions that prevailed in these close quarters, many infants—and even adults—died. Numerous missions only maintained their populations by regularly recruiting new groups of Indians, which of course greatly set back the missionaries' goal of acculturating mission residents. Small contingents of soldiers often stationed nearby helped bring in new Indians. They also pursued the substantial number of mission Indians who ran away.

Yet another response among some mission Indians was to revolt. Mission Indians who revolted sought to kill the Europeans and to rid themselves of all foreign influence in an effort to return to the perceived purity and benefits of precontact existence. Such uprisings are termed "nativist" or "revitalization" movements. The natives recognized that mission life was destroying their culture, and that nothing better would replace it. In such settings, revolts sometimes began when a local native preached a return to indigenous ways to rid them of death, injury, insult, and evil. Believers in such movements sometimes felt that they had become impervious to death and personal injury, or if killed, that they would rise again. If successful, they massacred all Europeans, destroyed the mission, and returned to their nomadic way of life. Often, however, Christian beliefs had so deeply influenced them that they incorporated some aspects of Christianity within an indigenous belief system to produce a mixed, or syncretic, system of values and worship.

An illustrative case is the Acaxee Rebellion of 1601 in northwestern Mexico. Colonists began to move into the region in the 1580s. The first Jesuit arrived in 1598 and cooperated with the settlers and a contingent of Spanish troops to make the Acaxees available for work on rural estates and mines. Spanish authorities pressured the Acaxees to give up their dispersed residential pattern and congregate in several communities. They then required the Acaxees to wear

A Mission Indian flutist in Central South America, c. 1750 *(David Block,*
Mission Culture on the Upper Amazon: Native Tradition, Jesuit Enterprise,
and Secular Policy in Moxos, 1660–1880, *Lincoln: University*
of Nebraska Press, 1994, p. 97. Ministerio de Educación, Cultura y Deporte.
Archivo General de Indias. MP, Estampas 201. Reprinted by permission.)

European clothing, cut their long hair, and cultivate the land. The Spanish
burned their idols and fetishes. The Jesuit priest in command retained traditional headmen in leadership positions.

The Acaxees initially cooperated with the colonial authorities who promised to protect them from raids by their traditional enemies. The Jesuits—two more arrived in 1601—conducted thousands of baptisms and worked to impose monogamous marriages, previously unknown among these desert peoples. The Acaxees became agriculturalists and mine workers, participating in the colonial market economy.

But the Acaxee regularly slipped out of the villages to worship traditional gods. Their elders warned of starvation and devastation unless the people restored the native gods to their customary place of honor. The Jesuits simultaneously pressured the village residents to further consolidate their settlements and to accept heightened control by the priests. In 1601, Perico, an Acaxee elder, organized a revolt. He referred to himself as God, Holy Spirit, and Bishop and said that he had descended from heaven to save his people from erroneous beliefs. He conducted baptisms and marriages and presided over masses. He even designated disciples.

Perico insisted that every vestige of the Spaniards and their culture had to be eradicated. He claimed that he could make the Spaniards blind, or even turn them into livestock, to facilitate their slaughter. The Jesuits managed to find refuge in a Spanish town, but over the next few weeks the Acaxee killed some 50 Spaniards and put churches and other structures to the torch. The insurgents carried banners made from ecclesiastical vestments. They also attacked Acaxees who refused to join the movement.

Colonial authorities initially sought to negotiate with the insurgents. But, ultimately, in 1603, the incoming governor led a combined force of local colonists and Indian allies in a systematic campaign against them. Hundreds of captives were summarily executed and many more sold into slavery. Perico was burned alive and about 50 of his lieutenants were hanged, effectively ending the uprising. Nonetheless, similar first-generation revolts continued among newly "reduced Indians" in that region throughout the seventeenth century.

Conclusion

The responses of semisedentary and nonsedentary peoples to the arrival of the Iberians shared several notable similarities the responses of the native societies of eastern North America to the arrival of the French, Dutch, and English. Flight was a frequent alternative, as peoples sought simply to evade Iberian impositions. Warfare was common and enduring, because neither side had the ability to quickly subdue the other. In some areas, relatively stable frontiers long endured. But some small native settlements might be present within the colonial zones. Intact indigenous groups at times incorporated beleaguered ones into their midst, or several peoples combined themselves into a new ethnic group. Some native groups provided food to maintain early Spanish colonies through difficult years. They also became long-term military and political allies of the Spanish because they appreciated that it was in their interest. Often, they used the colonists to assist them in their campaigns against rival groups. The Spanish also had to recognize native political and legal sovereignty in many cases, and participate in indigenous customs and rituals. In such situations, considerable biculturation transpired.

Even additional similarities prevailed. Sometimes colonists and native groups formed mutually advantageous alliances against their common enemies. The Europeans set up missions among many of these societies, though they differed greatly in their degrees of success. Cultural interchange was sporadic but very real; for example, even autonomous indigenous peoples incorporated aspects of Christian belief and worship into their cultures. Finally, through it all, native ethnic groups demonstrated remarkable cultural resilience and characteristically maintained their distinctiveness from the colonists.

Some of the native peoples who resisted Spanish advances, like their North American counterparts, came to appreciate that the rivalries among themselves had become counterproductive against these new enemies. The colonists played the Indian groups off against each other to their mutual disadvantage. Certain indigenous leaders began to promote broader coalitions, as also occurred in North America. The peoples of northern Mexico sought to organize a Chichimec League, while some Araucanians in Chile preached that all of their communities belonged to a common nation. But these efforts enjoyed only moderate success against the traditional divisions that prevailed among indigenous groups and the concerns of local leaders that their authority would become diminished.

Some important differences, however, distinguished the Latin American and North American experiences. Latin America had nothing comparable to the fur trade, which shaped native–colonist relations in so much of North America for a prolonged time. But the North American colonists made little use of native laborers in their enterprises, unlike their Latin American counterparts, who recruited or coerced many semisedentary people into becoming permanent workers for them.

Few new Spaniards migrated to areas inhabited by semisedentary and nomadic peoples after the initial settlements occurred. The wealth and resources of Mexico and Peru attracted most new arrivals. So unlike in North America, a certain stagnation developed in these peripheral Spanish American colonies. With few pure-blooded Spanish women present, settlers in these zones often mated with native women.

Similarly, while race mixture marked Latin America even in semisedentary zones, rather little transpired in North America. When it did, as in French Canada, the offspring might well be raised in the tribal setting of the mother and be fully incorporated into native society. Unlike in Latin America, where mixed-race people proliferated within the most settled colonial zones, in North America people of mixed ancestry were rarely found away from the frontier.

Overall, then, the semisedentary and nonsedentary peoples who occupied so vast an area in the Americas upon the arrival of the Europeans responded as creatively as did the sedentary societies, though in quite different ways. They displayed just as resolute a cultural identity. Further, in a number of cases, their characteristics and those of the environments they inhabited enabled them to resist incorporation into the colonial empires for long periods of time.

Select Bibliography

Block, David. *Mission Culture on the Upper Amazon: Native Tradition, Jesuit Enterprise, and Secular Policy in Moxos, 1660–1880.* Lincoln: University of Nebraska Press, 1994.

Clastres, Hélène. *The Land Without Evil: Tupí-Guaraní Prophetism.* Jacqueline Grenez Brovender, trans. Urbana: University of Illinois Press, 1995.

Clendinnen, Inga. *Ambivalent Conquests: Maya and Spaniard in Yucatan, 1517–1570.* Cambridge, England: Cambridge University Press, 1987.

Cook, Sherburne F. *The Conflict Between the California Indian and White Civilization.* Berkeley: University of California Press, 1976.

Farriss, Nancy M. *Maya Society Under Colonial Rule: The Collective Enterprise of Survival.* Princeton: Princeton University Press, 1984.

Guy, Donna J. and Thomas E. Sheridan, eds. *Contested Ground: Comparative Frontiers on the Northern and Southern Edges of the Spanish Empire.* Tucson: University of Arizona Press, 1998.

Hemming, John. *Red Gold: The Conquest of the Brazilian Indians, 1500–1760.* Cambridge, MA: Harvard University Press, 1978.

Hu-DeHart, Evelyn. *Missionaries, Miners, and Indians: Spanish Contact With the Yaqui Nation of Northwestern New Spain, 1533–1820.* Tucson: University of Arizona, 1981.

Jackson, Robert H. *Indian Population Decline: The Missions of Northwestern New Spain, 1687–1840.* Albuquerque: University of New Mexico Press, 1994.

Jackson, Robert H. and Edward Castillo. *Indians, Franciscans, and Spanish Colonization: The Impact of the Mission System on California Indians.* Albuquerque: University of New Mexico Press, 1995.

Jones, Grant D. *Maya Resistance to Spanish Rule: Time and History on a Colonial Frontier.* Albuquerque: University of New Mexico Press, 1989.

Marchant, Alexander. *From Barter to Slavery: The Economic Relations of Portuguese and Indians in the Settlement of Brazil, 1500–1580.* Baltimore: The Johns Hopkins University Press, 1942.

Patch, Robert W. *Maya and Spaniard in Yucatan, 1648–1812.* Stanford: Stanford University Press, 1993.

Powell, Philip Wayne. *Soldiers, Indians, and Silver: The Northward Advance of New Spain, 1550–1600.* Berkeley: University of California Press, 1952.

Radding, Cynthia. *Wandering Peoples: Colonialism, Ethnic Spaces, and Ecological Frontiers in Northwestern Mexico, 1700–1850.* Durham: Duke University Press, 1997.

Restall, Matthew. *The Maya World: Yucatec Culture and Society, 1500–1850.* Stanford: Stanford University Press, 1997.

Service, Elman R. *Spanish-Guaraní Relations Early Colonial Paraguay.* Ann Arbor: University of Michigan Press, 1954.

Endnotes

1   Nancy M. Farriss, *Maya Society Under Colonial Rule: The Collective Enterprise of Survival* (Princeton: Princeton University Press, 1984), p. 75.

2   Stuart B. Schwartz, *Sugar Plantations in the Formation of Brazilian Society: Bahia, 1550–1835* (Cambridge, England: Cambridge University Press, 1985), p. 47.

8

Enduring Connections Between the New World and the Old

All of the preceding chapters have considered the nature of the native peoples of the Americas and how they were affected by and responded to European colonization. The first part of this chapter examines the impact of the incorporation of the Americas into the environmental and economic frameworks of the Old World, a process commonly termed "The Columbian Exchange." For the first time, the Atlantic Ocean became a primary arena for the movement of people, diseases, animals, plants, and precious metals. This process transformed the environment of the Americas as much as it did the rest of the world. The following five sections consider the scope and impact of each of these emerging connections between the New World and the Old. A concluding section examines certain lasting patterns and trends in the history of Indian–European interactions in the colonial period.

Before the discovery of the Americas, Western Europe participated only episodically in the exchange systems of the Old World. Located on the western periphery of the three continents of Africa, Asia, and Europe that constituted this trade zone, Western Europe produced few commodities or manufactured goods that could compete in African or Asian markets. Hence it scarcely participated in the dynamic and flourishing trading networks centered in the Indian Ocean and the South China Sea. The complex economies of South Asia and China routinely shipped merchandise to East Africa, throughout Southeast Asia, and to the Spice Islands (modern Indonesia) and the Philippines.

The Movement of Peoples

The Americas had only minimal impact on the Old World in this exchange. Few Native Americans journeyed to Europe, and fewer still remained for very long. Europe certainly did not need people from America as settlers or laborers. Early explorers of the Americas, though, frequently kidnapped small numbers of young natives to take back with them. Once in Europe, they displayed the natives to the royal court and the public and also trained them to serve as translators in later voyages to the natives' regions of origin. Surrounded by dense populations of disease-carrying peoples in Europe's very different climate, many of these Indians became ill and died soon after their arrival.

A few European settlers who had married Indian women of high social status brought them to their European homes with the intention of lengthy stays. Pocahantas accompanied her husband, John Rolfe, to England, but soon took ill and died. Some women from the Aztec and Inca nobilities who held title to large estates—and sometimes to labor service—wed Spaniards. While most remained in their homelands, a small number travelled to Spain with their husbands. Some remained there for the rest of their lives, constructing mansions and transferring much of their wealth to their new country of residence. In Spain, they were readily incorporated into the national elite, and their descendants proudly displayed their Indian surnames. The Cano y Montezuma family, for example, circulated in the highest social circles in Mexico and Spain through the end of the colonial period, while retaining the entailed estates it had originally been assigned through the indigenous noble lineage. The family had its origins in the (fourth) marriage of Isabel, the daughter of the emperor Montezuma, with the companion of Cortés, Juan Cano.

The migration of people in the other direction, to the Americas, was massive. The vast territory of Spanish America attracted nearly 700,000 immigrants from the home country during the three colonial centuries, an average of around 2,000 a year. Most of these immigrants settled either in Mexico or Peru. Some 523,000 Portuguese came to Brazil, over half of them after 1700. Immigration to New France totaled around 100,000. New Netherland received a mere 20,000. British North America attracted large numbers of settlers, perhaps 750,000 up to the outbreak of the independence movement.

In the colonial period, far more Africans came to the Americas as slaves than Europeans as freemen. By 1800, some 7,500,000 Africans had arrived in the New World. The slave trade channelled them in overwhelming numbers to the two primary sugar plantation zones: Brazil (totalling around 2,500,000) and the Caribbean (totalling around 3,700,000). Substantial numbers of Afro-Latinos could be found in other settings as well. The total received in Spanish America by 1800 approached 950,000, with Mexico, Peru, Venezuela, and Chile among the colonies with substantial populations from Africa. But once in the Americas, African slaves could barely reproduce their numbers, while the Europeans enjoyed very high rates of population increase.

The Movement of Diseases

The previous chapters have examined the impact of epidemic diseases on the native peoples of the Americas in some detail. With no natural resistance to the diseases endemic to the Old World for centuries—smallpox, measles, typhus, malaria, yellow fever, and at least some strains of influenza—the Indians succumbed in overwhelming numbers to the waves of epidemics that accompanied the European arrival. Once systematic contact between the two peoples occurred, the population of the native society declined over the next 150 years. By that time, many indigenous ethnic groups retained merely a twentieth to a tenth of their precontact population, and some peoples had died off completely or had their few survivors incorporated into other native societies. After this century-and-a-half of devastation, the surviving native populations began a slow recovery.

Apparently, only one disease seems to have been transferred from the Americas to Europe: syphilis. Before the emergence of syphilis, Europe certainly had venereal diseases but none as debilitating or fatal. Syphilis was common enough in the Americas, and most evidence indicates that it migrated from there to Europe. However, syphilis was also present in South Asia, and the Europeans reached there about the same time that they reached the Americas. So the disease may have been transmitted to Europe from that part of the world instead.

The Movement of Animals

The Americas lacked the draft animals and the variety of comestible animals found in Europe. The cultures of the Old World, therefore, did not widely adopt the New World's creatures. Buffalo, llamas, and Guinea pigs were brought over as specimens, but only the turkey had any significant impact on the Old World. Even it remained a secondary poultry variety in Europe, unable to rival the traditional popularity of chickens, geese, and ducks.

In contrast, the numerous animals that accompanied Europeans to the New World transformed the indigenous way of life. All of the European groups brought cattle with them, and they proliferated in the Americas, benefitting from the abundant vegetation and the lack of predatory animals in most regions. The grassy plains of southern South America (the *pampas*) and of south central Colombia and Venezuela (the *llanos*) soon supported hundreds of thousands of wild cattle. But cattle proliferated in wooded and settled areas as well. The Indians of Massachusetts, the Carolinas, and Mexico, among others, complained to the colonists that cattle trampled their fields of maize. Colonists prized cattle more for their hides than for their flesh in most regions, for they were not yet bred for either abundant or tender beef. Beef in these centuries was a food for commoners, not for the elite. The major exceptions included the native tribes of the Argentine grasslands and southern Chile, who commonly slaughtered cattle to eat only the most tender parts of their carcasses. But they enjoyed few alternative sources of animal protein.

Sheep likewise thrived in the Americas. But, unlike cattle, sheep did not generally run wild; rather they were tended by shepherds and were raised commercially for their wool and mutton, the meat of preference among Iberians. Before the end of the sixteenth century, Mexico alone contained hundreds of thousands of sheep.

Favored by the extensive grasslands of the Americas, horses proliferated much like cattle and sheep. As earlier recounted, the Araucanians of Chile adopted the horse to improve their style of warfare against the Spanish. In North America, wild horses spread rapidly across the plains and transformed the way of life of the Indians there. By the time that Americans of European descent reached the western plains, the native peoples, who largely lived off hunting buffalo, had incorporated the horse into their culture—and mode of warfare—for more than a century.

Vibrant cowboy cultures flourished in colonial Latin America. The *gauchos* of Argentina, the *llaneros* of Venezuela, and the *charros* of northern Mexico all became familiar types and later strongly influenced national values and images. The *charros* of Mexico helped to shape the American cowboy way of life as the United States moved into its western territories in the last third of the nineteenth century. The Spanish origins of many American ranching terms—including corral, rodeo, mustang (from *mesteño*), and lariat (from *la reata*)—reflect this legacy.

Indian agriculturalists throughout Latin America incorporated two small animals as food sources: pigs and chickens. Neither threatened their crops, and both could be easily raised near houses. Both provided animal protein, which historically had been in short supply in the native diet. Natives also sold them for the small amounts of cash needed from time to time even in these small, rural societies.

The Movement of Plants

Substantial numbers of plants crossed the Atlantic with enormous impact. Certain weeds and grasses common to Europe spread across the Americas, modifying local landscapes by crowding out indigenous plants. These new weeds typically followed close on the environmental disruption caused by the invasion of animals from Europe. With the local flora damaged, these hardy, alien plants could impose themselves, sometimes dominating vast areas. In 1877, a naturalist visiting Buenos Aires and the region of Patagonia to its south identified 153 European plants inhabiting the area.

Wheat cultivation followed close upon the establishment of European settlements. Until well after the end of the colonial period, European-Americans consumed wheat bread exclusively, never eating maize products, while the opposite was the case among the Indians. Native communities in Latin America, however, did deliberately raise wheat on their own land, selling their harvests in colonial towns, where it had a sure market. These communities used the proceeds to make tribute payments and to settle other debts. The Spanish also introduced olive groves and vineyards to the Americas, but the Indian population rarely consumed the products of these cultivators. The natives continued to prefer indigenous intoxicants, particularly *pulque* (the fermented sap of the maguey cactus) in Mexico and *chicha* (maize beer) in the Andes.

Europeans brought several crops native to the Americas to the Old World and greatly increased food productivity, contributing to a substantial growth in population over the following several centuries. Maize, potatoes, sweet potatoes, beans, and manioc were also widely adopted in the Old World, in some cases even more so in Africa and Asia than in Europe. Other foods, such as squashes, peanuts, and tomatoes, were less central to the revolution in crop cultivation, but did enjoy some popularity, and were important in certain limited areas of the Old World.

With their ability to survive in harsher climates than other crops, maize and potatoes greatly expanded the amount of land under cultivation in Europe and China. Regions that were not conducive to the cultivation of such traditional staples as wheat, barley, and rice became highly productive once planted with maize or potatoes. On average, maize harvests rendered twice the calories per unit of land as did wheat. It also enjoyed a shorter growing cycle. Maize also became a vital feed grain for large animals throughout Europe. Vast upland areas in China unsuitable to rice cultivation flourished after the introduction of these Old World staples. At the end of the twentieth century, about 35 percent of the food grown in China is of American origin. China grows more maize than any other country in the world except the United States, and no country exceeds its production of sweet potatoes.

Though rejected as a food in the Old World for more than a century, potatoes gradually became popular. Eventually they came to dominate cultivation in certain large temperate zones, notably Ireland and Central Europe. As they provide abundant harvests on lands too inferior for the cultivation of grains, potatoes became the favored crop among people who subsisted on small plots with inferior soils.

Manioc, also known as cassava, became the primary crop cultivated in tropical zones. It thrives in a variety of environments and even in very poor soil. People from central Africa through to the Spice Islands in the Pacific Ocean adopted this starchy root, which also contains certain vitamins. The many varieties of beans native to the Americas proliferated throughout the Old World, never becoming the dominant crop in a major zone, but remaining important as a supplement due to their substantial amounts of protein. Peanuts and squashes became significant complementary foods throughout central Africa, and India has become the world's largest producer of peanuts. Tomatoes and chile peppers are grown in much of the continent. Africa became a major exporter of cacao, peanuts, vanilla, and pineapples, all of which originated in the Americas.

The peoples of the Americas also provided Europe with herbs and other plants of great medicinal value. They had a profound knowledge of the beneficial value of many plants. The great range of environments in the Americas provided the natives with a wide selection of greenery from which to draw. We know the most about the pharmacopoeia of the Aztecs. Montezuma supposedly kept an extensive herb garden.

In 1552, the Colegio de la Santa Cruz, a college for Indian youths established by Spanish friars, decided to sponsor the composition of an herbal, that is, a book that describes plants with medicinal value. An Aztec doctor, Martín de la

Cruz, composed the work in Nahuatl. Juan Badiano, an Indian scholar at the college then translated it into Latin, the formal language of learning in Europe. Illustrated in color, the book was dispatched to the royal court in Madrid and eventually found its way into the Vatican Library, where it was rediscovered early in the twentieth century.

The Columbian Exchange led to the vast ecological transformation of the Americas. In some areas of the Americas this occurred early in the colonial period. Understandably, most of this transformation took place in the regions most heavily settled by colonists.

The nonsedentary societies of the Americas did almost nothing to transform their environments. They depended on the plants and animals produced naturally within their territories for their sustenance, so hunting-and-gathering peoples intervened very little in their environments. Semisedentary peoples cut down brush and small trees and then burned them to obtain open areas and fertilizer for their agriculture. But they relied on the land regenerating itself so that they could perform the same process repeatedly . Hence they were careful not to permanently damage their natural settings, for they certainly would be the ultimate losers.

The sedentary peoples, of course, modified their lands quite extensively and quite intentionally. The Mesoamerican and Andean civilizations constructed raised fields and terraces along with other forms of agricultural engineering. But the lack of draft animals and the plow restricted their ecological interventions. With their rudimentary tools they apparently had difficulty breaking up lowlands densely covered with grasses for planting and may therefore have emphasized the cultivation of less heavily overgrown hillsides.

Though famines were known, especially in Mesoamerica, the sedentary peoples do not seem to have placed undue strain on the productive capacity of the land up to the arrival of the Europeans. Even subjugated provinces produced enough food to feed themselves and their imperial masters. Further, sedentary peoples operated effective, highly developed storage systems.

The arrival of colonists brought major changes to the environment. In Brazil the Portuguese traded with the natives for dyewood trees they cut down. Demand for dyewood trees was such that by the early 1600s the Portuguese crown became concerned about exhausting the supply and regulated cutting. When the colonists shifted to the cultivation of sugar after 1550, they took a more aggressive policy toward the extensive Atlantic forest that ran along much of the Brazilian coastline south of the Amazon. They burned down large sections to facilitate the creation of plantations, causing the forest to recede significantly from the coast in northeast Brazil and in greater Sâo Paulo.

The great animal herds that proliferated after introduction by the Europeans also caused damage and, in some cases, wholesale environmental transformation. In a well-documented case, the Valley of Mezquital, to the north of the Valley of Mexico, existed largely as a sedentary agricultural zone with extensive irrigation before the arrival of the Spanish. But in the second half of the seventeenth century, Spanish ranchers moved into the valley to graze large herds of sheep. These flocks grew rapidly in size over the next several decades and ate the native grasses down to their roots, leaving nothing to grow back. Weeds and scrub plants began to replace the previously lush foliage. With grazing limited, the sheep herds shrank notably in size. But even when most herds were decimated or had moved out of the valley, the environment did not recover. The sheep invasion had permanently transformed it into infertile scrubland.

English colonists in North America also drastically transformed their countryside. The Eastern Woodlands Indians typically waited for the land to regain coverage by foliage before they once again used an area for slash-and-burn agriculture. The English would have none of that. Rather, they quickly set up permanent communities and cleared much of the surrounding land to undertake an annual cycle of agriculture. Under this approach, they eradicated much of the woodlands. They cleared the forest to open up fields, but the English also cut it down to provide construction materials and firewood. A certain commerce existed as well for some of the finer woods.

William Cronon describes the consequences.

In summary, then, deforestation was one of the most sweeping transformations wrought by European settlement in New England. It aided the reduction of edge-dwelling animal species. Where forests were not completely eliminated, their species composition changed: trees such as white pines, white cedars, and white oaks became less common. Where forests were entirely destroyed, the landscape became hotter in summer and colder in winter. Temperatures in general fluctuated more widely. Snow melted more readily than it had before, and the ground froze more deeply. The water-holding capacity of the soil was reduced, and runoff was thereby increased and made more erratic.[1]

Similar levelings of forests occurred in the colonial South. There, settlers cut or burned down vast expanses of trees to open up land for the emerging rice plantation economy in early eighteenth-century South Carolina.

Finally, the Indians of eastern North America responded to economic incentives from European traders by trapping beaver and hunting white-tail deer to near extinction, with significant environmental consequences.

The Movement of Precious Metals

The transfer of Aztec and Inca gold and silver to Spain in the 1520s and 1530s sparked the economies of the home provinces of the returning *conquistadores* and displayed to the larger society the level of wealth that these American civilizations had achieved. But this one-time delivery of wealth was not enough to stimulate the larger Spanish economy in any notable fashion. Then in the 1540s and 1550s colonists in Mexico and Peru discovered major silver lodes as they explored the new territories. Immense amounts of wealth circulated in these colonies and poured into the home country in the second half of the sixteenth century—and continued to flow, though at differing rates, through the remainder of the colonial period. Between 1493 and 1800, about 85 percent of the world's silver production and some 70 percent of its gold production came from Latin America. Fully 70 percent of the silver mined in Latin America in the colonial period was shipped to Europe. The amount of silver available in Europe had tripled by 1650.

Spain quickly became the envy of its many European rivals, and its monarchs used this unprecedented wealth to finance extensive diplomatic and military undertakings in the rest of the continent. But Spain's economy could not build upon this continual infusion of specie to develop, and by 1600 it clearly lagged behind its major competitors in Western Europe: England, France, and the Netherlands. Spain's economy was already rather backward in the early sixteenth century. Its agricultural estates were not productive, nor did they make efficient use of labor. The country hardly had a manufacturing sector. Trade was restricted by many regulations, was not competitive with that of Spain's rivals, and was substantially dominated by foreigners. Inflation and rising wages were already becoming problems in the economy, as it failed to respond dynamically to growing demand. The unexpected infusion of so much wealth from the Americas actually exacerbated these problems. The economy did not modernize itself or significantly increase its output. Hence inflation worsened and Spain became even less competitive in the international trading system. Spain itself imported ever-increasing amounts of manufactured goods from other Western European countries, paying for them with the specie arriving regularly from the Americas.

The Spanish monarchy borrowed vast amounts of money from foreign bankers to finance its political ambitions. Over the next couple of centuries, Spain intervened regularly in wars and dynastic disputes throughout the continent, often with little success. International financiers did not hesitate to loan money to the Spanish government despite its poor record of accomplishment, because they could always place claims on future shipments of specie from America if the crown had trouble making its payments. And so it did. The government declared bankruptcy and renegotiated its loans in 1557, 1575, 1596, 1607, 1627, and 1647. It even devalued its coins in an effort to relieve the problem.

Even before the end of the sixteenth century, most of the specie Spain received from its colonies quickly left the country. J.H. Elliott relates:

> An official estimate of 1594 indicates that, out of an average annual remittance from the Indies of some ten million ducats, six million were leaving Spain each year—three million to meet the foreign expenses of the Crown, and three million to the account of private individuals. Instead of ten million ducats being injected into the Spanish monetary system, therefore, the figure is only four million, at the very most.[2]

The economies of the countries that received this exported specie did not suffer the same fate as Spain, for they were much more dynamic and multidimensional and used the silver coin to finance their growing trade with South Asia and the Far East. They needed to, for the Europeans faced a major obstacle in their economic relations with the advanced civilizations of Asia; they did not produce any item greatly desired in that part of the world, while they craved the cloths, ceramics, spices, and other fine goods produced in such abundance by the Eastern civilizations.

But fortunately for Europe, the advanced economies of China and the Indian subcontinent suffered from marked shortages of silver coin. European traders therefore paid for their purchases with silver specie they had obtained from Spain, which had been, of course, originally mined in the Americas. Thus from very early on, the first modern world trading system relied heavily on precious metals shipped from the New World. Estimates indicate that fully a third— and maybe up to half—of the silver produced in the Americas before 1800 ended up in China, with another third going to India and the Ottoman empire. American silver was even used in Southeast Asia to purchase the pepper and cloves shipped to Europe. Europe's overwhelming reliance on silver coin to finance this vital commerce continued through the end of the eighteenth century despite the persistent efforts of its trading nations to develop other exports.

One result of this long-term dependence was that the standard Spanish coin, the piece of eight, was known and accepted throughout the world. John J. TePaske elaborates.

> In fact, American silver was so ubiquitous that merchants from Boston to Havana, Seville to Antwerp, Murmansk to Alexandria, Constantinople to Coromandel, Macao to Canton, and Nagasaki to Manila all used the Spanish peso or piece of eight (real) as a standard medium of exchange; these same merchants even knew the relative fineness of the silver coins minted in Potosí, Lima, Mexico, and other sites in the Indies thousands of miles away.[3]

But not just European countries traded with East Asia. The major Spanish American colonies did so as well. Hence Mexico and (somewhat secondarily) Peru participated directly in the world economy, not just indirectly as the sources of the silver coin. Mexico and Peru managed to retain increasing percentages of the silver they produced. In the mid-seventeenth century, both colonies shipped only about a third of their minted coin to Spain. The rest remained, most of it used to construct buildings and infrastructure, and increased amounts dedicated to defense. But colonial merchants, many of whom had become independent of Spanish commercial houses, assembled substantial amounts of silver to back their extensive credit transactions—and to acquire Chinese goods directly from Manila, the capital of the Spanish colony of the Philippines. Shortly after the Spanish takeover of that city in the mid-sixteenth century, the crown had authorized Mexican merchants to send one or two ships a year out of Acapulco (depending on the specific era) loaded with silver to Manila, where the funds were used to purchase goods brought to the Philippines by Chinese merchants.

By the beginning of the seventeenth century, perhaps five million pesos were shipped annually from Mexico to Manila, despite government efforts intended to keep the amount much lower. Even Peruvian ships continued to participate for some years, though this was contrary to a government edict. And when Peruvian merchants ultimately had difficulty sending ships to Manila, they dispatched them to Acapulco, also illegally, to buy some of the abundant Chinese goods that landed there.

By Way of Conclusion—Enduring Patterns in the Americas

Numerous and distinctive native cultures interacted with the Europeans who settled in the Americas beginning in the late fifteenth century. These peoples had profound histories that shaped how they viewed and acted toward the newcomers. They likewise had long-established cultural, economic, and political relationships with each other, and these also informed the responses of each local society to Europeans. Overall, at least in the early decades of contact, the Indians sought to understand the Europeans in traditional terms and to utilize them to their own best advantage. The European colonists behaved in much the same way.

The level of agricultural development of the local peoples substantially shaped the character of the interaction between the natives and colonists. Sedentary peoples had dense populations organized into substantial settlements with considerable social and political elaboration and with sophisticated, widely spread religious and cultural systems. Semisedentary societies were less densely populated and somewhat more mobile, with less complex social and political overlays. The nomadic peoples had small populations and were extremely mobile, having no permanent settlements and little social or political elaboration.

The environment and immediate economic possibilities also affected the nature of colonial settlement and the colonists' expectations of the local peoples. More than any other factor, the highly lucrative fur trade shaped Indian-European relations in the northern half of eastern North America. The presence of massive silver deposits in northern New Spain compelled the Spaniards to pacify the indomitable nomadic peoples of this extensive region instead of merely ignoring them. The few colonists in the Yucatan, on the other hand, exported little and largely subsisted by raising cattle for themselves. Hence the Mayas continued to be autonomous throughout large parts of the peninsula, and the Spaniards took only a small number of them as laborers. In Portuguese Brazil, the Tupí remained independent and economically important for roughly the first half century of contact because of their central role in dyewood harvesting, easily the most important component of the early colonial economy. When the Portuguese subsequently moved to sugar plantation agriculture, they tried first to subjugate local peoples as forced laborers. When this proved unworkable, the colonists took a much more hostile approach as they turned massively to black slavery.

Many colonies depended on military alliances with native peoples against their European rivals or antagonistic indigenous societies. The history of the North American colonies is replete with such partnerships through the American

Revolution. The colonists of Mexico turned to client peoples from the central zone in their campaign against the nomadic societies of the desert north. The Spanish-Guaraní partnership against surrounding native peoples and the slave-raiding Portuguese colonists of São Paulo shaped the entire colonial period of Paraguayan history.

Time and again colonists in both Americas had to accommodate themselves to indigenous practices and priorities. Whether conducting trade, contracting for laborers, or securing a land transfer, European agents were required to participate in native rituals or to conduct themselves according to traditional ways to secure their ends. Further, except when a colony had clearly subjugated an indigenous people to its authority, judicial procedures and penalties commonly had to be negotiated when members of both societies were involved in a dispute or possible infraction.

Interethnic relationships and understandings were typically worked out informally and locally by the parties actually involved. No effective transcolonial "Indian policy" was ever implemented. Any overarching colonial statutes were enforced only if they were clearly in accord with the local situation and need. Otherwise, they were likely to be simply ignored. Colonial governments, whether in Virginia, Peru, or Bahia, rarely determined the character of native–colonist interaction. Informal personal and small group relationships played out on a day-in and day-out basis primarily shaped the course of Indian–settler relationships at the lcoal level.

None of the European colonizing powers implemented a consistent or effective approach to the native societies in the area it claimed. No Spanish, Portuguese, French, Dutch, or English government agency set or executed policy toward the indigenous peoples over the long term. For every rule or approach that prevailed in one part of an empire, an exception could be found in another. The French and Dutch respected Indian might and sovereignty where the fur trade was important, but did not hesitate to pursue warfare and removal when they coveted Indian lands. The Spanish incorporated native peoples into their colonial societies in central Mexico and even Paraguay, but for many decades absorbed rather few in the Yucatan and Chile, where they had to deal with autonomous polities who long maintained effective frontiers between themselves and the colonists. When the exceptional cases of the conquests of the Aztecs and the Incas are excluded, Spanish dealings with native peoples in the Americas much more closely resemble those of the other European colonizing nations.

The pressures that the Europeans placed on native societies differed greatly according to whether they were sedentary empires or semisedentary or nonsedentary tribes at the time the colonists arrived. The Spanish empire caused the Aztec and Inca civilizations (and empires) to fragment to their local component parts, which became more culturally and economically isolated than had ever been the case in precontact times. But quite the reverse was the case among the many nonimperial peoples of the Americas. In North America, the Iroquois Confederation became stronger in the early eighteenth century. Centralizing leaders emerged in other parts of North America, as well, calling for alliances among the different ethnic groups at an unprecedented level. In Mexico, the nomadic peoples of the north entered into something of a "Chichimec League," offering mutual support to each other. In Chile, during the prolonged resistance to Spanish expansion, the concept of an Araucanian nation emerged.

Exhibiting cultural flexibility and resilience and responding in what they understood to be their own best interests, the indigenous peoples responded creatively to the arrival of the Europeans. They incorporated many aspects of Western material culture into their way of life, but numerous essential patterns of native culture endured in vibrant fashion. They retained their ethnic identities and sought to remain autonomous communities, even when their numbers and lands became limited and they lived surrounded by colonists.

Numerous native peoples still lived quite intact and on the other side of frontiers when the colonial period came to an end in the Americas around 1800. But even they had to adapt to the presence of the Europeans. As just noted, stronger transethnic political alliances emerged among some of them. Others incorporated the remnants of devastated tribes into their midst. Native peoples acquired aspects of Western material culture through trade. Warfare became more deadly and devastating, as warriors utilized firearms and metal weapons in combat and as warfare became increasingly fought over material benefits, such as privileged access to trade or commodities. Now too often warfare involved large numbers of combatants disputing a community's continued existence rather than merely small groups seeking to capture enemies to redress damages to their lineages through blood feuds. With greater political centralization and the growing importance of warfare in indigenous life, the status of women diminished somewhat, as they had lost some of their customary political voice and influence.

The achievement of independence by the American colonies in and of itself had only measured impact on the indigenous peoples. In Latin America, most of the new nations were such weak political entities and the established elites were so divided that native societies were able to assert their claims to land, sometimes through direct seizure. The new nations generally asserted the equality of all citizens before the law and therefore abolished special jurisdictions and law codes for native peoples. Around the middle of the nineteenth century, the governments began to effectively require Indian communities to abandon collective ownership of their land in favor of individual proprietorship. The corporate identity of these societies suffered enormously along with their resource base. In North America, independence meant that the Indians could no longer appeal to the British government to counteract the demands of the settlers for access to Indian lands and the relocation of the indigenous population onto isolated reservations.

But even under these worsening conditions, the native cultures maintained distinctive ethnic identities and customs. Rather few among them sought incorporation into the dominant national cultures. Eventually, well into the twentieth century, their petitions reached more sympathetic ears and their enduring claims began to receive some legal redress.

Select Bibliography

Barrett, Ward, "World Bullion Flows, 1450–1800," in James D. Tracy, ed., *The Rise of Merchant Empires: Long-Distance Trade in the Early Modern World, 1350–1750* (Cambridge, England: Cambridge University Press, 1990), pp. 224–254.

Cronon, William. *Changes in the Land: Indians, Colonists, and the Ecology of New England.* New York: Hill and Wang, 1983.

Crosby Jr., Alfred W. *The Columbian Exchange: Biological and Cultural Consequences of 1492.* Westport, CT: Greenwood Press, 1972.

Crosby, Alfred W. *Ecological Imperialism: The Biological Expansion of Europe, 900–1900.* Cambridge, England: Cambridge University Press, 1986.

Cross, Harry E., "South American Bullion Production and Export, 1550–1750," in J. F. Richards, ed., *Precious Metals in the Later Medieval and Early Modern Worlds* (Durham, NC: Carolina Academic Press, 1983), pp. 397–423.

Dean, Warren. *With Broadax and Firebrand: The Destruction of the Brazilian Atlantic Forest.* Berkeley: University of California Press, 1995.

Elliott, J. H. *The Old World and the New, 1492–1650.* Cambridge, England: Cambridge University Press, 1970.

Frank, Andre Gunder. *ReOrient: Global Economy in the Asian Age.* Berkeley: University of California Press, 1998.

Krech III, Shepard. *The Ecological Indian: Myth and History.* New York: W.W. Norton, 1999.

Melville, Elinor G. K. *A Plague of Sheep: Environmental Consequences of the Conquest of Mexico.* Cambridge, England: Cambridge University Press, 1994.

Merchant, Carolyn. *Ecological Revolutions: Nature, Gender, and Science in New England.* Chapel Hill: University of North Carolina Press, 1989.

Schlesinger, Roger. *In the Wake of Columbus: The Impact of the New World on Europe, 1492–1650.* Wheeling, IL: Harland Davidson, Inc., 1996.

Silver, Timothy. *A New Face on the Countryside: Indians, Colonists, and Slaves in South Atlantic Forests, 1500–1800.* Cambridge, England: Cambridge University Press, 1990.

Super, John C. *Food, Conquest, and Colonization in Sixteenth-Century Spanish America.* Albuquerque: University of New Mexico Press, 1988.

TePaske, John J., "New World Silver, Castile and the Philippines, 1590–1800," in J. F. Richards, ed., *Precious Metals in the Later Medieval and Early Modern Worlds* (Durham, NC: Carolina Academic Press, 1983), pp. 425–445.

Viola, Herman J. and Carolyn Margolis, eds. *Seeds of Change: Five Hundred Years Since Columbus.* Washington D.C.: Smithsonian Institution Press, 1991.

Endnotes

1   William Cronon, *Changes in the Land: Indians, Colonists, and the Ecology of New England,* (New York: Hill and Wang, 1983), p. 126.

2   J. H. Elliott, *The Old World and the New, 1492–1650,* (Cambridge, England: Cambridge University Press, 1970), p. 65.

3   John J. TePaske, "New World Silver, Castile and the Philippines, 1590–1800," in J. F. Richards, ed., *Precious Metals in the Later Medieval and Early Modern Worlds* (Durham, NC: Carolina Academic Press, 1983), p. 425.

Bibliography

Adams, Richard E. W. *Ancient Civilizations of the New World.* Boulder, CO: Westview Press, 1997.

Adorno, Rolena. *Guaman Poma: Writing and Resistance in Colonial Peru.* Austin: University of Texas Press, 1986.

Anderson, Gary Clayton. *The Indian Southwest, 1580–1830: Ethnogenesis and Reinvention.* Norman: University of Oklahoma Press, 1999.

Andrien, Kenneth J. *Andean Worlds: Indigenous History, Culture and Consciousness Under Spanish Rule, 1532–1825.* Albuquerque: University of New Mexico Press, 2001.

Axtell, James. *Beyond 1492: Encounters in Colonial North America.* New York: Oxford University Press, 1992.

Axtell, James. *The Invasion Within: The Contest of Cultures in Colonial North America.* New York: Oxford University Press, 1985.

Barrett, Ward, "World Bullion Flows, 1450–1800," in James D. Tracy, ed., *The Rise of Merchant Empires: Long-Distance Trade in the Early Modern World, 1350–1750* (Cambridge, England: Cambridge University Press, 1990), pp. 224–254.

Berdan, Frances F. *The Aztecs of Central Mexico: An Imperial Society.* New York: Holt, Rinehart and Winston, 1982.

Block, David. *Mission Culture on the Upper Amazon: Native Tradition, Jesuit Enterprise, and Secular Policy in Moxos, 1660–1880.* Lincoln: University of Nebraska Press, 1994.

Boone, Elizabeth Hill. *Stories in Red and Black: Pictorial Histories of the Aztecs and Mixtecs.* Austin: University of Texas Press, 2000.

Boone, Elizabeth Hill and Tom Cummins, eds. *Native Traditions in the Postconquest World.* Washington, DC: Dumbarton Oaks Research Library and Collection, 1998.

Calloway, Colin G. *New Worlds for All: Indians, Europeans, and the Remaking of Early America.* Baltimore: The Johns Hopkins University Press, 1997.

Calloway, Colin G. *The American Revolution in Indian Country: Crisis and Diversity in Native American Communities.* Cambridge, England: Cambridge University Press, 1995.

Calloway, Colin G. *The Western Abenakis of Vermont, 1600–1800: War, Migration, and the Survival of an Indian People.* Norman: University of Oklahoma Press, 1990

Cayton, Andrew R. L. and Frederika J. Teute, eds. *Contact Points: American Frontiers from the Mohawk Valley to the Mississippi, 1750–1830.* Chapel Hill: University of North Carolina Press, 1998.

Chance, John K. *Conquest of the Sierra: Spaniards and Indians in Colonial Oaxaca.* Norman: University of Oklahoma Press, 1989.

Chance, John K. *Race and Class in Colonial Oaxaca.* Stanford: Stanford University Press, 1978.

Chaplin, Joyce E. *Subject Matter: Technology, the Body, and Science on the Anglo-American Frontier, 1500–1676.* Cambridge, MA: Harvard University Press, 2001.

Clastres, Hélène. *The Land Without Evil: Tupí-Guaraní Prophetism.* Jacqueline Grenez Brovender, trans. Urbana: University of Illinois Press, 1995.

Clendinnen, Inga. *Aztecs: An Interpretation.* Cambridge, England: Cambridge University Press, 1991.

Clendinnen, Inga. *Ambivalent Conquests: Maya and Spaniard in Yucatan, 1517–1570.* Cambridge, England: Cambridge University Press, 1987.

Cline, S.L, ed. *The Book of Tributes: Early Sixteenth-Century Nahuatl Censuses from Morelos.* Los Angeles: UCLA Latin American Center Publications, 1993.

Cline, S.L. *Colonial Culhuacan, 1580–1600: A Social History of an Aztec Town.* Albuquerque: University of New Mexico Press, 1986.

Coe, Michael, Dean Snow, and Elizabeth Benson. *Atlas of Ancient America.* New York: Facts on File, 1986.

Conrad, Geoffrey W. and Arthur A. Demerest. *Religion and Empire: The Dynamics of Aztec and Inca Expansionism.* Cambridge, England: Cambridge University Press, 1984.

Cook, Noble David. *Born to Die: Disease and New World Conquest, 1492–1650.* Cambridge, England: Cambridge University Press, 1998.

Cook, Noble David. *Demographic Collapse: Indian Peru, 1520–1620.* Cambridge, England: Cambridge University Press, 1981.

Cook, Sherburne F. *The Conflict Between the California Indian and White Civilization.* Berkeley: University of California Press, 1976.

Crane, Verner W. *The Southern Frontier, 1670–1732.* Ann Arbor: University of Michigan Press, 1964.

Cronon, William. *Changes in the Land: Indians, Colonists, and the Ecology of New England.* New York: Hill and Wang, 1983.

Crosby Jr., Alfred W. *The Columbian Exchange: Biological and Cultural Consequences of 1492.* Westport, CT: Greenwood Press, 1972.

Crosby, Alfred W. *Ecological Imperialism: The Biological Expansion of Europe, 900–1900.* Cambridge, England: Cambridge University Press, 1986.

Cross, Harry E., "South American Bullion Production and Export, 1550–1750," in J. F. Richards, ed., *Precious Metals in the Later Medieval and Early Modern Worlds* (Durham, NC: Carolina Academic Press, 1983), pp. 397–423.

Daunton, Martin and Rick Halpern, eds. *Empire and Others: British Encounters with Indigenous Peoples, 1600–1850.* Philadelphia: University of Pennsylvania Press, 1999.

Davies, Nigel. *The Ancient Kingdoms of Mexico.* Harmondsworth, England: Penguin Books, 1983.

Dean, Warren. *With Broadax and Firebrand: The Destruction of the Brazilian Atlantic Forest.* Berkeley: University of California Press, 1995.

Dennis, Matthew. *Cultivating a Landscape of Peace: Iroquois-European Encounters in Seventeenth-Century America.* Ithaca: Cornell University Press, 1993.

Dickason, Olive Patricia. *Canada's First Nations: A History of Founding Peoples from Earliest Times.* Norman: University of Oklahoma Press, 1992.

Dowd, Gregory Evans. *A Spirited Resistance: The North American Indian Struggle for Unity, 1745–1815.* Baltimore: The Johns Hopkins University Press, 1992.

Eccles, W. J. *The Canadian Frontier, 1534–1760.* rev. ed. Albuquerque: University of New Mexico Press, 1983.

Elliott, J. H. *The Old World and the New, 1492–1650.* Cambridge, England: Cambridge University Press, 1970.

Farriss, Nancy M. *Maya Society Under Colonial Rule: The Collective Enterprise of Survival.* Princeton: Princeton University Press, 1984.

Fiedel, Stuart J. *Prehistory of the Americas.* Cambridge, England: Cambridge University Press, 1987.

Flickema, Thomas, "The Siege of Cuzco," *Revista de Historia de América, 92* (July–Dec. 1981), pp. 17–47.

Frank, Andre Gunder. *ReOrient: Global Economy in the Asian Age.* Berkeley: University of California Press, 1998.

Galloway, Patricia. *Choctaw Genesis, 1500–1700.* Lincoln: University of Nebraska Press, 1995.

Gibson, Charles. *Tlaxcala in the Sixteenth Century.* Stanford: Stanford University Press, 1967 [1952].

Gibson, Charles. *The Aztecs Under Spanish Rule: A History of the Indians of the Valley of Mexico, 1519–1810.* Stanford: Stanford University Press, 1964.

Gleach, Frederic W. *Powhatan's World and Colonial Virginia.* Lincoln: University of Nebraska Press, 1997.

Griffith, Nicholas and Fernando Cervantes, eds. *Spiritual Encounters: Interactions Between Christianity and Native Religions in Colonial America.* Lincoln: University of Nebraska Press, 1999.

Griffiths, Nicholas. *The Cross and the Serpent: Religious Repression and Resurgence in Colonial Peru.* Norman: University of Oklahoma Press, 1996.

Gruzinski, Serge. *The Conquest of Mexico: The Incorporation of Indian Societies into the Western World, 16th–18th Centuries.* Eileen Corrigan, trans. Cambridge, England: Polity Press, 1993.

Gruzinski, Serge. *Man-Gods in the Mexican Highlands: Indian Power and Colonial Society, 1520–1800.* Eileen Corrigan, trans. Stanford: Stanford University Press, 1989.

Guilmartin, Jr., John F., "The Cutting Edge: An Analysis of the Spanish Invasion and Overthrow of the Inca Empire, 1532–1539," in Kenneth J. Andrien and Rolena Adorno, eds., *Transatlantic Encounters: Europeans and Andeans in the Sixteenth Century* (Berkeley: University of California Press, 1991), pp. 40–69.

Gutiérrez, Ramón A. *When Jesus Came, the Corn Mothers Went Away: Marriage, Sexuality, and Power in New Mexico, 1500–1846.* Stanford: Stanford University Press, 1991.

Guy, Donna J. and Thomas E. Sheridan, eds. *Contested Ground: Comparative Frontiers on the Northern and Southern Edges of the Spanish Empire.* Tucson: University of Arizona Press, 1998.

Haskett, Robert S. *Indigenous Rulers: An Ethnohistory of Town Government in Colonial Cuernavaca.* Albuquerque: University of New Mexico Press, 1991.

Hassig, Ross. *Mexico and the Spanish Conquest.* London: Longman, 1994.

Hassig, Ross. *War and Society in Ancient Mesoamerica.* Berkeley: University of California Press, 1992.

Hassig, Ross. *Aztec Warfare: Imperial Expansion and Political Control.* Norman: University of Oklahoma Press, 1988.

Hemming, John. *Red Gold: The Conquest of the Brazilian Indians, 1500–1760.* Cambridge, MA: Harvard University Press, 1978.

Hemming, John. *The Conquest of the Incas.* New York: Harcourt Brace Jovanovich, 1970.

Hu-DeHart, Evelyn. *Missionaries, Miners, and Indians: Spanish Contact With the Yaqui Nation of Northwestern New Spain, 1533–1820.* Tucson: University of Arizona, 1981.

Jackson, Robert H. *Indian Population Decline: The Missions of Northwestern New Spain, 1687–1840.* Albuquerque: University of New Mexico Press, 1994.

Jackson, Robert H. and Edward Castillo. *Indians, Franciscans, and Spanish Colonization: The Impact of the Mission System on California Indians.* Albuquerque: University of New Mexico Press, 1995.

Jaenen, Cornelius J., "Characteristics of French Amerindian Contact in New France," in David B. Quinn et al. *Essays on the History of North American Discovery and Exploration.* The Walter Prescott Webb Memorial Lectures n. 21. College Station: Texas A & M Press, 1988. pp. 79–101.

Jaenen, Cornelius J. *Friend and Foe: Aspects of French-Amerindian Cultural Contact in the Sixteenth and Seventeenth Centuries.* New York: Columbia University Press, 1976.

Jennings, Francis. *The Invasion of America: Indians, Colonialism, and the Cant of Conquest.* Chapel Hill: University of North Carolina Press, 1975.

Jones, Grant D. *Maya Resistance to Spanish Rule: Time and History on a Colonial Frontier.* Albuquerque: University of New Mexico Press, 1989.

Josephy, Jr., Alvin M., ed. *America in 1492: The World of the Indian Peoples Before the Arrival of Columbus.* New York: Alfred A. Knopf, 1992.

Kellogg, Susan and Matthew Restall, eds. *Dead Giveaways: Indigenous Testaments of Colonial Mesoamerica and the Andes.* Salt Lake City: University of Utah Press, 1998.

Kicza, John E., "Patterns in Early Spanish Overseas Expansion," *William and Mary Quarterly,* 3rd series, 49:2 (April 1992), pp. 229–253.

Knaut, Andrew L. *The Pueblo Revolt of 1680: Conquest and Persistence in Seventeenth-Century New Mexico.* Norman: University of Oklahoma Press, 1995.

Krech III, Shepard. *The Ecological Indian: Myth and History.* New York: W.W. Norton, 1999.

Kupperman, Karen Ordahl. *Indians and English: Facing Off in Early America.* Ithaca: Cornell University Press, 2000.

Kupperman, Karen Ordahl. *Roanoke: The Abandoned Colony.* Totowa, NJ: Rowman & Littlefield, 1984.

Larson, Brooke and Olivia Harris, eds. *Ethnicity, Markets, and Migration in the Andes: At the Crossroads of History and Anthropology.* Durham, NC: Duke University Press, 1995.

Leach, Douglas E. *Flintlock and Tomahawk: New England in King Philip's War.* New York: W.W. Norton & Co., 1966.

Lepore, Jill. *The Name of War: King Philip's War and the Origins of American Identity.* New York: Alfred A. Knopf, 1988.

Lockhart, James, ed. and trans. *We People Here: Nahuatl Accounts of the Conquest of Mexico.* Berkeley: University of California Press, 1993.

Lockhart, James. *The Nahuas After the Conquest: A Social and Cultural History of the Indians of Central Mexico, Sixteenth Through Eighteenth Centuries.* Stanford: Stanford University Press, 1992.

Lockhart, James. *The Men of Cajamarca: A Social and Biographical Study of the First Conquerors of Peru.* Austin: University of Texas Press, 1972.

Lucena Salmoral, Manuel. *America 1492: Portrait of a Continent 500 Years Ago.* New York: Facts on File, 1990.

Malone, Patrick M. *The Skulking Way of War: Technology and Tactics Among the New England Indians.* Baltimore: The Johns Hopkins University Press, 1993.

Mancall, Peter C. and James H. Merrell, eds. *American Encounters: Natives and Newcomers from European Contact to Indian Removal.* New York: Routledge, 2000.

Mandell, Daniel R. *Behind the Frontier: Indians in Eighteenth-Century Eastern Massachusetts.* Lincoln: University of Nebraska Press, 1996.

Marchant, Alexander. *From Barter to Slavery: The Economic Relations of Portuguese and Indians in the Settlement of Brazil, 1500–1580.* Baltimore: Johns Hopkins University Press, 1942.

Martin, Joel W. *Sacred Revolt: The Muskogees' Struggle for a New World.* Boston: Beacon Press, 1991.

McCaa, Robert, "Spanish and Nahuatl Views on Smallpox and Demographic Catastrophe in Mexico," *Journal of Interdisciplinary History, 25*:3 (Winter 1995), pp. 397–431.

Melville, Elinor G. K. *A Plague of Sheep: Environmental Consequences of the Conquest of Mexico.* Cambridge, England: Cambridge University Press, 1994.

Merchant, Carolyn. *Ecological Revolutions: Nature, Gender, and Science in New England.* Chapel Hill: University of North Carolina Press, 1989.

Merrell, James H. *Into the American Woods: Negotiators on the Pennsylvania Frontier.* New York: W.W. Norton & Co., 1999.

Merrell, James H. *The Indians' New World: Catawbas and Their Neighbors from European Contact through the Era of Removal.* Chapel Hill: University of North Carolina Press, 1989.

Milanich, Jerald T. *Florida Indians and the Invasion from Europe.* Gainesville: University Press of Florida, 1995.

Morgan, Edmund S. *American Slavery, American Freedom: The Ordeal of Colonial Virginia.* New York: W. W. Norton & Company, 1975.

Morris, Craig and Adriana von Hagen. *The Inka Empire and Its Andean Origins.* New York: Abbeville Press, 1993.

Morrison, Kenneth A. *The Embattled Northeast: The Elusive Ideal of Alliance of Abenaki-Euroamerican Relations.* Berkeley: University of California Press, 1984.

Nash, Gary B. *Red, White, and Black: The Peoples of Early America,* 3rd ed. Englewood Cliffs, NJ: Prentice-Hall, 1992.

Oberg, Michael Leroy. *Dominion and Civility: English Imperialism and Native America, 1585–1685.* Ithaca, NY: Cornell University Press, 1999.

Padden, Robert Charles, "Cultural Adaptation and Militant Autonomy among the Araucanians of Chile," *Southwestern Journal of Anthropology, 13*:1 (Spring 1957), pp. 103–121.

Patch, Robert W. *Maya and Spaniard in Yucatan, 1648–1812.* Stanford: Stanford University Press, 1993.

Plane, Ann Marie. *Colonial Intimacies: Indian Marriage in Early New England.* Ithaca, New York: Cornell University Press, 2000.

Powell, Philip Wayne. *Soldiers, Indians, and Silver: The Northward Advance of New Spain, 1550–1600.* Berkeley: University of California Press, 1952.

Radding, Cynthia. *Wandering Peoples: Colonialism, Ethnic Spaces, and Ecological Frontiers in Northwestern Mexico, 1700–1850.* Durham: Duke University Press, 1997.

Restall, Matthew. *The Maya World: Yucatec Culture and Society, 1500–1850.* Stanford: Stanford University Press, 1997.

Richter, Daniel K. *Facing East from Indian Country: A Native History of Early America.* Cambridge, MA: Harvard University Press, 2001.

Richter, Daniel K. *The Ordeal of the Longhouse: The Peoples of the Iroquois League in the Era of European Colonization.* Chapel Hill: University of North Carolina Press, 1992.

Rink, Oliver A. *Holland on the Hudson: An Economic and Social History of Dutch New York.* Ithaca: Cornell University Press, 1986.

Rountree, Helen C. *Pocahantas's People: The Powhatan Indian of Virginia Through Four Centuries.* Norman: University of Oklahoma Press, 1990.

Rountree, Helen C. *The Powhatan Indians of Viginia: Their Traditional Culture.* Norman: University of Oklahoma Press, 1989.

Rouse, Irving. *The Tainos: Rise and Decline of the People Who Greeted Columbus.* New Haven: Yale University Press, 1992.

Salisbury, Neal. *Manitou and Providence: Indians, Europeans, and the Making of New England, 1500–1643.* New York: Oxford University Press, 1982.

Sauer, Carl Ortwin. *The Early Spanish Main.* Berkeley: University of California Press, 1966.

Schlesinger, Roger. *In the Wake of Columbus: The Impact of the New World on Europe, 1492–1650.* Wheeling, IL: Harland Davidson, Inc., 1996.

Schroeder, Susan. *Chimalpahin and the Kingdoms of Chalco.* Tucson: University of Arizona Press, 1991.

Service, Elman R. *Spanish-Guaraní Relations Early Colonial Paraguay.* Ann Arbor: University of Michigan Press, 1954.

Sharer, Robert J. *The Ancient Maya,* 5th ed. Stanford: Stanford University Press, 1994.

Silver, Timothy. *A New Face on the Countryside: Indians, Colonists, and Slaves in South Atlantic Forests, 1500–1800.* Cambridge, England: Cambridge University Press, 1990.

Snow, Dean R. *The Iroquois.* Cambridge, MA: Blackwell, 1994.

Spalding, Karen. *Huarochirí: An Andean Society Under Inca and Spanish Rule.* Stanford: Stanford University Press, 1984.

Spores, Ronald. *The Mixtecs in Ancient and Colonial Times.* Norman: University of Oklahoma Press, 1984.

Starkey, Armstrong. *European and Native American Warfare, 1675–1815.* Norman: University of Oklahoma Press, 1998.

Stern, Steve J. *Peru's Indian Peoples and the Challenge of Spanish Conquest: Huamanga to 1640.* Madison: University of Wisconsin Press, 1982.

Super, John C. *Food, Conquest, and Colonization in Sixteenth-Century Spanish America.* Albuquerque: University of New Mexico Press, 1988.

Taylor, William B. *Drinking, Homicide, and Rebellion in Colonial Mexican Villages.* Stanford: Stanford University Press, 1979.

TePaske, John J., "New World Silver, Castile and the Philippines, 1590–1800," in J.F. Richards, ed., *Precious Metals in the Later Medieval and Early Modern Worlds* (Durham, NC: Carolina Academic Press, 1983), pp. 425–445.

Terraciano, Kevin. *The Mixtecs of Colonial Oaxaca.* Stanford: Stanford University Press, 2001.

Thomas, Hugh. *Conquest: Montezuma, Cortés, and the Fall of Old Mexico.* New York: Simon & Schuster, 1993.

Trelease, Allen W. *Indian Affairs in Colonial New York: The Seventeenth Century.* Ithaca: Cornell University Press, 1960.

Trigger, Bruce G. *Natives and Newcomers: Canada's "Heroic Age" Reconsidered.* Montreal: McGill-Queen's University Press, 1985.

Trigger, Bruce G. *The Children of Aateantsic: A History of the Huron People to 1660.* 2 vols. Montreal: McGill-Queen's University Press, 1976.

Trigger, Bruce G. and Wilcomb E. Washburn, eds. *The Cambridge History of the Native Peoples of the Americas: Volume I North America, Part 1.* Cambridge, England: Cambridge University Press, 1996.

Usner, Jr., Daniel H. *Indians, Settlers, and Slaves in a Frontier Exchange Economy: The Lower Mississippi Valley Before 1783.* Chapel Hill: University of North Carolina Press, 1992.

Vaughan, Alden T. *New England Frontier: Puritans and Indians, 1620–1675.* Boston: Little, Brown and Co., 1965.

Viola, Herman J. and Carolyn Margolis, eds. *Seeds of Change: Five Hundred Years Since Columbus.* Washington DC: Smithsonian Institution Press, 1991.

Wallace, Anthony F. C. *The Death and Rebirth of the Seneca.* New York: Vintage Books, 1972.

Weber, David J. *The Spanish Frontier in North America.* New Haven: Yale University Press, 1992.

White Richard. *The Middle Ground: Indians, Empires, and Republics in the Great Lakes Region, 1650–1815.* Cambridge, England: Cambridge University Press, 1991.

Wightman, Ann M. *Indigenous Migration and Social Change: The Forasteros of Cuzco, 1520–1720.* Durham, NC: Duke University Press, 1990.

Wilson, Samuel M. *Hispaniola: Caribbean Chiefdoms in the Age of Columbus.* Tuscaloosa, AL: University of Alabama Press, 1990.

Wright, Jr., J. Leitch. *The Only Land They Knew: The Tragic Story of the American Indians in the Old South.* New York: The Free Press, 1981.

Index

A

Acaxee Rebelion, 169–71
Acculturation
    to English ways, 130
    to Spanish ways, 60, 69, 75, 78, 93
Adelantado, 43, 45, 46
Adoption ceremony, 140
Agricultural products, demand for, 39
Agricultural revolution, America's, 5
Agriculture, 69
    reliance of sedentary societies on, 6
    of Seneca, 25
    swidden, 23–25, 152
Aguirre, Lepe de, 46
Alberta Maria de los Dolores, 80
Aldeias, 161
Algonquian people, 105
Alpacas, 6
American Southwest, 23
Andean zone, 5, 16, 30, 67
    chronology of central history up to
        European contact, 10 *fig.*
    important towns and ethnic groups
        in 500–1500, 20 *fig.*

organized states in, 8
revolts in, 91–92
Animals, 179. *See also* Horses.
    European, 103, 120, 176–77, 179
    European food, 84
    movement of, 176–77
Anti-Muslim feeling of European
        expansion, 35
Apaches, 102
Araucanians, 59, 164–65, 166, 185
Architecture
    Olmec, 11
    of sedentary societies, 6
Armies, 21
Astronomers, 13
Asunción, 60
Atahuallpa, 52, 55 *fig.*
Ayllón, Lucas Vázquez, 99
Ayllus, 14
Aztecs, 5, 30, 51, 184
    army of at war, 22
    cities of and warfare, 52
    civilization of, 72
    human sacrifice by, 14
    migration myth of, 12 *fig.*

population of, 50
royal lineage, 83
warrior attire of, 48 *fig.*

B

Bacon, Nathaniel, Jr., 131
Bacon's Rebellion, 131–32
Bandeirantes, 163–64
Beans, 5, 178
Beaver furs, trade in, 105. *See also* Fur
    trade.
Beringia, 4
Biculturation, 172
Black population, in Carolinas, 145
Black slavery, 144, 161, 175
Bows and arrows, 28
Brant, Joseph, 141, 143
Brazil, 37, 61, 152, 157–61, 175
Bubonic plague, 34
Buenos Aires, 161
Buffalo, 6, 103

C

Cabeza de Vaca, Alvar Nuñez, 162
Cacao beans, 16
Caciques, 83
Cahokia, 8
Calendars, 13
California, 103, 168
California Indians, 100
Calloway, Colin G., 147
Calpullis, 14
Canada
    French arrival in, 104–08
    population of French, 114
    west, 116–18
Canary Islands, conquest of, 36
Cannibalism, 14, 27
Canny, Nicholas P., 125
Cano y Montezuma family, 175
Captives, 28–29
Caribbean, 30, 175

forced labor in, 40–41
Spanish exploration in, 37–40
Caribs, 27
Carolinas
    black population in, 145
    English colonization of, 143–45
Cartier, Jacques, 104
Casas, Bartolomé, 37
Castas, 80
Castillo, Díaz del, 49, 50, 51, 53
Catari, Tomás. 92
Catholic church
    and expansion, 35
    missionaries of in Caribbean, 40
Catholicism, 94, 110
Cattle, 176, 183
Cattle ranching, in Yucatan, 153
Cavalry, 49, 50
    against semisedentary societies, 58
Cempoalans, 50
Central America, 23, 30
Champlain, Samuel, 105, 106, 107 *fig.*
Chance, John K., 78
Charros, 177
Chesapeake, English settlement in,
    126–32
Chicha, 177
Chichimec League, 184
Chichimecs, 63
Chickasaws, 146
Chickens, 177
Chiefs, of semisedentary peoples, 28
Chile, 164–65
Chile peppers, 178
China, 35–36, 178, 182
Chinampas, 8
Choctaw, 117, 118
Christianization of natives, 84–88, 155,
    156
Cieza de León, Pedro, 19, 69
City-states, 18
    ethnic, 70
    parishes organized along lines of, 86
Civil-religious hierarchy, 89
Civilization zones, 94
Clendinnen, Inga, 57

Clothes, European, 84
Cloth goods, European, 100
Cobo, Father Bernabé, 19
Cofradías, 88, 156
Collective land ownership, 14
Colonists, expectations of Spanish, 67–69
Columbian Exchange, 174, 179
Columbus, Christopher, 37
Comanches, 103
Community, primacy of, 27–29
Condolence raids, 111
Congregación, 75, 155
Conquistadores, 46, 63
Conversion, of natives, 69, 110, 135
Cook, Noble David, 74
Coronado, Francisco Vázques, 101
Cortés, Hernando, 41, 43, 50, 51, 52, 53, 54
Cowboy cultures, 177
Craft items, 27
Cronon, William, 180
Crossbows, 48
Cruz, Martín de la, 178
Cuauhtemoc, 54
Cuba, 42
Cultivation of crops, 5, 8
Cult of the saints, 89–90, 156
Cultural attainments of sedentary peoples, 8
Cultural change, 90–91
Cultural identity, urban, 78
Culture
    changes in material, 83–84
    lack of curiosity about native, 69
Culture zone, 72
Cuzcatlan, map of, 82 fig.
Cuzco, 11, 56

D

Demographic collapse of sedentary societies, 72, 74–75
de Soto, Hernando, 99
Díaz del Castillo, Bernal, 11

Die-off of natives, 40
Disease
    affecting Spanish, 58
    movement of, 176
    in North America, 99, 102, 109, 121, 122, 132, 146, 154, 159
Disease environment, in Americas, 74
Draft animals, lack of, 5
Draft laborers, 40
Durán, Diego, 22
Dutch. See Holland.
Dutch West Indies Company, 120
Dyewoods, 61, 157, 179, 183

E

Eastern North America, native peoples of, 97
Eastern Woodlands Indians, 23, 25, 31, 180
    practice of war among, 134
Ecological zones, in Andes, 16
Eliot, John, 135
Elliott, J. H., 181
Empires, 19–22
Encomenderos, 153
Encomienda, 41
England, 35, 180
    and New Netherland, 119
    in North America, 97, 99, 125
    rivalry with France, 112
    settlement in Jamestown and the Chesapeake, 126–32
    takeover of New France by, 141
Entradas, 42–43, 58, 63
Epidemic diseases, 31, 54
Ethnic provinces, 8
Europe
    in mid-fifteenth century, 34–35
    travel of Indians to, 175
European societies, nature of encounters with indigenous societies, 2
Export, production of profitable colonial, 39

F

Families
   arrival of Dutch, 120
   arrival of Puritan, 133
Famine, affecting Spanish, 58
Festivals, native, 88
Firearms, 35, 60, 84, 165
Fiscales, 88
Fishermen, European, 97
Forced labor, forms of in Caribbean,
      40–41
Fort Orange, 118, 119–20
Forts (presidios), 59, 63, 167
Fragmentation of sedentary imperial
      peoples, 72–73
France, 35
   avoidance of conflict with natives,
      108–09
   in Canada, 104–08
   Iroquois as enemies of, 105
   missionaries from, 109–10
   in North America, 97, 99, 122
   settlement along St. Lawrence,
      114–16
   warfare against Iroquois, 112–14
Franciscans, 101, 103–04,153
French-Algonquian alliance, 117
French and Indian War, 112, 140
French Protestants, 99
Frontier zone, 153–54
Full-settlement model, 41
Fur trade, 105, 116, 122, 145, 183
   Canada's dependence on, 114
   in Carolinas, 143
   Dutch, 119–20
   and Huron, 109–11

G

Gauchos, 177
Gender, task specialization by, 16, 25,
      29, 157
Geographical features, 5
Gibson, Charles, 70

Gilbert, Sir Humphrey, 126
Gold, 39, 180, 181
Gold rush mentality, 39
Gómara, López de, 50, 52, 53
Goods, distribution of, 16
Guachichiles, 167
Guamares, 167
Guaraní, 26, 60, 161–64, 168
Guaycurú, 162
Guerilla tactics, 165
Guzmán, Fernando de, 46

H

Headman, capture of and ruling
      through, 52
Headtowns, 73
Herbs, 178–79
Hispaniola, 39, 40
Histories, native, 1–2
Holland, 35
   in Fort Orange, 119–20
   and fur trade, 119–20
   in New Amsterdam, 118, 120–21
   in North America, 97, 99, 122
Horses, 103, 177
   in conquest of Americas, 45, 49, 50
   used by natives, 59, 165, 167
Huamanga, 81
Hudson, Henry, 118
Huguenots, 99
Human sacrifice, 14
Hundred Years War, 35
Hunting societies, North American,
      100
Huron, 105
   fur trade and, 109–11

I

Imperial centers, of sedentary
      societies, 51
Incas, 6, 30, 51, 184
   civilizations of, 72

heirs to throne of, 69
method of empire expansion, 19–21
population of, 50
problems in warfare against
    Spanish, 57
royal lineage of, 83
India, 37, 182
Indian cultures of Latin America in
    1500, 7 *fig.*
Indian peoples in eastern North
    America, 98 *fig.*
Indians
    enslaved, 158, 159
    in Europe, 175
    urban, 78–80
Indian slave trade, 144
Indian warfare, precontact, 111
Indigenous provincial organization,
    retention of, 70–72
Indigenous societies, nature of
        encounters with European
        societies, 2
Influenza, 40, 74, 176
Infrastructure, 18
Inquisition, of Maya, 155
Interprovincial trading network,
    establishment of, 72–73
Ireland, English in, 125–26
Iroquois confederation, 27, 105, 116,
    184
    attacks on Huron by, 111
    and Dutch, 119–20
    in eighteenth century, 137–43
    French warfare against, 112–14
Irrigation projects, 73
Isabel, 175

J

Jaenen, Cornelius J., 108
Jamestown, 126–32
Jemison, Mary, 140
Jennings, Francis, 133
Jesuits, 103, 109–10, 168, 171

K

King Philip's War, 135, 136
Kinship groups, 17, 29, 162–63

L

Labor
    exploitation of native, 102
    for Spanish, 70
Laborers, free, 78
Labor service, 18, 76–78, 154, 157–58,
    163, 172
Land
    competition over, 130, 131–32, 135,
        144–45
    lack of for population growth, 93
    Mayan corporate ownership of, 156
Landa, Diego de, 155
Language, changes in, 90–91
Landholding patterns, 14–19
La Salle, Robert, 117
Lautaro, 164
Leitch, J. Wright, Jr., 147
Léry, Jean de, 159
Lima, 69
Lineage, 27–29
Llamas, 6
Llaneros, 177
Lockhart, James, 51, 86, 89

M

Mahicans, 119
Maize, 5, 6, 31, 178
Malaria, 176
Malone, Patrick M., 111, 134
Mamelucos, 62
Manco Inca, 54–56
Mandell, Daniel R., 137
Manioc, 5, 157, 178
Manpower
    for expeditions of conquest, 43, 45

recruitment of to hold conquered areas, 58
Mapuches, 59–60
Marketing traditions, 81–82
Markets, 16
Maya, 27, 153–56, 183
  politics of, 7
  and Spanish conquest, 57–59
  writing system of, 13
Measles, 40, 74, 176
Men
  role of in sedentary societies, 16
  role of in semisedentary societies, 25
Mendoza, Pedro de, 60
Merchants, native, 81
Merrell, James H., 145
Mescaleros, 103
Mesoamerica, 6, 16, 21
Mestizaje, 80
Mestizo, 60, 78, 80, 163
Metacom, 135, 136
Metallurgy, 6
Metal tools, 84, 100
  lack of, 5
Mexica, 30
  great migration of, 15
Mexico, 6, 21, 30, 51, 165–67, 182
  chronology of central up to European contact, 9 *fig.*
  conquest of, 50
  important sites in valley of on even of European contact, 17 *fig.*
  mining camps in northern, 62–63, 69
  Olmecs of, 8
  organization into states, 7
  settlement in northern, 100
  settlement of Spanish colonists in, 67
Mexico City, 68
Micmac, 115
Migration of groups, 30, 73
Military alliances with native peoples, 183–84
Military men, native, 81

Military technological advantage of Europeans, 47–49
Millenarian movement, 86
Ming dynasty, 36
Mining camps, in Mexico, 62–63, 69
Minuit, Peter, 120
Miscegenation, 80
Missionaries, 69
  French, 109–10
  Puritan, 135
Mission Indians, 169
Missions, 104, 163, 167–71, 172
Mississippi mound builders, 27
Mississippi River valley, 116–18
Mixed-blood offspring, 80, 116, 147, 163, 172
Mohawks, 114, 119, 134, 136
Monarchs, 18
Montezuma, 52
Montezuma, Doña Isabel, 83
Morgan, Edmund S., 126
Municipalities, native identification with, 73
Muskets, introduction of, 111
Mutiny, on expeditions of conquest, 46

N

Narragansetts, 134
Narváez, Pánfilo, 99
Nash, Gary B., 144
Natchez, 117, 118
Native die-off, 93
Native population on the eve of European contact, 30–31
Natives
  Christianization of, 84–88
  in Cuba, 42
  description of by Columbus, 37
  rapid die-off of, 40
  religion of, 101
  response to colonial regime of, 81–83
  tensions with Dutch, 120–21

use of horses by, 59, 165, 167
warfare style of semisedentary, 58
west of the Appalchians, 145–48
Navahos, 102
Neolin, 141
New Amsterdam, 118
New England, Puritan settlement in,
132–37
New Mexico, 101
New Netherland, 118
Nonsedentary (nomadic) peoples,
29–30, 152, 165–67, 179, 183
conquest of, 62–63
Norse, in Americas, 4–5
North America, 30
semisedentary societies in, 23
North-South orientation of American
continents, 5–6
Numerical systems, 13

O

Olive groves, 177
Olmec civilization, 7, 8
architecture of, 11
Oñate, Juan, 101
Opechancanough, 130, 131
Ottoman empire, 34, 35
Otumba, battle of, 53

P

Pacific coast, 23
Paraguay, 60, 161–64
Passing, 80
Pastoralism, 84
Patriarchal cultures, 16
Paulistas, 163
Peanuts, 178
Peoples, movement of, 175
Pequots, 134
Pequot War, 134
Perico, 171
Permanent council, 8

Permanent retainers, 153
Personal retainers, 40, 41, 77
Peru, 182
settlement of Spanish colonists in,
67
Petition to the king, 71–72
Pigs, 177
Pilgrims, 133
Pineapples, 178
Pizarro, Francisco, 45, 50, 52, 69
Plants, movement of, 177–80
Pocahontas, 175
Political organization of empires in
1700 South America, 68 fig.
Poma de Ayala, Guaman, 87
Ponce de Léon, Juan, 97
Pontiac, 141
Pontiac's Rebellion, 141
Population, 30
Aztec, 50
decline of native, 163
of Europe, 34
of Hispaniola, 40
impact of growth in, 92–93
loss of, 74
Population density, 27
Portugal, 35, 37, 152
in Brazil, 157–61
conquests in South America, 44
fig., 61
in North America, 97
in Paraguay, 161–64
Potatoes, 5, 6, 178
Potosí, 92
Powhatan, 127, 129, 131
Praying Indians, 136
Praying towns, 135
Precious metals. See Gold, Silver
Presidios, 59, 103
Priests
native, 81
Spanish, 86
Property rights, of royal lineage, 83
Protestant Reformation, 35
Pueblo Revolt, 102
Pueblos, 23, 100, 101, 102, 121

Pulque, 177
Puritans
    missionary, 135
    settlement in New England, 132–37

R

Race mixture and its recognition,
        80–81, 116
Raleigh, Sir Walter, 126
Recollets, 109, 115
Religion
    dismantling of native, 73, 101
    localism in celebration of, 88
    of natives, 37, 69
    public, 88
Religious systems, 13
Religious zeal, 35
Repartimiento, 40
Reserve Indians, 114
Revolts, native, 91–92
Rojas, Doego de, 58
Rotary draft labor service, 18, 19, 76
Rountree, Helen C., 131

S

Saints
    Catholic emphasis on, 110
    cult of the, 89–90, 156
Salisbury, Neal, 135, 136
San Agustín, 99
Sancho, Pedro, 11
Santiago, 164
Santidade, 159–61
Schwartz, Stuart B., 160
Scientific advances, 13
Secota, 26 fig.
Sedentary imperial societies, 6–22,
        179, 183
    conquest of, 47–57
    demographic collapse of, 72, 74–75
    Spanish settlements in, 67–69

Semisendentary societies, 23–29,
        57–62, 152, 164–65, 179, 183
Seneca, 112, 140
Sheep, 176–77, 179–80
Sheepherding, 103
Ship design, improved, 34
Silver, 39, 69, 100, 180–83
Slash and burn, 23–25, 152, 162, 180
Slave raiding, 163–64
Slavery
    in Canary Islands, 36
    in Caribbean, 41
    Indian, 77, 134, 139, 144
Smallpox, 40, 54, 74, 155, 164, 176
Smith, Captain John, 129
Sodalities, religious, 88–89
South America, 23, 26
Southwest, American, 100–104
Spain, 35, 152, 161–67, 181
    in American Southwest, 100–104
    in the Caribbean, 37–41
    and conquest of sedentary imperial
        societies, 47–57
    early efforts at exploration by, 36
    in eastern North American, 97–100
    form of warfare conducted by,
        47–50
    and nonsedentary peoples, 62–63
    organization of expeditions of
        conquest by, 41–47
    and semisedentary peoples, 57–62
Spanish-American cities, 79 fig.
Squanto, 133
Squash, 5, 178
Stern, Steve J., 81
Sugar, 39, 157, 179, 183
Sweet potatoes, 178
Swidden agriculture, 23–25, 152
Swords, 58
Syphilis, 176

T

Tainos, 39–40
Taki Onqoy, 86

Tarascans, 167
Temple-mound builder cultures, 8
Tenochtitlan, 11, 69
    siege of, 53–54
Teotihuacan, 11
TePaske, John J., 182
Terraciano, Kevin, 94
Terracing projects, 73
Texas, 70
Time, concept of, 14
Tlaxcalans, battle against, 49, 50
Tobacco, cultivation of, 130
Tomatoes, 178
Tovar, Juan de, 15
Trade, 16
    across frontier zone, 153
    long-distance, 155
Trading system
    first true worldwide, 2, 182
    traditional native, 81–82
Trelease, Allen W., 119
Tribes of Eastern North American on
        eve of European contact, 24
        fig.
Tribute payments, 21, 70, 76–78, 102
    Spanish demand for, 40
Trigger, Bruce G., 105
Tupac Amaru, 57
Tupac Amaru revolt, 92
Tupians, 61, 157, 159–61, 183
Tupinambá, 27
Turkey, 176
Tuscarora, 139–40
Typhus, 176

U

Urban complexes, 8, 11
Ursúa, Pedro de, 46
Utes, 102

V

Valdivia, Pedro de, 59, 164

Vanilla, 178
Vargas, Diego, 102
Vicuñas, 6
Vineyards, 177

W

Wallace, Anthony F. C., 25
Wampanoags, 136
War chiefs, permanent, 60, 147
Warfare, 19–22
    among Eastern Woodlands Indians,
        134
    of semisedentary peoples, 28
Weapons, of Europe vs. America,
        47–49, 58
Weeds, 177
Wheat, 60, 84, 165, 177
White, Richard, 117
Women
    in Canada, 114
    on expeditions of conquest, 45
    in Guaraní society, 60, 162–63
    in marketplaces, 82
    and native revolts, 91
    in native society, 147
    role of in sedentary societies, 16
    role of in semisedentary societies,
        25, 26–27
    working among Spanish, 78
Writing systems, 13

Y

Yamasees, 144
Yucatan Peninsula, 153–54

Z

Zacatecos, 167